1

Adult Aphasia

Under the advisory editorship of
Hayes A. Newby

Adult Aphasia

Assessment and Treatment

Jon Eisenson

California State University,

San Francisco

Prentice-Hall, Inc., Englewood Cliffs, New Jersey

Printed in the United States of America

ISBN: 0-13-038646-4

Library of Congress Catalog Card Number: 73-2373

10 9 8 7 6 5

ACKNOWLEDGMENTS

Excerpts appearing throughout this book are reprinted from the following sources:

Weinstein, E. A., Lyerly, O. G., Cole, M., and Ozer, M. N. 1966. Meaning in jargon aphasia. *Cortex*, 2:2, 181–182, 186.
Head, H., *Aphasia and Kindred Disorders of Speech*. New York: Cambridge University Press, 1926, pp. 27, 145–146, 164, 209–211, 257–258, 428–429.
Friedman, D. 1961. On the nature of regression in aphasia. *Archives of General Psychiatry*, 55, 252–256. Copyright 1961, American Medical Association.
Schuell, H., Jenkins, J. J., and Jimenez-Pabon, E., *Aphasia in Adults*. New York: Harper & Row, 1964, pp. 161, 199, 213, 339.
Ritchie, D., *Stroke: A Study of a Recovery*. New York: Doubleday & Co., 1961; London: Faber and Faber, Ltd., 1961, pp. 26–28, 30, 35–36, 38, 162, 183. Copyright © 1960 by Douglas Ritchie. Reprinted by permission of Doubleday & Company, Inc. and Faber and Faber Ltd.
Pribram, K. H., *Languages of the Brain: Experimental Paradoxes and Principles in Neuropsychology*. Englewood Cliffs, N. J.: Prentice-Hall, Inc., 1971, pp. 358–360. Copyright 1971. By permission of Prentice-Hall, Inc., Englewood Cliffs, N. J.
De Renzi, E. and Vignolo, L. A. 1962. The Token Test. *Brain*, 85, 670–672.
Holland, A. L. 1970. Case studies in aphasia rehabilitation using programmed instruction. *Journal of Speech and Hearing Disorders*, 35, 388–389.
Luria, A. R., *Traumatic Aphasia*. The Hague: Mouton & Co., 1970, pp. 48–50, 51, 375–376, 381, 458.
Packer, H. L. 1972. Professor Packer gives views on politics, law, and wine. *Stanford Law School Journal*, May 11. Reproduced by permission of Professor Packer.

PRENTICE-HALL INTERNATIONAL, INC., *London*
PRENTICE-HALL OF AUSTRALIA, PTY. LTD., *Sydney*
PRENTICE-HALL OF CANADA, LTD., *Toronto*
PRENTICE-HALL OF INDIA PRIVATE LIMITED, *New Delhi*
PRENTICE-HALL OF JAPAN, INC., *Tokyo*

To HILDRED SCHUELL, for

her contribution to aphasiology

and for many years of friendship.

Contents

Preface

Adult Aphasia: Assessment and Treatment is intended for aphasiologists, especially those concerned with the rehabilitation of language functions in patients who have incurred cerebral insults and have suffered language impairment. In a field in which the literature is growing in an almost geometric progression, it is obviously impossible to survey all that is available and deserving of citation in any one year, much less over the period of more than a century since aphasia was identified as a syndrome. In attempting to survey even the literature of the past quarter century, I was able to appreciate the significance of the "Alice in Wonderland" experience—one had to run as fast as possible just to stand still. Difficult decisions had to be made as to relevant citations, and those citations finally chosen reflect the author's judgment of what best represents the positions presented in the book according to the subject matter in each chapter. Selection implies prejudice, but in no instance was the prejudice personal.

Recent major publications on aphasia, including Schuell, Jenkins, and Jiminez-Pabon's *Aphasia in Adults* (New York: Harper & Row, 1964), Luria's *Traumatic Aphasia* (The Hague: Mouton, 1970), and Critchley's *Aphasiology* (London: Edward Arnold, 1970), simplified one aspect of the task of determining the contents of the present text. The Schuell *et al.* and Critchley books include excellent historical surveys of aphasia, and so obviated any need for the inclusion of such a review. This volume's emphasis, in keeping with my background and training as a clinical psychologist and speech pathologist as well as an aphasiologist, is on the psychological aspects of aphasia. Thus, modifications in personality and intellectual functioning and their implications for recovery from the complex of symptoms that comprises the syndrome of aphasia are treated more extensively in this text than in others published in the last 10 to 15 years. Even in these respects, I must indicate my indebtedness to the contemporary contributions of J. Hughlings Jackson, even though they were available more than a hundred years ago, and to Kurt Goldstein's publications since the 1920s.

The reader who is acquainted with the *Handbook of Speech Pathology and Audiology*, edited by L. E. Travis (New York: Appleton-Century-Crofts, 1971), may occasionally have a déja vu experience with some of the materials in the present text. *Adult Aphasia: Assessment and Treatment* did, indeed, have its genesis in the three chapters on adult aphasia written by this author for the *Handbook*. Although some of the materials originally included in the *Handbook* have been reproduced in this volume with little or no change, most of them were updated and considerably expanded. In all, perhaps 10 to 15 percent of the *Handbook* materials is included in this writing. I am grateful to Appleton-Century-Crofts for permitting this arrangement.

I am also grateful to the publishers and investigators whose writings are cited or quoted directly. I hope that my interpretations of these authorities are true to their intention as well as to the surface meanings. For critical reading of the manuscript, I am indebted to the advisory editor, Hayes A. Newby. For typing and lending a variety of support when needed, a large debt of gratitude is due to Mrs. Lillian Klock, secretary and administrative assistant extraordinary.

I

Background

1

The Nature of Aphasia: Introductory Considerations

What is most apparent in the behavior of persons with acquired aphasia is that they suffer from an impairment of their previous level of ability to use language. Aphasic persons cannot readily say what they would like to say, or write what formerly they would have had no difficulty in writing. Almost always we can observe that most aphasic persons also have difficulty in the comprehension of language. Typically, the aphasic person's difficulties in language production and comprehension have a relatively sudden and dramatic onset. So, we may offer a preliminary definition that aphasia is a general impairment of language functioning associated with localized cerebral pathology. The pathology (lesion) is almost always in the left hemisphere for right-handed persons as well as for a majority of those who are left-handed. In Chapter 2 we shall consider in detail the relationship between handedness, site of lesion, and aphasia.

Basic Considerations Concerning Language and Language Functioning

To help us in our understanding of the language and related impairments associated with brain lesions, we shall review briefly some concepts about the nature of language, the symbol code employed by human beings to communicate their thoughts and to express their feelings in spoken and written forms. We regard speech—the ability to use linguistic symbols—as a function peculiar to and characteristic of human beings.[1]

Symbols, with the possible exceptions of those which are onomatopoetic and thus suggestive of their meanings, are arbitrary arrangements of discernible stimuli. Most frequently they are sounds (auditory events) or sights (visual events), but they may be tactile events (the braille used by the blind) which derive their meanings through a process of association involving a community of persons. We shall accept the definition of White (1949, p. 25) that "a symbol may be defined as a thing [an event] the value or meaning of which is bestowed upon it by those who use it."

Language consists of an arrangement or system of symbols employed by beings who are capable of making associations between essentially arbitrary representations and events to express their thoughts, their wishes, and their feelings. Ordinarily, and except for the profoundly deaf, the congenitally brain damaged, and the severely mentally retarded, the first linguistic system acquired consists of special arrangements (a system) of orally produced and aurally received symbols. This system, regardless of what the particular language features may be according to the nation or people who use it, has certain characteristics (design features) which Brown (1965, p. 248) summarizes as follows: "Fewer than one hundred sounds which are individually meaningless are compounded, not in all possible ways, to produce some hundreds of thousands of meaningful morphemes, which have meanings that are arbitrarily assigned, and these morphemes are combined by rule to yield an infinite variety of sentences, having meanings that can be derived. All of the systems of communication called language have these design features."

Brown's concise statement of the features of a language system include several terms—*sounds, morphemes,* and *rules*—which we need to define.

Sounds refer, of course, to speech sounds, those produced by the organs of articulation and vocalization. Each spoken language has a number of speech sounds or *phonemes*.[2] Phonemes are identifiable by the characteristics or distinctive features that are a product of the way they are produced. The phoneme /p/ is characterized by lip closure which "suddenly" and momentarily completely stops the flow of breath and then, as in the word *pa*, is followed by a sudden (plosive) release of breath. The /p/ is produced without accompanying

---

[1] We are aware that two chimpanzees have been trained to employ codes that, in a very limited way, approximate human symbol behavior. (See Gardner, R. A., and Gardner, B. T., "Teaching Sign Language to a Chimpanzee," *Science*, 1969, 165, 644–672, and Premack, D., "Language in Chimpanzee?", *Science*, 1971, 172, 808–822, for expositions of these remarkable achievements.)

[2] With the exception of Oriental languages that employ ideograms, e.g., *kanjis* in Japanese, most linguistic systems that have a written language have some correspondence between the written and spoken forms, between the sounds of the language and their written (orthographic) representations. The correspondence varies from language to language. Contemporary Spanish is more consistent in letter-to-sound correspondence than is contemporary English. The English language has 26 letters in its alphabet. However, varying with the dialect, at least 40 sounds (phonemes) are used by speakers of English.

vocalization. The phoneme /a/—the sound of *ah*—is produced with open mouth, tongue relatively flat, and with accompanying vocalization. The phoneme /b/ is like /p/ except that the former is produced with accompanying vocalization. Thus we may describe /p/ as a voiceless, bilabial stop and /b/ as a voiced, bilabial stop. The /p/ and /b/ differ by one distinctive phonemic features, that of voicing.

Phonemes may be defined as distinctive sound elements of a word which, although they have no meaning when produced as isolated (individual) sounds, produce meaningful messages when they occur in context, for example, the difference between *pit* and *bit*, or *pat* and *put*. A phoneme represents a cluster of characteristics of a speech sound that permit us, acoustically, to differentiate it from other speech sounds, and so for words and meanings when the sounds are produced in contextual utterance. Variations of phonemes resulting from contextual utterance are referred to as *allophones*. For example, the *t* in *two* is somewhat different from the *t* in *at times, hit that, pets, put through*, and the two *t*'s in *turtle*. Despite these differences, however, the similarities in place or position of the tongue tip and the manner of release of the tongue tip from articulatory contact position are sufficiently similar for us to discern that we are listening to words all of which include *t* sounds.

Morphemes are the minimum units of meaning within a word. Some single morphemes may constitute complete words, such as *less, not, go,* and all single-syllable words. Some morphemes may be identified as prefixes or suffixes and so contribute to the meaning of a word, such as *un*tidy, *in*take, precious, prince*ly*. Morphemes such as prefixes and suffixes and other affixes do not stand alone (i.e., occur as separate words) and so are referred to as *bound*. Morphemes that do stand alone are referred to as *free*. The word *blends* has the free morpheme *blend* and the bound affix *s* to indicate plural; the word *prefix* has the free morpheme *fix* and the bound form *pre*. Some bound morphemes have relatively consistent meanings, such as *un, pre, tri, ous*. However, a form such as *s* may indicate plural, possession, or tense, according to the word to which it is an affix.

The elements of an utterance, whether they are sounds, morphemes, or a sequence of words (a contextual utterance), do not occur at random but according to the *rules* (grammar) that govern each linguistic system. Some sound sequences do not occur in any identified language, many occur in most languages, and some are peculiar to a particular language. There are sequences which occur in some word positions and not in others. In English the combination *nd* is not found in initial positions but does occur in final positions, as in *end*, and medially, as in *bands* or *ending*. Similarly, *dl* will not be found initially but does occur finally or medially, as in *ladle* and *paddled*. The sequence *dv* is reserved by English speakers for foreign-sounding words, such as the name of the composer Dvořák. The sequence *kl* may occur initially, medially, or finally, as in *club, cycling*, and *freckle*.

The structure and order of words within an utterance—a statement or a question—are governed by the rules to which we conventionally refer as grammar or syntax. The acquisition of most of these rules, normally accomplished by most children as early as age 3, permits the eventual production and understanding of utterances with "an infinite variety of meaning." In some forms of aphasia and in disturbances which may be related to aphasia, the patient appears to be suffering from a disruption or impairment of his previously acquired ability to use the underlying rules of his linguistic system in communicative behavior.[3]

SPEECH AND LANGUAGE

Speech is a human, species-specific medium that employs a linguistic code (a language). Through the medium of speech we are able to express thoughts and feelings and to understand the thoughts and feelings of others who employ the same code. This concept of speech is implied in Critchley's (1970, p. 3) definition: "Speech should be restricted to the expression and reception of ideas and feelings by way of verbal symbols (i.e., words, or any other verbal tools which we may come to regard as units of speech)." Thus, the signs and finger spelling of the deaf as well as the oral-verbal products of the normal-hearing constitute the units of spoken language, or speech. When we write, however, we are using a code of a code as well as employing instruments external to the human body. Thus, writing is not speech but a written secondary associated linguistic code. In some linguistic systems, such as Japanese and Chinese, the two codes are separate. In most linguistic systems that have a written code, there is direct correspondence between the written and spoken systems.

Aphasic persons are defective in speech primarily because they are impaired in their previously acquired ability in the use of their linguistic code. They may also be defective in speaking because of associated neuropathologies which directly impair their control of their articulatory mechanism. Deaf persons who become aphasic may be impaired in their ability to comprehend (decode) or produce (encode) appropriate sequences of symbols (signs and finger spellings) of their visual code. Parallel forms of difficulty in written language, while to some degree varying with the individual patient, are usually present in aphasic persons. For blind aphasics the equivalent difficulties would be in impairments in producing and reading braille print.

LEVELS OF LANGUAGE USAGE: PROPOSITIONAL AND
NONPROPOSITIONAL SPEECH

When we employ linguistic symbol formulations to communicate a specific idea or to elicit a specific response, we are dealing with propositional language. When

---

[3] Linguists use the term *competencies* to refer to all the knowledge we acquire about a linguistic system and *performance* to refer to how we express (produce) the formulations that are derived from our linguistic knowledge.

the formulations are spoken, we are using *propositional speech*. In a proposition, as the term was originally used by Hughlings Jackson,[4] not only the words but also the background situation and the manner in which the words are used, how they relate and refer to one another within the verbal formulation, become important and indicate the essential nature and significance of the utterance. Thus, "You go to hell" produced by a speaker who is angry or irritated has a different significance from the same sequence of words spoken by a fundamentalist minister in answer to the question, "Reverend, what will happen to me if I continue to be a sinner?" Utterances such as "a lousy bitch" may be used propositionally to designate a flea-ridden female dog. However, when used to express a feeling or an attitude about a person, usually even without regard for the sex of the person, the utterance is nonpropositional.

Propositional utterances call for a creative formulation of words with specific and appropriate regard to the situation and do not come "ready made" or preformulated for the speaker. Jackson distinguished linguistic formulations as constituting either *superior* or *inferior* speech. Propositional utterances are superior speech formulations. Inferior speech includes the use of emotionally charged utterances (swearing, strongly affective terms of like and dislike), expletives, cliché "remarks," established verbal series (counting, the alphabet, days of the week, months of the year), verbal social gestures such as those used in greetings and departures, and thoroughly memorized content such as poems and songs. In general, inferior speech constitutes utterances that are "triggered" in preestablished formulations and are generally, rather than specifically, appropriate to a situation. When we apply the distinctions between propositional or superior speech and nonpropositional or inferior speech, we may observe that aphasic persons are considerably more impaired in the former than in the latter. Thus we may observe, as did Jackson, that aphasic persons are not as lacking for words as they are in the formulation and production of propositional utterances. Aphasic persons are much better able to express their feelings, especially if they are strong feelings, than they are able to express or communicate their thoughts.

WORDS, CONCEPTS, AND MEANINGS

Concepts are generalizations about experiences. Concepts are the mental products which result from a succession of experiences with events which are considered by the respondent to be the same or similar in one or more essential respects. The *constellation of essential respects* constitutes the generalization which underlies the concept.[5] Concepts for normal persons are presumably subject to continued modification according to individual ongoing, direct or

---

[4] Later in this chapter we shall expand and apply the concept of propositional speech in relation to Jackson's (1879) position on the nature of aphasic involvements.

[5] J. B. Carroll ("Words, Meanings, and Concepts," *Harvard Educational Review*, 1964, 34, 178–190) considers a concept to be "the abstracted and often cognitively structured classes of 'mental' experiences learned by organisms in the course of their life histories."

vicarious, experiences. Except for most proper names, vocabulary (lexicon) items are verbal representations of concepts. To the degree to which some proper names (e.g., Mary, Joe, Tom, Dick, Harry, Jonah) are likely to predispose or prejudice one's reactions to the utterance, these too may be said to have conceptual implication.

Although we may be able to form concepts without words, the words of our individual lexicons are the incorporations of concepts for which we have had associated verbal experiences. A single word-form may stand for one or more concepts, which may or may not be related. Homonyms, such as *reign* and *rain,* *read* and *reed*, are examples of audible word forms which have different and unrelated meanings. Other single word-forms, such as *board* and *race*, have both related and unrelated meanings. *Water* is an example of one of many English words that have several meanings and concepts which, for the most part, are related to the most common or core meaning of the word. Other such English words are *run, head,* and *chief. Dry* may refer to things which are not sweet, or to degrees of sweetness as well as to degrees of wetness. Thus, a *dry* drink is one which, however wet, is relatively *not sweet.*

Except when a single word constitutes a complete utterance, the meaning of a word is determined by the utterance as a whole as well as by the overall environment (circumstances) in which the utterance is produced. The meanings of single-word utterances are determined by the overall nonverbal circumstances and/or by the verbal circumstances of a preceding speaker. We may return to Jackson's postulation that we communicate in propositions, that the sentence rather than the word is the basic unit for the expression of our meanings when we engage in verbal behavior.

There is considerable research evidence to support the observation that aphasic patients, as a total population, show a vocabulary reduction which is inversely related to the frequency of word usage. That is, the words most difficult to retrieve (available to the aphasic according to recognized lexical need) are those which occur least frequently in the language (Wepman, Bock, Jones, and Van Pelt, 1956). We believe that this observation may be applied to the individual aphasic, in that word usages—the meaning and manner in which a word is employed by the individual—are related to the reduction in vocabulary available or retrievable "on demand" in inverse relationship to *his* particular frequency of usage. Thus, the individual's most common (frequent) use of a word is more likely to be retained than his least frequent use of the word. So, presumably, for most speakers the use of *dry* for *not wet* is more apt to be retained than the use of *dry* for *not sweet.* However, it is conceivable that a given individual may prove to be an exception because he was and is *a given individual* and not a generalization of individuals.[6]

---

[6] For a discussion of the broad implications of the relationship of word frequency to the concept of aphasia see Howes, D., "Application of the Word-Frequency Concept to Aphasia," in DeReuck, A., and O'Connor, M., eds., *Disorders of Language*, London: J. & A. Churchill, 1964.

Reduction in comprehension appears to be related to frequency of word usage along the same lines as reduction for expression (Schuell, Jenkins, and Landis, 1961, p. 3). That is, the less frequent the meaning of a particular word, and the more abstract the meaning, the greater the likelihood that there will be failure of comprehension. We can project this generalization for the individual on the basis of frequency of word usage and frequency of meaning for words with multiple meanings. However, because each individual has his own lexicon of meanings for words as well as words themselves, exceptions are to be expected according to each person's particular use and experience with his total lexical inventory.

NONINTELLECTUAL USE OF WORD FORMS

Most intelligent human beings learn to use language with sufficient facility and proficiency to elicit specific responses or to express specific ideas according to the needs of varying situations. This is not all, however. Most human beings also learn to use language symbols without regard to specific ideas or without the intention of eliciting specific responses. Words spoken under the influence of strong emotion—anger, fear, and hate—as well as words of a more tender emotion, are *nonspecific* and *nonsymbolic*. The same word form, then, may have both abstract and specific (symbolic) meaning as well as nonabstract and nonsymbolic meaning. Some English words of Anglo-Saxon origin are rarely used except in nondenotative, nonsymbolic ways. It is possible, however, to utter any word, or any group of words, in a manner which makes it devoid of intellectual significance. This point is emphasized because we regard an aphasic person as one for whom intellectual and abstract meanings are, in conventional communicative situations, considerably more impaired than his ability to express affect (feelings and emotions).

Nonintellectual speech is not confined to emotional utterances. As we indicated in our earlier discussion of inferior language, other forms of nonintellectual or reduced intellectual speech include *automatic, serial-content,* and *social-gesture speech. Automatic speech* consists of linguistic material which has been repeated so often *in a given order* that the content has been memorized. Familiar verses, prayers, and songs are examples of speech content which initially may or may not have had intellectual significance but which became automatic and nonintellectual through repetition. Words of a song are usually automatic only when the melody as well as the words are produced. If the melody is intentionally inhibited, it will generally be found that voluntary effort is necessary to recall the words of the song.

Serial-content speech consists of a series of words which have been learned and memorized in a given order. The alphabet, numerical sequences, and arithmetic tables are examples of serial-content speech. Automatic and serial-content speech may become modified and require voluntary control when it becomes necessary to begin at other than the habitual starting point.

Social-gesture speech is another form of linguistic content in which individual words and their specific symbolic significance are relatively unimportant. In the use of such verbal social gestures as "How are you?" and "Pleased to meet you," we pay little attention to the specific symbolic or denotative meanings of the words. At best, these words have "area meanings." Social-gesture words are appropriate in broad ways to the situations in which they are used. In general, several possible choices may be equally appropriate to the same situation. For example, when two acquaintances meet, it is not of great importance whether one greets the other with "Hello"; "How are you?"; or "How do you do?" It is usually equally unimportant whether the response to the greeting is "Fine, thank you"; or "How are you?"

Emotional utterance, automatic-content, serial-content, and social-gesture speech are examples of linguistic word forms and word usages which remain relatively intact for most aphasic patients. These, as we have indicated, are nonpropositional or inferior language utterances.

LANGUAGE AND THINKING

As we shall soon note in our review of definitions and concepts of aphasia an issue that arises repeatedly is whether the aphasic person is impaired primarily in his thinking, and so in the use of language, or is impaired primarily in the use of language, and so in his thinking. If it is the latter, then the assumption·is that thinking is impaired because thinking is mediated through language. Evidence, which we shall review in Chapter 3, suggests strongly that for many aphasics there are decrements in intelligence even when language need not be employed in the intellectual task. We shall suggest a position to which we shall return later that functional intelligence is reduced in many persons, including those with only relatively slight residual manifestations of aphasia. However, when conditions are optimal and "noise" factors are controlled, recovered aphasics in particular, and many with more obvious aphasic impairments, are able to function close to their premorbid intellectual level, *especially when they are not called upon to explain their thinking in language.*

Disturbances Frequently Associated with Aphasia

There are several disturbances of intake and production, and of behavior, not limited to language, that are frequently associated with aphasic involvements. We shall review several of these and indicate their implications for the understanding of the overall changes that are part of the involvements in persons who are aphasic.

AGNOSIAS: RECOGNITION IMPAIRMENTS

Henry Head (1926) wrote, "before it is possible to determine the behavior of a supposed aphasic to tests which depend on reading or comprehension of spoken words, we must be certain that he is capable of appreciating the significance of sights and sounds." The term *agnosia* is attributed to Freud (1891), who applied the term to states in which the individual is able to receive sensory impressions but is unable to recognize (appreciate) their significance. Such impairments of perception have serious implications for language if they involve auditory or visual modalities or, in the case of blind persons, for the tactile modality. In assessing for agnosias we must make certain that due allowance is made for the possibility of sensory defect or limitation. Thus, hearing loss *per se*, or visual loss or defect, including that for visual field limitation, must be accounted for and considered before an assessment of agnosia is made. It is also essential that the patient being assessed is not in so severe a state of confusion that he does not know what behavior is expected of him. Most tests for *agnosias* call for some form of *matching to sample* through a single sensory modality at a time.

The nature of the examining procedure may serve to confuse patients with cerebral damage and so mislead examiners as to the presence of agnostic impairments. A patient may, in fact, not believe that the examiner really expects him to perform a simple matching task, and so may fail to perform at all.

Acoustic Agnosia. *Acoustic agnosia*, a disturbance of discriminative hearing, is regarded by Luria (1966*b*, pp. 103–107) as a fundamental source of speech disturbance. According to Luria, this disturbance arises because of impairment in the analytic-synthetic activity of the auditory cortex and is manifest in defective analysis of the speech-sound (phonemic) system of the language. The patient's errors for speech-sound discrimination increase as differences between sounds decrease. Thus more errors are likely to occur when discrimination needs to be made between sounds such as *t* and *p*, or *t* and *d*, than between *s* and *m*, or *k* and *r*. Luria considers acoustic agnosia to be the basis for auditory or temporal acoustic aphasia.

Auditory Agnosia. The term *auditory agnosia* is broader in its implications than is acoustic agnosia. Auditory agnosia refers to disturbances in the recognition of sounds or combinations of sounds without regard to the individual's ability to evaluate them. The disturbance may be for nonsymbolic (nonlanguage) sounds such as mechanical or animal noises; for human, nonlinguistic sounds (coughing, sneezing, hand clapping); or for sounds which are associated with spoken symbols (phonetic units, words, or groups of words). A patient who hears sounds which he cannot recognize will not be able to evaluate the auditory stimuli. An individual with *auditory verbal agnosia* is not able to understand oral language.

We may test for auditory agnosias by having a patient imitate sounds, or in some other way, as by pointing, indicate the source or origin of a sound. Verbal agnosias may be tested by repetitions of words or, on a higher level, by eliciting an appropriate motor response to a word or a group of words. A person who can point to the parts of his body when they are named reveals that he both recognizes and understands the words he hears.

A special form of auditory agnosia is *amusia*. Auditory musical agnosia (amusia) refers to a disturbance in a previously existing ability to recognize music. It is not to be confused with so-called tone-deafness, or with a lack of singing ability which may be present even among nonaphasic persons. If amusia is actually found to exist in a patient, the disturbance may impair the person's ability to respond appropriately to inflectional and intonational changes in speech (dysprosody). On the whole, however, amusia is not one of the more frequent disturbances related to aphasia.

Visual Agnosia. *Visual agnosia* is a disturbance of recognition of situations through visual intake. The individual may sense that he is seeing something but may not be able to recognize what he sees. Visual agnosias may be specific for objects, representations, geometric forms, colors, letters, words, or other special configurations. It is unlikely, however, that an individual will have an agnosia for pictures and not for objects; for letters, and not for words; or for single words and not for words in context.

The importance of determining whether an individual has visual agnosia before deciding whether he has alexia is evident. If letters, or groups of letters, cannot be recognized, they cannot be evaluated as symbols. It is essential, therefore, that a patient's ability to recognize visual configurations be determined before a decision is made as to possible reading difficulties (dyslexia).

Tactile Agnosia. *Tactile agnosia* is a disturbance in the ability of an individual to recognize objects through the sense of touch. For the blind person, who has been trained in braille reading, tactile agnosia will impair reading ability. For other than the blind, there is little implication in this disturbance for language dysfunction.

APRAXIA—IMPAIRMENT OF VOLUNTARY MOVEMENTS

The concept of *apraxia* was introduced by Liepmann (1900) to distinguish between motor disorders based on impairment of voluntary movement and those resulting from paralysis, ataxia, and pathologies directly affecting muscle tone. The term *apraxia* as we shall use it will refer to impairment of voluntary and purposeful movements (acts) which cannot be accounted for on the basis of motor weakness. Apraxic patients often are able to execute an act on an "involuntary" basis which they seem unable to perform voluntarily. Thus, a patient may lick his lips on the basis of an inner urge, or even light and smoke a cigarette and yet not be able to imitate such acts or to execute them on direction or command by another person. We must, of course, make certain that a patient understands a command or direction before we attribute his failure to an inability to execute purposive movements to accomplish an act.

We are, of course, primarily concerned with apraxic involvements that directly implicate language functions—the apraxias of the articulatory mechanism and for the movements in writing. Liepmann (1913) argued that some forms of motor, or so-called Broca's aphasia, have their etiology in a disturbance of the kinesthetic engrams (kinesthetic plans or "schemes" of movement) which form the mental framework or basis for each motor act. The patient who cannot produce words he seems able to understand may be suffering from a failure to recall the order of articulatory activity from an amnesia for verbal production, rather than from impairment of the inner formulation of the utterance.[7] Similarly, a patient may be unable to write because of an impairment for the plan or scheme for the movements to produce the sequence of letters he has in mind.

Although we shall not try to unravel the knot of where aphasic involvements begin and apraxia leaves off, we do wish to share the clinical impression that apraxic patients show greater impairment with propositional than with non-propositional language. Impairments also increase as the patient needs to appreciate the *intention of another person* in the execution of an act.

The relationship of the propositional level of the act is emphasized by Denny-Brown (1958) in his concept of *ideational apraxia*.

It is obvious that the more hypothetic the nature of the request, the more imaginary the circumstances, and the more the requested movement is a mimesis of the real thing, the more vulnerable it is to such disease. The patient is unable to *pretend* to drink from a glass of water, or even to pretend to drink from an empty glass, yet can perform without difficulty when presented with a glass with water in it. This is the distinction between the vulnerability of propositional performance versus spontaneous or emotional performance that Jackson pointed out in relation to disturbances of speech.

. . . in its highest elaboration, mimetic and propositional behavior is related to conceptual organization of space, objects and persons in the dominant hemisphere. Such behavior is more highly vulnerable to pathologic changes than is direct physiologic reaction to external events.

Articulatory apraxia, we should note, may occur without any accompanying aphasic involvements. As Critchley (1970, p. 214) observes: "Articulatory apraxia . . . can exist alone, that is, without any impairment of symbolic formulation and expression. When this is the case, it probably represents the 'cortical dysarthria' of older writers, stemming from a unilateral lesion of the brain."

---

[7]See Luria (1966a, pp. 178–211) for a review of concepts of apraxia and the distinction between apraxias, dysarthrias, and aphasias.

DYSARTHRIA

Dysarthrias refer to impairments of articulatory (speech) movements that are etiologically associated with neuropathology. The neuropathology may be of central origin or one directly affecting the peripheral musculature. Thus, Darley, Aronson, and Brown (1969) consider the term dysarthria to be "a collective name for a group of speech disorders resulting from disturbances in muscular control over the speech mechanism due to damage of the central or peripheral nervous system. It designates problems in oral communication due to paralysis, weakness, or incoordination of the speech musculature. It differentiates such problems from disorders of higher centers related to the faulty programming of movements and sequences of movements (apraxia of speech) and to the inefficient processing of linguistic units (aphasia)."[8]

Although our concept of dysarthria does not limit its etiology to cerebral pathology but includes lower motor neuron involvements, dysarthrias in aphasics are almost always related to cerebrocortical damage. Functionally, we may accept Bay's concept that dysarthria is a nonlinguistic disorder that may or may not accompany aphasia. It is primary motor disturbance of the articulary muscles which directly impairs speech production (Bay, 1967). The dysarthric patient may slur individual sounds, or omit sounds, and may have difficulty in the production of contextual utterance. Unlike the apraxic patient, however, he does not suffer from an impairment of the plan or scheme of movements required for the production of an utterance.

Aphasic (Linguistic) Impairments

PARAPHASIA

Freud (1891) defined paraphasia as a disorder of speech "in which the appropriate word is replaced by a less appropriate one, which, however, still retains a certain relationship to the correct word." Freud was mindful that the verbal behavior of the aphasic is not without its underlying psychodynamics, and so he compared the verbal errors of the aphasics with those made by many normal persons under conditions of stress, fatigue, and distraction (divided attention). Critchley (1970, p. 9) defined paraphasia as "the evocation of an inappropriate sound in place of a desired sound or phrase." We consider paraphasia to be any error of commission modifying the individual word (sound and morpheme substitution) or of word substitution in the spoken or written

---

[8] Darley *et al.*, based on a computer analysis of the specific speech symptoms of dysarthric patients, delineate five types of dysarthria associated with different neuropathologies. These are flaccid dysarthria in bulbar palsy, spastic dysarthria in pseudobulbar palsy, ataxic dysarthria in cerebellar disorders, hypokinetic dysarthria in parkinsonism, and hyperkinetic dysarthria in dystonia and chorea.

production of a speaker or writer. Paraphasic errors are not limited to persons who are aphasic. For the aphasic, however, organic rather than psychodynamic factors are presumed to be primarily responsible for the linguistic distortions.[9] The following are some samples of paraphasic errors in the spoken and written efforts of a 53-year-old male patient.

Paraphasic errors in oral sentence repetition (note perseverative nature of errors):

(The car sped swiftly down the road.)
The car would spit sweetly down the load.

(Persistence is essential to success.)
Mesastense is instans to sesatins.

The patient was presented with the following paragraph. Errors in the patient's oral reading are indicated within parentheses.

The crown (crowd) and glory of a useful (ufless) life is character (krakatic). It is the noblest (modest) possession of man. It forms a rank in itself (insist), an estate (state) in the general good will, dignifying (degnatates) every station and exalting (farfaletis) every position (fashiner) in society (sasintly). It exercises (esresides) a greater power than wealth, and is a valuable (voluble) means (meez) of securing (shuraze) honor (harmat).

Errors in writing to dictation:

Dictated Word	Patient's Writing	Possible Explanation of Error
tell	tale	association—e.g., "tell a tale"
saw	salt	phonetic similarity
campaign	parade	association, a parade for a political campaign
occur	concur	phonetic similarity
was	why	syntactic association, as in a "why was . . .?" sentence

In the errors produced by the patient, we can see the effects of the process of association and the failure to inhibit such association because of the relaxation of attention. We believe this observation to be consistent with the generalized position of Jakobson and Halle (1956, p. 76): "Every form of aphasic disturbance consists in some impairment, more or less severe, either of the faculty for selection and substitution or for combination and contexture."

---

[9] We should not, however, overlook the possibility that for a given speaking situation, underlying psychodynamics may explain the specific paraphasic production. In his *Psychopathology of Everyday Life* (1938, p. 69), Freud said: "What we observe in normal persons as slips of the tongue gives the same impression as the first step of the so-called 'paraphasias' which manifest themselves under pathologic conditions."

NEOLOGISMS

When a speaker uses a neologism, he has literally "invented" a new word. This form of verbal creativity is sometimes done for special effect by poets and frequently by writers of advertising copy. *Neologisms* may be regarded as a form of paraphasia in which an expected (conventional) word is replaced by a new one, the meaning of which is not apparent in the utterance. Some aphasics have "pet" neologisms, words or phrases used frequently and without apparent differentiation as to possible referent. Other neologisms, however, may comprise combinations of words or of morphemes which do indicate intent and meaning. Thus the word "spork" may be evoked for *spoon* and *fork*. This type of neologism, a product of semantic association, is likely to occur as a specific attempt at naming and not become part of an aphasic's habitual verbal behavior.

Neologisms, as we suggested in our discussion of paraphasia, may arise as a result of a process of association between the appropriate word and other "parameters" of the word. Thus the word *flower* may evoke *flose* as a contamination of flour (a homonym and a phonetic association, and rose, a semantic association. Similarly, *scent* may evoke *sment* as a contamination of scent and smell.[10]

JARGON

Some aphasics produce a relatively free flow of unintelligible utterance. Critchley (1970, p. 9) defines jargon aphasia as "a type of speech impairment whereby the patient emits a profusion of utterance most of which is incomprehensible to the hearer, though perhaps not to the speaker." The key words in this definition are *profusion* and *incomprehensible*. It is our impression, however, that the apparent jargon is not devoid of underlying meaning. By analyzing a sample of jargon speech of an aphasic, we were able to find some surprisingly "lawful" and regular sound and morpheme substitutions and so "break the code" of the jargon utterance.

Weinstein, Lyerly, Cole, and Ozer (1966) present the following example of jargon abstracted from an interview with a 34-year-old Marine sergeant who had incurred a head injury in an automobile accident.

Doctor: Now, how did your accident happen?
Patient: . . . I'm not sure, I think I just started getting trouble with colds and they found out I was tied up with some virus affair that the Army had and uh used me as a means to a cure that or . . . to put out a spread to it.

[10]We may also view these "contaminations" as a product of linguistic (stimulus) generalization. A word as a stimulus event may evoke many possible associations. A normal person, under normal conditions, is able to inhibit inappropriate responses (exercise vigilance) and overtly produce one appropriate to the situation. When responses are not inhibited, as in "normal" slips of the tongue, a neologism may be produced. Persons with brain damage are less able to exercise vigilance and so produce their forms of neologisms.

Doctor: And what's the name of the hospital?

Patient: Uh . . . patients or etimology, one of the two, I'm not sure, sir. I've been in part where you had the majority of them on the floor and some of them were not.

Doctor: Were you in an automobile accident?

Patient: Not to my knowledge I wasn't.

Doctor: I notice you have a couple of black eyes and a scar on your head. How did that happen?

Patient: Uh these, sir, I got through care of uh skin refractions uh some day while I was taking care of. I believe it was uh some areas that they were sending people into in Havana and all around they had some of these temperate discolorations and stuff like that. . . .

Doctor: Do you have any trouble in putting your thoughts into words or figuring out what you mean?

Patient: No, I don't think I did. Uh I may have had at one time but it seems like I'm pretty much along the general lines of everyone else [laughs], so I didn't do much straining to go in any particular way. My children are being raised . . . in their own country . . . thing started out.

Doctor: Do you have any trouble with your memory?

Patient: Uh . . . no, only . . . only possibly pertaining to child usage of any of the instruments, tools or anything like that.

The "jargon"-producing patient seems to be unaware that he is not communicating satisfactorily. "Jargon" productions are actually more fluent than normal speech and much more fluent than most aphasic speech in that they do not include halts, hesitations, and self-corrections. Weinstein *et al.* note that:

The jargon patient feels that he is communicating satisfactorily and so does not show the halts, hesitations and corrections that mark standard aphasic speech. Much of what is said to him he interprets as concerning himself; hence the many rambling self-references and the pervading "officialese." Questions about illness and problems are likely to bring out the social idiom which constituted the patient's premorbid "problem solving language." The bizarre but unhesitating responses that are given in word association are attempts at self-referential usages in metaphorical, idiomatic or "humorous" speech. . . .

In jargon, one retains the structure if not the substance of meaningful speech. Some sense of significance is felt even from nonsense rhymes or neologisms if they are put in a grammatical sequence. The demonstrated relationship between jargon and colloquialisms, stock phrases, clichés and officialese indicates that a sense of meaning is gotten from a particular style of speech and anticipated response from the social environment that this language entails. The utterances of the jargon patient are bizarre to the listener who is trying to interpret them in the framework of referential speech. What is considered as jargon is to some extent variable in terms of the degree to which the listener is aware of the patient's problems and preferred social idiom.

ECHOLALIA

The term *echolalia* refers to the tendency of an aphasic to repeat without modification (verbal transformation) an utterance addressed to him by another speaker. The echolalic product may constitute a complete sentence, or the final phrase or word of a sentence. Sometimes the echolalic product is repeated several times without evidence of comprehension. We consider echolalia to be a form of verbal perseveration.

PERSEVERATION

The term *perseveration* refers broadly to any morbid tendency to maintain a mental set or to repeat an act not appropriate to the situation to which a response is required. When a perseverative response is overt, an act is repeated which was originally organized by the respondent as a plan to meet a previous situation. The repeated act reflects an inability on the part of the responding individual to reorganize his behavior to meet the new situation or an inability to perceive that a new situation is present. Verbal perseveration is expressed in the production of utterances which may have been evoked as an appropriate response to a context other than the one to which the utterances continue to be made. Perseveration responses may also occur as original and maintained errors rather than as carryovers from preceding situations. Such errors are most likely to be made when the aphasic is confronted with difficult new contexts, in states of fatigue, when situations change rapidly, and perhaps most generally in states of anxiety when the patient feels the need to say something despite his inability at the moment to say what is required. Under comparable conditions, a parallel phenomenon may be observed in the written products of the aphasic.

Additional Common Terminology for Aphasic Disorders

As we shall note in our later discussion of classification of aphasic disorders (Chapter 5), aphasiologists vary considerably in their terminology for language disorders. In the following discussion we shall present and define terms for which there is fairly common acceptance by contemporary aphasiologists. Unless otherwise defined or explained, the definitions given will be the working ones for our later discussions. Despite an attempt of aphasiologists during the 1930s and 1940s to use the prefix *a-* for severe forms of aphasic disorders and *dys-* for moderate forms, the present practice is to use the single prefix *a-* for all degrees of disorder with modifying adjectives, mild, moderate, or severe, to express degree. The terms *dysprosody* and dyslexia seem to be exceptions in this practice.

AUDITORY APHASIA

Auditory aphasia refers specifically to disturbances in the comprehension of audible speech which normally is received and evaluated through hearing. Perhaps more often than we might suspect, auditory aphasic disturbances become apparent only as the quantity or complexity of speech is increased.

Occasionally, it will become readily apparent only when the patient is fatigued. Sometimes a patient's difficulty in auditory comprehension is manifest only when there is a fairly rapid change in the nature or content of what he hears.

ANOMIA OR NOMINAL APHASIA

Anomia or *nominal aphasia* is probably the outstanding and most frequent subtype of productive disturbance. Anomia refers to the patient's difficulty in evoking an appropriate term *regardless of its part of speech*. The defect is most likely to be evident in the effort to evoke nouns (nominal words) only because nouns constitute the bulk of most vocabularies. As the patient recovers, anomia is most likely to be a residual disturbance. Most patients, unless they also have considerable evaluative difficulty, are able to recognize and repeat words readily which they cannot evoke easily. A patient with anomic difficulty, consciously or unconsciously, may learn to substitute a synonym or a phrase with approximate meaning for an elusive word, or he may engage in circumlocution, or use a gesture as a verbal substitute. This technique is not the special property of the aphasic patient. Normal speakers use it when, under some temporary pressure, they cannot readily find the most appropriate word to express an idea although, subjectively, the word seems to be at "the tip of the tongue." Typical anomic errors are the substitution of "in class" or "related" items for the term required for the situation. Thus, a patient may refer to a knife as a fork, or use the term plate for cup. One patient's anomic errors, shown below, indicate that he probably understood the questions asked, but had difficulty in "zeroing in" on his answers.

(On what do you sleep?)
Alarm clock, wake up.

(What's ink for?)
To do with a pen.

Anomia may be tested by directing a patient to name objects or pictures, by having him supply words to complete sentences, by requiring the patient to supply a synonym for a word or a phrase, or by asking the patient to summarize in his own words content he has heard or read.

ALEXIA

Alexia is a disturbance in the comprehension of written symbols. Alexic difficulties are difficulties in *silent reading*. These difficulties, as is the case with auditory aphasia, sometimes become obvious only when the patient is required to read comparatively difficult material or long, unbroken pages. Occasionally, the difficulty is apparent chiefly in the evaluation of "small words"—articles, prepositions, conjunctions—and others which are used semantically as connectives or to indicate relationships of words (ideas) within a sentence. Sometimes it will be found that the rate of reading is impaired. A once proficient reader may read accurately but laboriously, and with a feeling of insecurity about his ability. Alexic disturbances may be tested by presenting a patient with written material varying in length and complexity which he is directed to read silently. When he is finished reading, the patient is then required to answer questions or to carry out directions based on the reading.

AGRAPHIA

Agraphia, or writing disturbances, may be manifest in all writing, or in the writing of nominal words, as in anomia, or in faulty grammar, or by the omission of articles, prepositions, conjunctions, and other words that serve as connectives or to indicate relationships of parts of a sentence. These errors may appear in writing to dictation, in spontaneous writing, and even in direct copying.

The following are examples of the writing errors of a 61-year-old patient who had suffered a spontaneous cerebral insult. We may note errors of spelling and substitutions and omissions of functional words.

Copying: (This month is August.)
The month in Augrest.

(Mexico is south of the United States.)
Macos is south Uinetest States.

In answer to the question, "What do you eat for breakfast?" the patient wrote: "I eggs and eat and drink coffee breakfast" (agrammatism).

Another patient, a 59-year-old male college graduate with a history of hypertension, made the following spelling errors: *campian* for *campaign* and *forgien* for *foreign*. For the word *tip* he wrote *pit*, *put*, and finally *tip*. The sentence, *Most girls like to sew*, was written: "Mostly girls like to sew." The sentence, *Mexico is south of the United States*, was written: "Mexico is south by U. S."

AGRAMMATISM

Agrammatism is defined by Critchley (1970, p. 16) as "an aphasic disorder which impairs syntax rather than vocabulary." Typically, agrammatism is characterized by the patient's errors or omissions in the use of functional words—articles, prepositions, and conjunctions—which serve to establish contextual relationships (grammatical context) of spoken and written content. Jakobson (1956) views agrammatism as a type of contiguity disorder characterized by the following: (1) a reduction in the variety of sentences, (2) loss (failure) to observe syntactical rules, (3) dissolution of ties of coordination and subordination, (4) loss of words that have purely grammatical functions and use of inflectional endings.

All these impairments are not necessarily found in patients with agrammatism. Goodglass and Berko (1960) believe that some aphasics may have considerably more difficulty in the use of inflectional endings than with overall adequacy for language production. They suggest: "In some aphasics, the syntactic and inflectional aspects of grammar may be impaired independently of each other."

In severe form, agrammatism may be expressed as *telegrammatism*. All functional words and grammatical markers may be omitted. In written form the verbal product at best resembles how economic motivation might influence our writing of a telegram. However, a product such as the one we presented as an example of agraphia, "I eggs and eat and drink coffee breakfast," is more typical of agrammatic production than an economic telegraphic writing or oral verbalization.

ACALCULIA (ARITHMETIC DISTURBANCES)

Acalculia or arithmetic disturbances may be present on a twofold basis: (1) because of actual difficulty on the part of the patient in dealing with arithmetic processes, or (2) because of related difficulty in the oral or written production of symbols involved in calculation. If the latter is the case, the difficulty is really one of word finding (anomia) rather than of acalculia.

Frequently we shall find that an aphasic patient may do well in simple arithmetic computation, especially if he is permitted to write his responses. This apparently well-retained ability can probably be explained by the automaticity with which most of us do simple arithmetic. The arithmetic tables have become automatic for most adults, so that many of our computations are carried out without the need for quantitative conceptualization or reasoning. Despite this general finding, we occasionally come across an aphasic who cannot perform simple arithmetic operations accurately but who can do fairly well in numerical problem-solving situations.

DYSPROSODY

Dysprosody refers to changes of accent, cadence, rhythm, and intonation of speech (Monrad-Krohn, 1947). In English, dysprosody is likely to impair the expression of affect much more than the semantic or ideational content of the utterance. Thus, emotional expression may be impaired. On the ideational side, subtle changes or implications which are conveyed through inflection and intonation may be beyond the capacity of the aphasic with dysprosody. The patient with dysprosody may have difficulty, except for word order, in indicating and distinguishing between declarative and interrogative utterances. In languages such as Chinese, where inflection determines the basic meaning of the individual "word," a speaker with dysprosody may be much more severely impaired than would one whose native language is English. We are inclined to accept the position of Bay (1964, p. 129) that dysprosody may be a component of *dysarthria* in so far as the prosodic components of speech are part of the motor aspects of articulatory production. In Chinese dialects, as well as in other East Asian languages, errors of "melody" might well constitute anomias, in that they implicate the essential conceptual-semantic component of word selection.

Most patients with dysprosody—and many manifest this as a residual of aphasia—speak without the color normally provided by vocal inflection and intonation. Thus, they may sound as if they were speaking a second language for which they have a mastery of vocabulary and grammar, but not of intonation.

The Nature of Aphasic Involvements

We opened this chapter with a preliminary definition of aphasia. We shall now return to the question of the nature of aphasic involvements by way of a review of definitions from the mid-nineteenth century to date. We shall not, however, attempt to review or consider all definitions or in any way attempt to cover the history of aphasia. Students interested in such a historical review may consult Volume I, Chapters I–VII of Henry Head's *Aphasia and Kindred Disorders of Speech* (1926, 1963), and Schuell, Jenkins, and Jiminez-Pabon, *Aphasia in Adults* (1964), Chapters I–III, for a brief consideration including contemporary positions. Critchley's chapter on "The Origins of Aphasiology" (Critchley, 1970) is an interesting essay on early recognition of language disorders going back to Aristotle's observations.

A REVIEW OF DEFINITIONS AND CONCEPTS

Since the mid-nineteenth century, when aphasia became an identifiable problem, concepts of aphasia have differed according to the nature of the underlying disturbance. A key question, still unresolved, is whether the disturbance is one of symbolic disorder and thinking, and so of language, or basically one of language, and so of thinking. These positions will be brought out in several of the definitions and descriptions of aphasia and aphasic involvements which we shall present in their historical order.[11]

Paul Broca (1861) defined aphemia (aphasia) as a loss of speech consequent to lesion of the frontal lobe of the brain.[12]

J. Hughlings Jackson (1879), a contemporary of Broca, considered aphasia to be an impairment of linguistic formulation and expression. Jackson, as we indicated earlier, directed attention to the differences between the kind of

---

[11] In Chapter 2 we shall consider implications of the definitions in relationship to localization theory and the concepts of aphasia held by the definer.

[12] Specifically, the lesion was localized in the second or third (usually third) frontal convolution. We should note that Broca used the term speech rather than language. This indicated Broca's concern at the time with articulated language production (speech) rather than with oral language comprehension.

speech (language content) that remains relatively available (retrievable) for most aphasic patients and the nature of speech content that is most impaired for the patient. These differences, Jackson pointed out, were related to the intellectual level and the manner in which the linguistic formulations are used. When linguistic symbols are employed in formulations (utterances) to communicate a specific idea or to elicit a specific response appropriate to a situation, we are dealing with a *proposition*. In propositional formulations, we may recall, both the words and the manner in which the words are related and refer to one another within the utterance become important.

Jackson was among the first to stress the need to understand the patient's premorbid personality in order to appreciate the modifications that occur as sequelae of brain damage and the overall aphasic involvements. Thus, Jackson the neurologist and aphasiologist was also very much the psychologist in his approach to aphasic persons. Jackson's observation that the aphasic person becomes "lame in his thinking" will be considered later in our extended discussion of intellectual functioning (Chapter 3).

Sigmund Freud published his views on aphasia in 1891, when he was 35 years old. His thinking was influenced by Darwinian evolutionary theory and, specifically in regard to aphasia, by the writings of Hughlings Jackson. Freud's concept of the central apparatus for speech "is that of a continuous cortical region occupying the space between the terminations of the optic and acoustic nerves and the areas of the cranial and certain peripheral motor nerves in the left hemisphere. It probably covers . . . all the convolutions forming the Sylvian fissure" (Freud, 1891, p. 67). Freud held that "all aphasias originate in interruptions of association; i.e., of conduction. Aphasia through destruction or lesion of a centre is to us no more and no less than aphasia through lesion of those association fibres which meet in that nodal point called a centre" (pp. 67–68).

Freud viewed aphasic disturbances as evolutionary retrogressions. The results of cortical pathology "represent instances of functional retrogression (disinvolution) of a highly organized apparatus, and therefore correspond to earlier states of its functional development. This means that under all circumstances an arrangement of associations which, having been acquired later, belongs to a higher level of functioning, will be lost, while an earlier and simpler one will be preserved" (p. 87).

Freud's views of aphasia had little positive influence on his contemporary colleagues concerned with aphasia. Freud is ignored in the historical survey in Volume I of Henry Head's writings on aphasia (1926). The omission is especially significant because of the emphasis Head gives to the contributions made by Jackson. Freud, as we recall, expressed his indebtedness to Jackson with regard to his thinking on aphasia.

Pierre Marie (1906) held that the essence of aphasia—the *sine qua non* of the involvement—was in deficits of intellect related to the impairment in the use of language. Basically, this is for the comprehension of language as is typically observed in patients with temporal lobe lesion (Wernicke's aphasia). Marie regarded the aphasia described by Broca as dysarthria. True aphasia, according to Marie, is a combination of impairment in the comprehension of language and associated mental decrement. Cole (1968), in a review of Marie's position, indicates that the intellectual deficit emphasized by Marie may be the same as the impairment for language comprehension.

Henry Head (1926) expanded Jackson's concept of aphasia and considered aphasia to be disturbances of "symbolic formulation and expression." This broadened concept implies that all functioning in which some form of symbolization is involved is impaired in aphasic persons. Later we shall consider Head's classification of aphasic disorders which reflect his concept of aphasia.

Head had some reservations about Jackson's use of the proposition and its implications. Head explained (1926; 1963, pp. 209–210):

It is with the greatest reluctance . . . that I venture to change his nomenclature; for I believe that under the uncouth word "propositionising" is included what I understand by "symbolic formulation and expression." This Jackson contrasted habitually with what he called "lower forms" of speech and thought. But the question as to what constitutes a proposition is so disputable, that it is better to avoid a term which is liable to be misunderstood and to lead to controversy. Moreover, it is doubtful whether the term is strictly accurate, even in Jackson's sense, and it certainly does not cover all the abnormalities observed in cases of aphasia and kindred disorders. . . .

I would therefore suggest that the functions affected in such pathological conditions can be grouped under the descriptive phrase "symbolic formulation and expression." But I am anxious that this term should not be thought to define the limits of the disorder. I should have preferred to adopt some entirely neutral appellation and to indicate its meaning by enumerating one after the other the various activities found to be affected on clinical examination. I have combined under the general heading of "symbolic formulation and expression," the disorders of language produced by a unilateral lesion of the brain, because in the majority of instances the gravest disturbance is shown in the use of such symbols as words and figures. But any form of mental behaviour is liable to suffer which demands perfect reproduction and use of any symbol between its initiation and fulfilment. I do not believe that it is possible to include within one categorical definition all those activities which experience shows to be affected; and yet from a physiological point of view they form a group of defects as definite as those of sensation.

Although *Kurt Goldstein's* principal writings in English were published during and after World War II, his thinking and his position were based on observations of World War I military personnel and civilian patients he studied prior to 1950. Goldstein's position (Goldstein and Scheerer, 1941; Goldstein, 1942, 1948) emphasized the changes in the way an individual thought and behaved as a consequence of brain damage. The aphasic individual was viewed as one whose behavior revealed a change from the ability to employ an *abstract attitude*—to perceive generalizations and deal in concepts, and to separate and project himself from the "demands" of the immediate present to broader and nonimmediate considerations–toward one of concretism. Such behavioral changes are expressed in language, but basically, according to Goldstein, are manifestations of intellectual change associated with cerebral damage *and* aphasia. The essence of the change is in a tendency toward concretism, so that the individual's "thinking and acting are directed by the immediate claims that one particular aspect of the object or situation in the environment makes."

DEFINITIONS OF APHASIA: POST-WORLD WAR II

We have selected only a few of the historically important definitions or concepts of aphasia from the mid-nineteenth century to the first quarter of the twentieth century.[13] We shall now consider several more contemporary definitions and their implications for understanding modifications in language and behavior that are associated with cerebral pathology. As an introductory statement, we may say that aphasia is a general impairment of language functioning associated with *localized cerebral pathology*. Implied in this statement is the generally accepted assumption that there are other pathologies of the central nervous system, including those of the cerebral cortex, that are associated with language dysfunction. Impairments may be temporary, as in severe fatigue, or as a reaction to alcohol or some drugs. They may be chronic, as a result of the prolonged effects of alcohol or drugs, or as a result of widespread of diffuse lesions associated with processes accompanying senility, or as a consequence of infections of the brain. We need also be aware that there are impairments of the peripheral sensory and motor mechanisms that create difficulties for the reception and/or production of language–difficulties in hearing, seeing, articulation, and writing–that may be separate problems or ones that occur in addition to those of cerebrocortical origin. These distinctions are brought out in the definitions that follow.

Penfield and Roberts (1959, p. 92) define aphasia as "that state in which one has difficulty in speech, comprehension of speech, naming, reading and writing, or any one or more of them; and it is associated with misuse and/or perseveration of words, but is not due to disturbance in the mechanism of articulation (as in pseudobulbar palsy) or involvement of peripheral nerves, nor due to general mental insufficiency."

Osgood and Miron (1963, p. 8), after reviewing several contemporary and historical definitions of aphasia, offer the following: "Aphasia is a nonfunctional impairment in the reception, manipulation, and/or expression of symbolic content whose basis is to be found in organic damage to relatively central brain structures. Such a definition would include all modalities and forms of linguistic signs, but would exclude such things as perceptual disorganization, disturbance in learning, in abstracting and problem-solving, and purely sensory or motor impairments–except as they specifically involve language symbols. This clinical

---

[13] We shall return to some of these definitions and concepts of aphasia in Chapter 3.

distinction, of course, does not mean that aphasia should be studied without reference to simultaneous nonaphasic symptomatology or that language behavior is in any sense separable from behavior in general."

E. Bay prefers a comparatively narrow concept of aphasia which is limited to the presenting "surface" features of the impairment. According to Bay (1967): "Aphasia should be limited to troubles which primarily and immediately concern language as a specific human property. Such troubles are revealed by erroneous interpretation of a verbal message (on the receptive side), and, on the expressive side, by faulty use of language as demonstrated, for instance, by the appearance of verbal paraphasias."

APHASIA: A DEFINITION BY CONSENSUS

Without further belaboring the matter of definition, we would like to point out that agreement among aphasiologists and clinicians in recognizing or identifying aphasic patients is likely to be much greater than their agreement as to definitions of aphasia or to the *essence* of aphasic involvement. Therefore, based on our own experience, we consider the following observations to be of primary importance.

1. At some stage in their involvement, persons designated as aphasic present evidence of impairment for intake of sequential verbal events as well as for verbal sequential output. Intake disturbances are often labeled as memory or attention-span defects. Output sequential disturbances are manifest in syntactical defects for formulations that are appropriate and relatively specific to the situation.

2. On a probability basis, aphasic involvements are in general expressed in a reduced likelihood that a given linguistic formulation will be understood (appropriately decoded and evaluated), or produced (appropriately formulated and expressed) in kind and manner consistent with the situation (events associated with the linguistic formulation). In general, the more intellectual and abstract the expected linguistic response, the less likely it is that the response will occur.

Based on these fundamental observations about the verbal behavior of aphasic patients, we may then present the following as a restatement-definition of aphasic language disorders. *Aphasia is an impairment of language functioning of persons who have incurred localized cerebral damage that results in a reduced likelihood that an individual involved in a communicative situation will understand or produce appropriate verbal formulations.* The greater the degree of adjustment required on the part of the brain-damaged individual to determine the adequacy and appropriateness of the verbal formulation in the communicative interchange, the greater the likelihood that he will experience difficulty. Thus, verbal expressions of strong feeling, emotion, or any other *set linguistic formulation*—in general any established sequential utterance—are better retained and evoked than are those utterances which call for specific formulation and, not infrequently, reformulation according to the special demands of the communicative situation. Written language impairments (reading and writing) often parallel those for oral language. In addition, impairments in arithmetic processes may be present.

This expanded definition includes the concept of Henry Head (1926) that aphasia is a disturbance of "symbolic formulation and expression" and the Hughlings Jackson's (1879) observation that subpropositional language (established word series as in counting statements of strong affect, etc.) tends to be better retained by aphasic patients than high-level, more "intellectual" propositional language—the language we use for our thinking and the expression of our thoughts.

The "localized cerebral pathology," to which several references have been made, will be considered in some detail in Chapter 2. For the present, we wish merely to emphasize the need to distinguish between the implications of diffuse and bilateral damage associated with progressive brain disease in the person who is suffering from dementia and the effects of localized cerebral pathology in the hemisphere dominant for language. The latter pathology is associated with aphasia. The pathology of the dement is, we believe, associated with intellectual deterioration and so with modifications in thought as expressed in language. We are mindful, however, that not all students of aphasia will accept this position and that the implications of the relationship between language and thinking—and the impairments of one as manifest in the impairments of the other—are deserving of more consideration. This consideration will be given to the subject in Chapter 3.

Aphasia and Aphasic Involvements: The Individual Aphasic

Up to this point we have discussed aphasia without emphasizing as we should that aphasic involvements happen to persons and are not disembodied impairments. We may, if we wish, try to separate the disturbances of language and thinking and the implications of such disturbances on the personality of the individual. However, we prefer to look upon the aphasic individual as one whose impairments are so interrelated that although we are mindful at some times of the manifestations of linguistic impairments, at other times of the modifications in cerebration—the "crippled thinking"—and are impressed on still other occasions with the modifications in personality, we are nevertheless dealing with an individual with dynamics and processes that are complex, interrelated, and disturbed. The aphasic is what he is at the time we see and relate to him as a result of all that he was, and all that happened to him when and after he incurred this pathology. Thus, we must always bear in mind that the involvements of aphasic persons can be understood only if we begin with the basic appreciation that aphasia constitutes a complexity of disturbances. The aphasic individual had habits, attitudes, and abilities, as well as capacities not yet translated into abilities, and personality, before he became impaired. If the individual is an adult, he had learned and developed strategies for responding to illness, to incapacities, to frustration, and to the myriad of influences that human beings are exposed to, long before he became aphasic. How he is likely to respond to the immediate effects of aphasic involvements we believe will depend to a large extent on the kind of person he was before he became aphasic. Aphasic involvements are likely to bring about modifications in the patient's premorbid personality, almost never in the direction of improvement. They are not, however, likely to produce a new personality unrelated in any way to the individual's premorbid state and manner of behaving. A well-adjusted individual who becomes aphasic probably has a better chance of ultimate adjustment than a neurotic individual who becomes aphasic. The latter is likely to become a neurotic aphasic with a reduced chance of recovery from either his neuroticism or his aphasic disturbances.

References

Bay, E. 1964. Principles of classification and their influence on our concepts of aphasia. In *Disorders of Language*, DeReuck, A., and O'Connor, M., eds. London: J. & A. Churchill, pp. 122–142.

_____. 1967. The classification of disorders of speech. *Cortex*, 3:1, 26–31.

Broca, P. 1861. Remarques sur le siege de la faculté du langage articale suivé d'une observation d'aphemie. *Bulletin Société Anatomique de Paris*, 36 (August), 331.

Brown, R. 1965. *Social Psychology*. New York: Free Press.

Carroll, J. B. 1964. Words, meanings and concepts. *Harvard Educational Review*, 34, 178–190.

Cole, M. 1968. The anatomical basis of aphasia as seen by Pierre Marie. *Cortex*. 4, 2, 172–183.

Critchley, M. 1970. *Aphasiology*. London: Edward Arnold.

Darley, F. L., Aronson, A. E., and Brown, J. R. 1969. Differential diagnostic patterns of dysarthria. *Journal of Speech and Hearing Research*, 12:2, 246–269.

Denny-Brown, D. 1958. The nature of apraxia. *Journal of Nervous and Mental Diseases*, 126, 9–32.

Freud, S. 1891. Zur Auffasung der Aphasien. Translated by Stengel, E. 1953. *Freud on Aphasia*. New York: International Universities Press.

_____. 1938. Psychopathology of everyday life. In *The Basic Writings of Sigmund Freud*, Brill, A. A., ed. New York: Modern Library.

Gardner, R. A., and Gardner, B. T. 1969. Teaching sign language to a chimpanzee. *Science*, 165, 644–672.

Goldstein, K. 1942. *After Effects of Brain Injury in War.* New York: Grune & Stratton.

———. 1948. *Language and Language Disturbances.* New York: Grune & Stratton.

Goldstein, K., and Scheerer, M. 1941. Abstract and concrete behavior. *Psychological Monographs,* 53, 2.

Goodglass, H., and Berko, J. 1960. Agrammatism and inflectional morphology in English. *Journal of Speech and Hearing Research,* 3:3, 257–267.

Head, H. 1926. *Aphasia and Kindred Disorders of Speech.* New York: Cambridge University Press and Macmillan. Reprinted by Hafner Publishing Co., New York, 1963.

Howes, D. 1964. Application of the word-frequency concept to aphasia. In *Disorders of Language,* DeReuck, A., and O'Connor, M., eds. London: J. & A. Churchill, pp. 47–78.

Jackson, J. H. 1879. On affections of speech from disease of the brain. In *Selected Writings,* Vol. 2. New York: Basic Books, 1958, pp. 184–204.

Jakobson, R. 1956. Two aspects of language and two types of aphasic disturbances. In *Fundamentals of Language,* Jakobson, R., and Halle, M. The Hague: Mouton, Part II, pp. 55–82.

Jakobson, R., and Halle, M. 1956. *Fundamentals of Language.* The Hague: Mouton.

Liepmann H. 1900. Das Krankheitsbild der Apraxie. *Monatsschrift Psychiatrie und Neurologie,* 8, 182–197.

———. 1913. Motorische Aphasie and Apraxie. *Monatsschrift Psychiatrie und Neurologie,* 34, 485–494.

Luria, A. 1966a. *Higher Cortical Functions in Man.* New York: Basic Books.

———. 1966b. *Human Brain and Psychological Processes.* New York: Harper & Row.

Marie, P. 1906. La troisième circonvolution frontale gauche ne joue aucun rôle spéciale dans la fonction du langage. *Semaine Médicale,* May 23. Reproduced in Marie, P., *Travoux et Memoires,* Tome I. Paris: Masson et Cie. (1926).

Monrad-Krohn, G. 1947. Dysprosody or disordered melody of speech. *Brain,* 70, 405–415.

Osgood, C., and Miron, M. 1963. *Approaches to the Study of Aphasia.* Urbana: University of Illinois Press.

Penfield, W., and Roberts, L. 1959. *Speech and Brain Mechanisms.* Princeton, N. J: Princeton University Press.

Premack, D. 1971. Language in chimpanzee? *Science,* 172, 808–822.

Schuell, H., Jenkins, J., and Jiminez-Pabon, E. 1964. *Aphasia in Adults.* New York: Harper & Row.

Schuell, H., Jenkins, J., and Landis, L. 1961. Relationship between auditory comprehension and word frequency in aphasia. *Journal of Speech and Hearing Research,* 4, 30–36.

Weinstein, E. A., Lyerly, O. G., Cole, M. and Ozer, M. N. 1966. Meaning in jargon aphasia. *Cortex*, 2:2, 165–187.

Wepman, J., Bock, R., Jones, L., and Van Pelt, D. 1956. Psycholinguistic study of aphasia: A revision of the concept of anomia. *Journal of Speech and Hearing Disorders*, 21, 468–477.

White, L. 1949. The symbol: The origin and basis of human behavior. Reprinted from *The Science of Culture*, New York: Farrar, Strauss and Cudahy, Chap. II.

2

Neuropathology of Aphasia: Neurological Correlates

Etiology

Although aphasiologists are not in complete agreement about the precise nature of aphasic disturbances, there is agreement that the underlying cause of aphasia is cerebral damage incurred as a consequence of disease or injury of the dominant (usually left) hemisphere. Although we need have no reservation that all aphasic individuals have incurred brain damage, the converse does not necessarily hold. Not all persons who incur brain damage, even of the dominant hemisphere, necessarily become manifestly aphasic.[1] However, some persons who have incurred cerebral insult, even though not manifestly aphasic, may demonstrate intellectual and behavioral modifications as sequelae to their damage. These will be considered in Chapter 3.

The possible causes of cerebral damage with which aphasic disturbances are associated are many and varied. They include direct trauma by externally applied force, tumors, cerebral vascular lesions (embolisms, thromboses, aneurysms, hemorrhages), infectious diseases affecting brain tissue, and degenerative diseases invading the brain. Of the factors just enumerated, the vascular disturbances, embolisms, hemorrhages, and thromboses are the most frequent

[1] Perhaps a more conservative statement might be that some persons who incur damage to their dominant cerebral hemispheres make such rapid spontaneous recoveries that by the time they are assessed, there are no objectively manifest evidences of language involvement.

etiological associates. Brain damage resulting from head injuries, and brain penetrations from high-velocity missiles, are increased factors during war, for both the civilian and military populations. For the most part, this cause of brain damage implicates a higher proportion of younger (below 30 years of age) than of older members of the population. As of now, it also implicates males considerably more than females.

Among the population at large, aphasic involvements are most frequently associated with pathologies of middle cerebral artery within the left hemisphere. The reason for this becomes apparent by an examination of Figure 2–1. We may note that the middle cerebral artery and its branches "nurtures" the areas of the cortex that include overlapping representations for the ear, throat, mouth, and tongue.

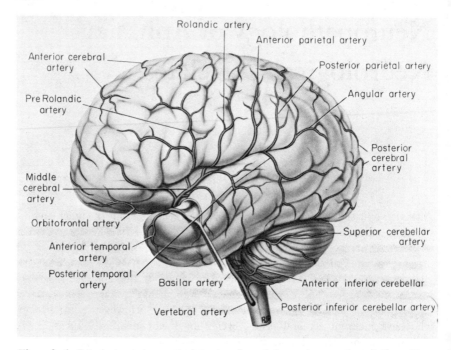

Figure 2–1. Principal arteries on the lateral surface of the cerebrum and cerebellum. (From Truex and Carpenter, *Human Neuroanatomy*, 6th ed. Baltimore: Williams and Wilkins, 1969.)

Cerebral Dominance, Laterality, and Language Functions

CEREBRAL DOMINANCE

Cerebral dominance—the processing and control of functions by a localized area within one of the hemispheres of the brain—is more clearly differentiated in man than in subhuman primates. The greatest differentiation is found for language functions where findings, which we shall review later, indicate that regardless of the individual's handedness, the vast majority of persons have dominance localized in the left cerebral hemisphere. For functions other than language, hemispheric specificity for perceptual functions is relative and is generally in keeping with the scheme represented in Figure 2–2.

The data for Figure 2–2 came from experimental investigations by Sperry and his associates. The subjects, for reasons of pathology, had to undergo surgical separation of the corpus callosum, the large set of association fibers that connects the two hemispheres. Such subjects may be said, literally, to have two separate brains rather than two connected cerebral hemispheres.

Although cerebral dominance for language is usually lateralized in the left hemisphere, for some individuals the expression of preference involved with the intake and motor production of language may be mixed or dissociated. Thus, even for persons who are clearly right-handed, left-eyedness can be readily demonstrated in some instances. For left-handed persons, dissociation is more frequent. A majority of left-handed persons are also left-cerebral dominant for language.[2]

TABLE 2–1
Difference in Percentage of Patients without Injury Before 2
Years of Age and with Aphasia after Operation on the
Left and Right Hemispheres

Hand	Left Hemisphere			Right Hemisphere			Significance of Difference
	Total No.	No. with Aphasia	Percent	Total No.	No. with Aphasia	Percent	
R[a]	157	115	73.2	196	1	0.5	< 0.001
L[b]	18	13	72.2	15	1	6.7	< 0.001
Total	175	128	73.1	211	2	0.9	< 0.001

[a]Including predominantly right.
[b]Including predominantly left.
From Penfield, W., and Roberts, L. *Speech and Brain Mechanisms*, Princeton, N. J.: Princeton University Press, 1959, Table VI B, p. 93. Copyright © 1959 by Princeton University Press.

In the discussion that follows we shall review some of the observations and research findings since World War II on localization of language function and the relation and implications of cerebral dominance to laterality preferences.

Penfield and Roberts (1959, p. 102) reported on 522 patients who were operated on for treatment of focal cerebral seizure. These cases were reviewed from evidence of handedness and evidence of aphasia after surgery. They conclude: "With exclusion of cases of cerebral injury prior to the age of two years, there is no difference in the frequency of aphasia after operation on the left hemisphere between the left- and right-handed." Table 2–1, from Penfield

---

[2] Later we shall consider in some detail the relationship of cerebral dominance to language functions for subgroups of left-handed persons.

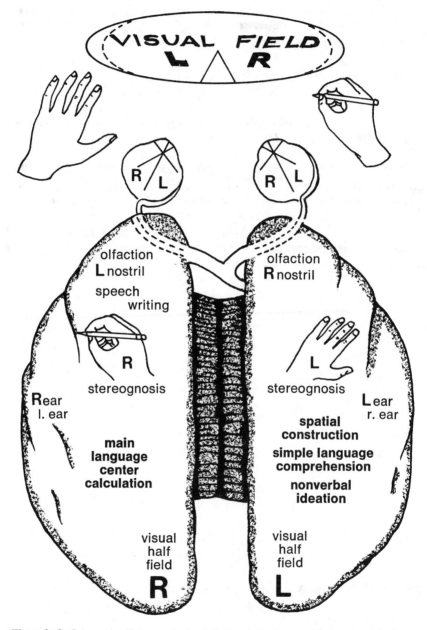

Figure 2–2. Schematic diagram of visual fields, optic tracts, and associated brain areas, showing left and right lateralization in man. (From Sperry, R. W., Perceptual and reading disorders. In *Early Experience and Visual Information Processing in Perceptual and Reading Disorders*, Publication ISBN 0-309-01765-3, Committee on Brain Sciences, Division of Medical Sciences, National Academy of Sciences–National Research Council, Washington, D.C., 1970.)

and Roberts, summarizes the observations for patients whose injuries were incurred after 2 years of age.

On the basis of a study of 225 World War II patients with head-penetrating wounds which were associated with aphasia, Russell and Espir (1961, p. 170) concluded that, with rare exceptions, wounds causing aphasia are almost always on the *left* cerebral hemisphere. "Left-cerebral dominance is therefore almost invariable, but the reasons for this are not clear."

Osgood and Miron (1963, p. 49) come to a similar conclusion. They say: "There now seems to be no question that there is 'localization' of language functions in the gross sense that one hemisphere, usually the left, is dominant. Aphasia is only rarely associated with lesions in the right hemisphere." Similar observations are reported by Goodglass and Quadfasel (1954), Ettlinger, Jackson, and Zangwill (1956), and Hecaen and Angelergues (1964). An excellent review of this subject may be found in the contribution by Milner, Branch, and Rasmussen (1964) in the symposium on Disorders of Language. Table 2–2 compares the Penfield and Roberts (1959) findings with those of Russell and Espir (1961) and Hecaen and Ajuriaguerra (1964).

The studies we have viewed and cited are on varied populations relative to age, nature of cerebral insult, and language. It is clear that regardless of handedness, aphasic involvements are usually associated with left-cerebral-hemisphere damage. Nevertheless, some investigators report an incidence of up to 10 percent of aphasia in right-handed persons following right-cerebral insult and higher incidence in left-handed patients (Milner *et al.*, 1964, p. 204; Goodglass and Quadfasel, 1954).

LEFT-HANDEDNESS AND APHASIA

Our previous references to studies on the relationship of handedness to cerebral dominance permit us to accept the conclusions of Goodglass and Quadfasel (1954) that there is neither a direction nor necessary relationship between hand preference and cerebral lateralization (dominance) for language. As indicated earlier, right-cerebral dominance is occasionally found in right-handed persons, and left-cerebral dominance occurs more often in left-handed persons than does right dominance (Subirana, 1964). Stated more generally and for the population at large, we may observe that left cerebral dominance occurs more frequently than right-handedness, and, conversely, right-cerebral dominance is much less frequent than left-handedness.[3]

Hecaen and Sauget (1971), in their investigation of cerebral dominance in left-handed subjects, found that left-handed persons do not represent a homogeneous group. Their study enabled them to make distinctions between

[3] We may well find that handedness (preferred hand), however convenient, is not as good an indicator of laterality as preferred ear. Studies of dichotic listening (competitive, simultaneous listening to like signals) suggest that ear preference is a reliable indicator of cerebral dominance for language functions (Curry and Rutherford, 1967; Kimura, 1967; Knox and Boone, 1970, and Shankweiler and Studdert-Kennedy, 1967).

TABLE 2–2
Comparative Data of Three Studies on the Relationship between Handedness and Cerebral Dominance for Language for Persons with Unilateral Brain Lesions

Source	Type of Lesion	Left Lesions				Right Lesions			
		Left Hand		Right Hand		Left Hand		Right Hand	
		n	With Aphasia	n	With Aphasia	n	With Aphasia	n	With Aphasia
Penfield and Roberts (1959)	Varied, surgical excisions	18	13	157	115	15	1	196	1
Russell and Espir (1961)	Head-penetrating wounds	24	9	288	186	24	4	221	3
Hecaen and Ajuriaguerra (1964)	Varied, retro-rolandic	37	22	163	81	22	11	130	0
Total		79	44	608	382	61	16	547	4
Percent			55.7		62.8		26.2		0.7

familial left-handers (persons with left-handed siblings or other left-handed relatives) and others who did not have other left-handed members in their family constellations. Although Hecaen and Sauget consider their observations and conclusions to be tentative because of the small number of subgroups in their investigation,[4] three main points stood out:

1. Familial left-handers appear to have bilateral cerebral representation for language and cognitive functions.

2. Familial left-handed subjects, in contrast with those who are right-handed, appear to have "a less marked intrahemispheric localization of the neurological mechanisms underlying higher cortical functions. In all probability, such relative diffusion of the neuronal structures subserving these abilities is variable and dependent on the particular functions under consideration" (Hecaen and Sauget, 1971, p. 44).

3. "In spite of these differences, the functional hemispheric asymmetry found in right-handed subjects is also found in left-handed subjects, although to a less strong and consistent degree. In left-handers, the pattern of disorganization due to unilateral brain damage includes some features that are generally found after lesions of the opposite hemisphere as well; this is never observed in right-handers" (Hecaen and Sauget, 1971, p. 45).

An added significant observation that is generally supported by other studies (see discussion of prognostic factors for recovery) is that in left-handers there is usually a rapid recovery of defects associated with the lesions.

As a summary statement, Hecaen and Sauget (1971, p. 46) conclude, "we suggest that cerebral ambilaterality is not a characteristic of all left-handers, but only of those who belong to the so-called 'familial' type."

AMBIDEXTERITY

Bilateral (ambidextrous) persons present a small but interesting population. Clinical observations strongly suggest that the *truly ambidextrous*, as distinguished from the ambinondextrous, may have bilateral representation for language functions. The possibility that most left-handed individuals are not too readily distinguished from the bilateral ambidextrous deserves serious consideration. Certainly, most left-handed (sinistral) individuals have more dexterity with their right hands than right-handed (dextral) individuals have with their left hands. With regard to aphasia, the evidence suggests that the ambidextrous may be considered as part of the population of the sinistrals. In general, we accept the conclusion of Milner *et al.* (1964, p. 205): "This suggestion of a considerable margin of safety in the cerebral organization of left-handed and ambidextrous patients again accords well with the notion of a more bilateral representation,

[4] The subject population included 73 left-handed persons, of whom 26 had right-sided lesions and 47 had left-sided lesions, and 487 right-handed subjects, 194 with right-sided lesions and 293 with left-sided lesions. All lesions were verified to be unilateral.

and there may well be considerable individual differences in this respect which find no places in our all-or-none scoring."

Cerebral Control (Dominance) for Nonlanguage Functions

In our discussion thus far we have been careful to use the term *cerebral dominance* in relationship to the functions of language. We have intentionally avoided any suggestion that the left hemisphere, which is usually dominant for language, is also generally dominant for all functions under cerebral control. Similarly, we should not assume that persons who have right-hemisphere dominance for language have overall right-hemisphere dominance for cerebrally controlled functions. The position we take and recommend is that cerebral dominance, or perhaps better, dominant cerebral control, is related to function. There are some functions, such as the appreciation of spatial relationships, which seem to be under right-hemisphere control, at least as judged by the effects of damage to the right cerebral hemisphere (Hecaen, 1967). In broadest terms, we can accept the position that the right hemisphere is usually dominant for nonverbal behavior and the left for verbal behavior. Thus, the kinds of functions that are assessed by the performance items of the Wechsler scales, such as the Wechsler Adult Intelligence Scale, are more likely to show impairment correlated with right-hemisphere damage. Except for language functions, however, the difference in impairment of function is usually not as severe or as clear-cut in relation to hemisphere of damage. Nevertheless, we can still accept the tentative conclusion of Meyer (1961) that "the most consistent claims are that patients with the left-hemisphere lesions (dominant side) are relatively poor at verbal tasks, while those with right-sided lesions . . . are relatively poor at practical tasks. . . ." We need to appreciate that effects of brain damage are not invariable. Further, the implications of brain damage are not manifest in precisely the same way in each individual. Assumptions that hold for experimental populations as a whole may not hold for each individual within the population. Reitan's (1966) review of problems relating to psychological correlates of brain lesions is recommended reading for aphasiologists. Reitan (1955), Heilbrun (1956), Meyer (1961), Teuber (1962), and Weinstein (1962) have significant studies on interhemispheric differences in functions resulting from brain lesion.

Right-Brain Damage and Higher Intellectual Functions

Before concluding the discussion on the differential roles of the two cerebral hemispheres, we should like to direct attention to the possibility that right-brain damage may have implications for language functioning when such functioning is related to high-level intellectual processes.[5]

In an unpublished study the author compared a group of 46 adults with right-brain damage with a group of 46 non-brain-damaged adults. The groups were matched on the basis of age and number of years of formal education. The age range of the subjects was from 18 to 66 years. All were literate in English on at least the eighth-grade school level. All cases were cleared for psychiatric manifestations and aphasic involvements. The subjects were administered a test battery of vocabulary and sentence-completion items of the Stanford-Binet (Terman-Merrill Revision, Form L) and a specially adapted series of vocabulary items from the Institute of Educational Research Test Inventory (CAVD). These test items permitted comparisons of productive and recognition vocabularies and the ability to complete sentences (presented incomplete written formulations) with either concrete or relatively abstract words. It was also possible to make comparisons between sentences that provide a multiple-choice opportunity for selection and completion and sentences for which no such choice was provided. In general, the results indicated a higher level of performance for the control (non-brain-damaged) subjects than for the experimental (right-brain-damaged) group. Small and not statistically significant differences were found for the number of correct "definitions" on the vocabulary items (25.5 compared with 24.7). A larger and significant difference was found on 15 selected vocabulary items from the CAVD battery (visual recognition vocabulary). The control subjects had an average of 11.6 correct choices compared with 10.2 for the brain-damaged subjects. The greatest differences, and from our point of view those with the most important implications, were found for the sentence-completion items. On the Minkus sentences of the Stanford-Binet test, which require the use of abstract words for correct completion, the control subjects completed an average of 2.3 sentences correctly compared with an average of 1.4 sentences for the brain-damaged subjects. Similar findings were obtained for the CAVD sentences, for both the no-choice and multiple-choice items. For the no-choice or open-end sentences, the control subjects had an average of 10.4 correct completions compared with 9.0 for the brain-damaged (experimental group). For the multiple-choice items, the controls had an average of 11.5 correct completions compared with 9.6 for the experimental group. The differences between groups for both sentence items is statistically significant (0.05 and 0.01 levels, respectively). Of added interest is the finding that larger differences were found for sentence completion when abstract rather than

---

[5] Detailed considerations of the functional differences between the cerebral hemisphere may be found in Mountcastle, V. B., ed., *Interhemispheric Relations and Cerebral Dominance*, Baltimore: Johns Hopkins Press, 1962. *Brain Mechanisms Underlying Speech and Language* (Millikan, C. H., and Darley, F. L., eds., New York: Grune & Stratton, 1967, is recommended reading for positions on the nature of language and cerebral functioning.

concrete words were required. This difference was found for both open-end and multiple-choice sentences.[6]

There are several possible interpretations of these findings. One interpretation might be involved with superior or extraordinary language functions, particularly as such functions call upon the ability of the individual to deal with (comprehend) relatively abstract and established language formulations to which he must respond. An alternate interpretation is that, in a nonspecific way, the right hemisphere contributes to all intellectual functions. Damage impairs and reduces the level of contribution. Another possible interpretation is that any cerebral damage reduces intellectual functioning with implications for language in less specific and certainly less apparent ways than patent aphasic involvements.

A general implication of our findings is made by Critchley (1970, p. 365):

Perhaps we still tend to overlook the possible role of the right half of the brain to the faculty of speech. Some aphasiologists . . . are beginning to suspect that appropriate testing of a sufficiently searching character might well elicit defects within the sphere of language which are too subtle for ordinary routine techniques to bring to light. This idea may be accepted as yet another example of minimal dysphasia. Neuropsychologists need to pay closer attention to the linguistic capacities and incapacities of right-handed victims of right-brain disease.

Critchley notes several functions which are affected by right-brain damage. These include dysarthrias, creative literary work, word-finding difficulties, and difficulties in the full understanding of pictorial material. So, we may conclude either that right-brain-damaged persons may suffer from "latent aphasia" (Boller, 1968) or that right-cerebral damage, in a nonspecific way, impairs language skills at a level at which they are associated with higher abstract mental processes. Specific to language disorders, Critchley (1970, p. 367), suggests that our notion of aphasia "may be extended so as to embrace a conception of a spectrum of speech-defect depending upon the intrinsic difficulty of the test situation. Such a continuum may be regarded as ranging from the 'normal' subject at one extreme, through a linguistic pattern of non-dominant and hemisphere-defect, to culminate at the other limit, in a frank aphasia from disease of the dominant half of the brain."

[6] The difference between the groups for the no-choice sentences requiring abstract words for completion had a t value of 1.99, significant at the 0.05 level. The difference between the groups for the sentences calling for concrete words had a t value of 1.67 and was below the 0.05 level for statistical significance. The differences, however, were in the same direction. An extension of this study was published in *Language and Speech* (Eisenson, 1962).

Anatomical Differences of the Hemispheres

It is clear from our discussion thus far that functionally, or perhaps better dysfunctionally, as far as language is concerned, man's two cerebral hemispheres are different. Are there any anatomical differences that may explain or at least be correlated with these functional differences? Von Bonin (1962, p. 6) sums up the available evidence by these observations:

> The left hemisphere has a slightly greater specific gravity than the right one. This would mean that there is a little more cortex on the left side. That fits in with the fact that the Sylvian fissure is a little bit longer, that the insula is longer and higher on the left side, that there is a doubling of the sulcus cinguli more frequently on the left side, and that the calcarine fissure has a hook more often on the left than on the right side.
>
> But all these morphological differences are, after all, quite small. How to correlate these with the astonishing differences in function, such as the speech function on the left side, is an entirely different question, and one that I am unable to answer.

Geschwind and Levitsky (1968), on the basis of postmortem findings of 100 adult brains, report marked anatomical asymmetries between the upper surfaces of the human right and left temporal lobes. Of special significance to us is that the differences involve an area of the brain which includes the primary auditory cortex and the auditory association cortex. Lesions in this area are etiologically associated with auditory (classical Wernicke's) aphasia.

Cerebral Localization for Language Functions

Information on cerebral localization for language functions has come to us by way of the pathology of dysfunction. Positive statements about localization are still assumptions and inferences. The underlying implications in the use of the term *localization of function* are that a healthy state, and so presumably normal functioning of a particular area of a brain, is essential to the execution of a particular function in a manner deemed normal. With regard to language, the assumption and implication for localization is that there are areas of the brain which are essential for particular functions, such as articulation, speech perception, reading, and writing.

We shall avoid any detailed presentation, except for a brief historical review, of positions before World War II relative to localization of function. There are still some "strict" or fine localizationists who accept the position exemplified by Nielsen (1947) as to specific correlations between relatively small areas of the brain and related functions. On the other hand, the position that all areas of the brain have equipotentiality for language function does not seem tenable.

EARLY LOCALIZATIONISTS

Present-day localization theory relative to aphasic disturbances had its origin in the presentation by *Paul Broca* of two papers in Paris in 1861.[7] At first Broca postulated that a lesion in the second or third frontal convolution was associated with aphasia of the motor (expressive) type. Later, Broca fixed the third convolution as the site of the lesion associated with expressive (spoken) disturbances of language function. This is the area which is included in Brodmann area 44.[8]

Other names prominent among the early localizationists and "diagram makers" are Bastian and Wernicke. Bastian (1887) went beyond Broca and localized areas for auditory and visual functions. Wernicke (1874) located and described an auditory center in the temporal convolution.

TWENTIETH-CENTURY LOCALIZATIONISTS

J. M. Nielsen is foremost among twentieth-century exponents of strict localization of cerebral functions. He is, however, not as rigid and pedantic a localizationist as Henschen. Nielsen (1941, p. 227), for example, admits: "Anatomy and physiology are still incompletely coordinated so far as the cerebral cortex is concerned." Although aware that " ... logic would seem to stipulate that each area of a certain structure must have a function differing from that of other areas with different structures ... ," Nielsen (1941, p. 229) observes that certain areas of the brain (e.g., area 19 of Brodmann) " ... [are] certainly divided physiologically." Nielsen (1941, Chap. 10) suggests several explanations for the apparent inconsistencies in localization theory. These include (1) the possibility that " ... even though the distribution of the cortical cells is the same throughout an anatomic area, the organization of the cells may be different in various portions of the same area," (2) neurons establish different connections with use in order to subserve different purposes in the more minute and precise sense, and (3) an area can serve one purpose as a result of one method of training and another purpose as a result of different training.

Despite these reservations, Nielsen accepts localization theory in a comparatively strict sense both in his textbook (1941) and in his more specialized book on disturbances related to aphasia (1947). He lists and describes specific cortical areas and specific dysfunctions which are associated with lesions in these areas.

---

[7] An English translation of the original Broca article by J. Kann appeared in the *Journal of Speech Hearing Disorders*, 1950, 15, 16–20.

[8] Brodmann divided and "diagrammed" the human cerebral cortex into areas according to cellular distribution. These have come to be known as Brodmann's cytoarchitectonic areas.

Henschen, whose text on clinical pathology is referred to by Nielsen (1941, p. 306) as "a priceless classic," allowed for no leeway in his structural viewpoint. On the basis of 60 of his own cases and 1500 taken from the literature, Henschen (1926) worked out what he considered to be unfailing one-to-one relationships between defective cortical area and linguistic disturbance. He also specified centers for arithmetic and music.

OPPOSITION TO STRICT LOCALIZATION

Opposition to the concept of strict localization of language function in specific cortical areas was not absent during the time of Broca and his followers. *J. Hughlings Jackson*, a chronological contemporary of Broca, was an early and outspoken opponent of narrow and rigid concepts of localization. Jackson emphasized the viewpoint that a knowledge of pathological conditions which disturb and impair language function does not provide information *per se* as to how the function is normally controlled in the healthy individual. Further, Jackson insisted that aphasic disturbances could not be understood without a knowledge of the patient who suffered the disturbances. He stressed the importance of observing the live aphasic patient rather than studying the autopsy findings of those who did not survive.

Jackson (1915 and 1931) did not deny that Broca's area was frequently damaged in patients who suffered from aphasic disturbances, especially when motor speech involvements were manifest. He refused, however, to localize language function in Broca's area alone, and stressed the notion that language was a psychological rather than a physiological function. Jackson emphasized that for language as well as for other intellectual functions the brain operates as a functional unit.

The concept that a destructive lesion can never be responsible for positive symptoms, and the much-quoted principle that "to locate the damage which destroys speech and to locate speech are two different things," were stressed by Jackson. Destruction, Jackson held, produces negative symptoms. Positive symptoms associated with destructions of cortical tissue are to be attributed to the effects of the released activity of the lower centers.

Among other contemporaries of Broca who opposed strict localization were Pierre Marie in France, Arnold Pick in Czechoslovakia, and W. R. Gowers in England. All three agreed with Jackson that while localized lesions could not be held responsible for language and speech disturbances, lesions in certain cortical areas can more readily disturb speech than can lesions in other areas.

The English neurologist *Henry Head* (1926) continued along the clinical, psychological paths of Hughlings Jackson. Head pointed out that the capacity to use language in any form is the result of physiological activities of certain parts of the brain cortex. All forms of language usage develop from the " . . . simple

acts of speaking and comprehension of spoken words." Aphasia is defined as
". . . a disorder of symbolic formulation and expression." Symbolic formulation
and expression is characterized as a mode of behavior in which some verbal or
nonverbal symbol plays a part between the initiation and the execution of the
act. Destruction of brain tissue is likely to result in an interference of normal
fulfillment of some specific forms of behavior. The reaction which follows is an
expression of the organism as a whole to the new situation.

Although Head emphasized the function of the brain as a whole, he observed
that, in the event of pathology, certain types of aphasic language dysfunction
can probably be associated with lesions in broadly outlined areas of the brain.
For example, impairments in the capacity to understand the deeper significance
of words and the wider meaning of a sentence as a whole (semantic aphasia)
seem to be associated with lesions of the supramarginal gyrus. Similarly, Head
postulated other likely areas of lesion associated with such subtypes of aphasia
as the verbal, syntactical, and nominal. Head emphasized that aphasic disturbances are not discrete and noted that for the aphasic person there is a
generalized defect in intellectual expression which requires symbolic formulation. The degree of defect is likely to be related directly to the propositional
level of the expression.

MODIFIED LOCALIZATION THEORY

Psychological influences, especially those of Gestalt psychology and the
neuropsychology of Karl Lashley (1958) have had considerable impact on
concepts of cerebral function and cerebral localization. Clinical observations of
neurologists and neuroanatomists which were the bases for localization theory
up to the first quarter of the twentieth century have had to give way or at least
be reconciled with new approaches and techniques for making and recording
observations and the treatment of data gathered on live patients as well as from
postmortem studies. In addition, the interests of linguists, psycholinguists, and
psychologists in the problems of language and language impairment have resulted
in contributions and new ways of viewing and understanding language and
associated higher mental processes as related to cerebral function.

As a result of their clinical and psychological study emphasizing standardized
testing procedures, *T. Weisenburg*, a neurologist, and *K. McBride*, a psychologist,
arrived at a comparatively moderate position with regard to cerebral localization
of function. They accepted relatively fixed localization for such motor and
sensory functions as motion, vision, hearing, and smell. With regard to
intellectual functions such as language usage, however, they said (1935,
p. 467): " . . . it is impossible to localize language. In the majority of individuals
language permeates the thought processes to such an extent that the one cannot
be separated from the other; and for the present at least it is impossible to give
an adequate explanation of intelligence, much less to localize it. That it is the
result of the activity of the entire brain, however, there is no doubt."

Weisenburg and McBride did not deny that lesions in certain parts of the brain are more likely to be associated with aphasic disturbances than are lesions elsewhere. Although they avoided specific localization, they observed that (1935, p. 468): " . . . in about 95 percent of the cases the lesion must be in the dominant hemisphere; and that it must implicate the anterior and to a less extent the posterior part of the brain within certain limits, including the lower portion of the pre-central convolution and probably the adjoining part of the frontal lobe, the lower portion of the parietal lobe, the upper part of the temporal lobe, and the anterior part of the occipital."

Weisenburg and McBride, as we have noted, divided their patients into four clinical types on the basis of predominant linguistic disturbances. For patients whose greatest difficulty is in expression, they found the lesion to be in the anterior or motor part of the brain; for patients with predominantly receptive (comprehension) difficulty, they found the posterior part of the brain to be more involved than in the expressive group, and a likelihood that the anterior part of the brain was also involved, but less severely than for the expressive patients. Patients with almost equal amounts of expressive and receptive difficulties were found to have more extensive and more permanent involvements of both anterior and posterior parts of the brain. Amnesic patients—those whose difficulty was in recall of names with relatively good ability to recognize the names not able to be recalled—were found to have no definitely localizable lesions.

Although *Kurt Goldstein* is likely to be regarded as an antilocalizationist, his clinical observations and many of his writings tend to contradict this opinion. Geschwind (1964), writing about Goldstein's position, observes: "His contribution as a localizer in the classical sense is in fact highly significant although rarely taught." Goldstein's position rejected narrow classification and the inadequacies of the rigid classical schemes. Among Goldstein's stated objections to classical (strict and rigid) localization theory are the following (1948, p. 47):

The so-called classic theory of localization is based mainly on the material gained from postmortems. It should be observed that the objections against the theory stem first from a more careful consideration of the pathologic-anatomic data. There are so-called negative cases: on the one hand, absence of symptoms in a lesion affecting an area which was considered characteristic of this locality; on the other hand, appearance of symptoms without the presence of a correspondingly localized lesion.

Goldstein, however, did more than present a negative attitude toward localization. He discussed in his writings some of the positive factors that made strict localization theory difficult for him to entertain (1948, p. 48): "It is very difficult, indeed, to evaluate the degree of damage; it is not only dependent on the direct destruction of the nerve cells but also on the condition of the glia, blood vessels, etc. Further, we have no idea of the relationship between a definite anatomic condition and a specific performance. *We are far from being able to decide whether the preserved tissue is still functioning sufficiently to allow for a certain performance or not.*"

On the question of the inconsistency of symptoms as related to localized brain injury, Goldstein said (1948, p. 48): "Whether certain symptoms will appear or not on account of a local injury certainly depends on many factors other than locality; i.e., on the nature of the disease process, on the damage of all or only some structures of the cortex, on the condition of the rest of the brain, on individual differences in cooperation of both hemispheres, . . . on the state of circulation in general, on the functional reactions of the organism to the defect . . . on the psycho-physical constitution of the personality, etc."

An important point relative to the effects of a lesion is made by Goldstein. He points out: "A lesion of a special locality in different cases may vary very much regarding the degree to which the substratum in general is affected, and particularly its different striata. Such a selective character of the process may be of paramount significance for the development of symptoms" (1948, pp. 47–48).

Goldstein's interpretation of localization is best understood in terms of Gestalt psychology, which emphasizes the function of the organism as a whole and the effects of a specific performance only as it is related to the organism functioning as a whole. With this in mind, it becomes possible to appreciate Goldstein's concept of cortical localization: " . . . *each performance is due to the function of the total organism in which the brain plays a particular role.* In each performance, the whole cortex is in activity, but the excitation in the cortex is not the same throughout" (1948, p. 50).

From the above, it would appear that Goldstein did not reject cortical localization. Actually, he redefined localization in terms which were consistent with his own thinking. For Goldstein, localization is acceptable only insofar as an individual performance is considered. The role of a given cortical area is significant according to the particular influence it exerts on the excitation of the cortex as a whole, and so as to the total dynamic process which occurs as a result of the functioning of the entire nervous system.

With this concept of localization, Goldstein was able to accept and define symptom complexes as being related to definite areas. Indeed, for practical purposes, Goldstein and Weisenburg and McBride are in agreement. Goldstein accepted the likelihood that a motor (expressive) language disturbance will usually be correctly localized in the expanded Broca's region of the left hemisphere and that sensory (receptive) disturbances will usually be correctly located in the temporal lobes.

CONTEMPORARY CONCEPTS OF LOCALIZATION OF CEREBRAL FUNCTIONS

A. R. Luria's approach to localization of function, although rooted in Pavlovian neurophysiology, often strikingly resembles Kurt Goldstein's. In his *Higher Cortical Functions in Man* (1966, p. 35) Luria writes: "We therefore suggest that *the material basis of the higher nervous processes is the brain as a whole* but that *the brain is a highly differentiated system whose parts are responsible for different aspects of the unified whole.*"

Luria is emphatic that his view of the organization of higher mental functions is opposed both to narrow localization and equipotentialism for brain function. He accepts Vygotsky's position that (Luria, 1966, p. 36): "Higher mental functions may exist only as a result of interaction between the highly differentiated brain structures and that individually these structures make their own specific contributions to the dynamic whole and play their own roles in the functional system."

Basic to the understanding of Luria's concept of localization of cortical function is the Pavlovian position that holds that (Luria, 1966, pp. 97–98):

Sensation incorporates the process of analysis of signals while they are still in the first stages of arrival. . . . According to this view, from the very beginning the sensory cortical divisions participate in the analysis and integration of complex, not elementary, signals. The units of any sensory process (including hearing) are not only acts of reception of individual signals, measurable in terms of thresholds of sensation, but also acts of complex analysis and integration of signals, measurable in units of comparison and discrimination. The sensory divisions of the cortex are the apparatuses responsible for this analysis, and indications of a lesion of these apparatuses are to be found, not so much in a lowering of the acuity of the sensations, as in a disturbance of the analytic-synthetic function.

Figure 2–3 gives Luria's conception of four cortical zones for the analytic systems.

The functions of the left temporal cortex and especially of the superior temporal gyrus (the secondary divisions of the auditory cortex), its contribution to the perception of sound as well as to the motor aspects of speech, and to aphasic involvements in the event of pathology, are explained by Luria as follows (Luria, 1966, p. 101):

All that has been said regarding the structure of the sounds of a language and regarding the hearing of speech is of decisive importance to the understanding of the nature of the work that must be done by the *secondary divisions of the auditory cortex of the left hemisphere*, those divisions that . . . are closely associated with the cortical apparatuses of kinesthetic (articulatory) analysis.

The work of these divisions consists of the *analysis* and *integration of the sound flow by identification of the phonemic signs of the objective system of the language*. This work must be carried out with the very close participation of articulatory acts which . . . constitute the efferent link for the perception of the sounds of speech. It consists of differentiating the significant, phonemic signs of the spoken sounds, inhibiting the unessential, nonphonemic signs, and comparing the perceived sound complexes on this phonemic basis.

The vulnerability of the left temporal cortex and its implications for aphasic involvement may be appreciated by Luria's statement that "a lesion of these cortical divisions, therefore, must cause, not the simple loss of acuity of hearing,

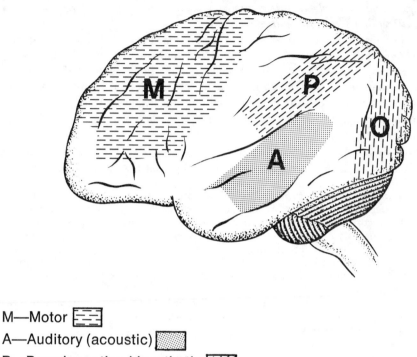

M—Motor
A—Auditory (acoustic)
P—Proprioceptive-kinesthetic
O—Optic-visual

Figure 2–3. Representation of four analytic centers essential for speech (after Luria).

but the disintegration of the whole complex structure of the analytic-synthetic activity underlying the process of the systematization of speech experience" (1966, p. 103).

The implication of lesions of the superior temporal region of the left hemisphere for aphasic involvements has been appreciated since Wernicke's time. The concept of impairment of phonemic analysis and the relationship of speech-sound discrimination to articulation is stressed by Luria as well as by investigators in the Haskins Laboratory (Liberman, Cooper, Harris, and MacNeilage, 1963). Figure 2–4 presents Luria's data on the site of lesion for 800 patients who presented symptoms of impairment for phonemic discrimination.

A summary of Luria's concept of cortical localization for language functions, and for aphasic disturbances, is presented in Table 2–3.

Hecaen and Angelergues (1964) analyzed data based on observations of 214 right-handed patients who had incurred lesions of the left hemisphere. The lesions were varied but were predominantly of tumor and traumatic origin. All of the observations were verified either by postmortem examination or by surgery. Their data were analyzed for intensity of aphasic symptoms, type of symptoms, and site of lesion. They note that in relation to location and extent of lesion, "only isolated temporal lesions and, to a lesser degree, parietal lesions provoke a high average of aphasic symptoms." The greatest intensity of aphasic symptoms was attained in massive lesions involving the fronto-parietal-temporal and parieto-temporal-occipital regions. Figure 2–5 presents a diagrammatic representation of type of aphasic disturbance in relation to site of lesion. It may be noted that with the exception of an absence of articulatory disturbances for lesions of the posterior region, a variety of disturbances may be associated with lesions in the three crucial areas of the cortex. We should also note the high degree of disturbances for verbal comprehension associated with lesions of the temporal and parietal regions.

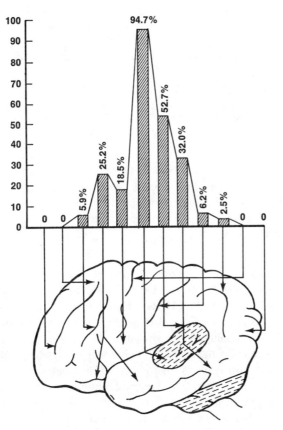

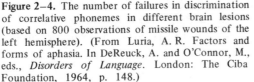

Figure 2–4. The number of failures in discrimination of correlative phonemes in different brain lesions (based on 800 observations of missile wounds of the left hemisphere). (From Luria, A. R. Factors and forms of aphasia. In DeReuck, A. and O'Connor, M., eds., *Disorders of Language*. London: The Ciba Foundation, 1964, p. 148.)

TABLE 2–3
Classification of Types of Aphasia

Aphasia	Disturbed Function	Speech Defect	Brain Lesion[a]
1. Sensory	Acoustic analysis	Phonemes	Posterior-temporal
2. Amnestic	Retention of audio-speech traces	Repetition of series	Centro-temporal
3. Afferent	Kinesthetic analysis of speech movements	Articulemes	Posterior motor speech area
4. Efferent	Kinetic analysis of successive speech movements	Articulation	Anterior motor speech area
5. Semantic	Simultaneous organization of speech components	Logico-grammatical	Temporo-parietal
6. Dynamic	"Inner speech"	Lack of spontaneity for active propositionalizing	Frontal

[a]Each zone of the cerebral cortex makes a specific contribution; damage to any zone impairs functions of all zones and the brain cortex as a whole.
From Luria, A. R., ".Factors and Forms of Aphasia," in DeReuck, A., and O'Connor, M., eds., *Disorders of Language*. London: The Ciba Foundation,1964, pp. 143–167.

From our discussion of the work of Luria and Hecaen, it becomes apparent that cerebral localization for language functions has by no means been abandoned. The approaches represented by these investigators provide a basis for a new way to view and interpret aphasic symptoms and to correlate symptoms with determined lesions.

The investigations by *Geschwind* and his associates should be viewed in the light of the possibilities for "finer" localization than was the trend in the period immediately after World War II. Geschwind (1967) studied naming errors (anomia) which occurred on "confrontation," in situations in which a patient had difficulties in naming things shown to him rather than in free-flowing, spontaneous speech. On the basis of his observations Geschwind differentiated a group of patients with lesions in the region of the dominant angular gyrus who were characterized as having *classic anomia* (failure to produce a response, verbal paraphasias, circumlocutions, etc., but ability to choose correct name if presented to patient) from a second anomic group that was characterized by an inability to match a stimulus to its spoken name. The lesions for this group are those which isolate or produce *disconnections of sensory regions* from the speech area, "probably from the left angular gyrus in particular."

Quite a different position from Geschwind's is taken by *K. Pribram* (1971, p. 374), who argues that:

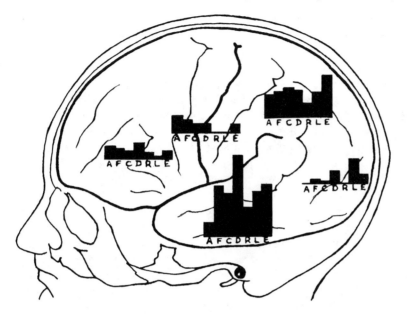

Figure 2–5. Diagrammatic representation of the average degree of disturbance of various language modalities which occurs when there is an isolated lesion of various lobes (front, rolandic, parietal, temporal, and occipital).

A: Articulatory disturbances
B: Difficulties in the fluency of speech
C: Disturbances of verbal communication
D: Disturbances of naming
R: Disturbances of repetition
L: Disturbances in reading
E: Disturbances of writing

(From Hecaen, H., and Angelergues, R., Localization of symptoms in aphasia. In DeReuck, A. and O'Connor, M., eds., *Disorders of Language*. London: The Ciba Foundation, 1964, pp. 223–246.)

Man's brain brings sign and symbol together in propositional language. Evidence from language disturbances produced by brain lesions and stimulation suggests that linguistic acts derive from the operations of a multifaceted cortico-subcortical system in which junctional patterns derived from sensory input have unusually ready access, through an overlap of connections, to those involved in motor mechanisms. The existence of this brain system makes possible propositions: communications about the truth, the symbolic rightness or wrongness, of significant perceptions. The accrual of such propositional communications constitutes a human language.

Pribram's statement represents his philosophy of the nature of language as well as of the pathologies of language represented in aphasic involvements. Pribram emphasizes the importance of *systems within the hemisphere*, and directs attention to his position that aphasias are a result of breakdowns between so-called lower centers in the subcortex and those in the cortex. He is opposed to the concept that aphasic involvements are the likely result of cortico-cortical connections. Pribram cites evidence that in nonhuman primates "the primary functional connections of the cerebral cortex are subcortical rather than cortico-cortical" (Pribram, 1971, p. 360). Nevertheless, he presents diagrams that indicate that in cases of marked aphasia, lesions of the frontal area of the brain produce expressive impairments while lesions of the posterior portions of the brain are likely to produce expressive and receptive impairment. Pribram notes (p. 359) that "the complexity of aphasic disorders tends to be greater with lesions involving posterior portions of the dominant hemisphere."

Geschwind's and Pribram's positions were selected as representative of the philosophies of contemporary neurologists and neurological scientists who have available to them new techniques and approaches for studying the effects of cerebral lesions. These were not available to neuropathologists in the late nineteenth century and the first half of this century. Despite the new and sophisticated approaches, we still need to exercise reserve and caution about definitive statements relative to the immediate and residual effects of brain lesion on language functioning and associated impairments. Statements made for groups of individuals do not necessarily apply to a given individual. The aphasic, as a person and a personality, continues to deserve individual study to assess the specific effects brain damage will have on him. Some of these possible effects will be considered in the next two chapters.

References

Bastian, H. C. 1887. On different kinds of aphasia, with special reference to their classification and ultimate pathology. *British Medical Journal*, 2, 931–936, 985–990.

Boller, F. 1968. Latent aphasia: Right and left "nonaphasic" patients compared. *Cortex*, 4:3, 245–256.

Critchley, M. 1970. *Aphasiology*. London: Edward Arnold.

Curry, F. K. W., and Rutherford, D. R. 1967. Recognition and recall of dichotically presented verbal stimuli by right- and left-handed persons. *Neuropsychologia*, 5, 119–125.

Eisenson, J. 1962. Language and intellectual modifications associated with right cerebral damage. *Language and Speech*, 5:2, 49–53.

Ettlinger, G., Jackson, C., and Zangwill, O. 1956. Cerebral dominance in sinistrals. *Brain*, 79, 569–588.

Geschwind, N. 1964. The paradoxical position of K. Goldstein in the history of aphasia. *Cortex*, 1:2, 214–224.

———. 1967. The varieties of naming errors. *Cortex*, 3:1, 97–112.

Geschwind, N., and Levitsky, W. 1968. Human brain: Left-right asymmetries in temporal speech region. *Science*, 161, 186–187.

Goldstein, K. 1948. *Language and Language Disturbances*. New York: Grune & Stratton.

Goodglass, H., and Quadfasel, F. 1954. Language laterality in left-handed aphasics. *Brain*, 77, 521–548.

Head, H. 1926. *Aphasia and Kindred Disorders of Speech* (2 vols.). New York: Cambridge University Press and Macmillan. Reprinted by Hafner Publishing Co., New York, 1963.

Hecaen, H. 1967. Brain mechanisms suggested by studies of parietal lobes. In *Brain Mechanisms Underlying Speech and Language*, Millikan, C., and Darley, F., eds. New York: Grune & Stratton, pp. 146–166.

Hecaen, H., and Ajuriaguerra, J. 1964. *Left-handedness.* New York: Grune & Stratton.

Hecaen, H., and Angelergues, R. 1964. Localization of symptoms in aphasia. In *Disorders of Language*, DeReuck, A., and O'Connor, M., eds. London: J. & A. Churchill, pp. 223–246.

Hecaen, H., and Sauget, J. 1971. Cerebral dominance in left-handed subjects. *Cortex* 7:1, 19–48.

Heilbrun, A. 1956. Psychological test performance as a function of lateral localization of cerebral lesion. *Journal of Comparative Physiology and Psychology*, 49, 10–14.

Henschen, S. 1926. On the function of the right hemisphere of the brain in relation to the left in speech, music, and calculation. *Brain*, 49, 110–123.

Jackson, J. H. 1915. Selected writings of J. Hughlings Jackson, Head, H., ed. *Brain*, 38, 1–90.

———. 1931. *Selected Writings of J. Hughlings Jackson*, Taylor, G., ed. London: Hodder and Stoughton.

Kimura, D. 1967. Functional asymmetry of the brain in dichotic listening. *Cortex*, 3:2, 163–168.

Knox, A. W., and Boone, D. R. 1970. Auditory laterality and tested handedness. *Cortex*, 6:2, 164–173.

Lashley, K. 1958. Cerebral organization and behavior in the brain and human behavior. *Proceedings for Association in Research in Nervous and Mental Disease*, 36, 1–18.

Liberman, A., Cooper, F., Harris, K., and MacNeilage, P. 1963. A motor theory of speech perception. *Journal of the Acoustical Society of America*, 35, 1114.

Luria, A. 1964a. Neuropsychology in the local diagnosis of the brain damage. *Cortex*, 1:1, 3–18.

———. 1964b. Factors and forms of aphasia. In *Disorders of Language*, DeReuck, A., and O'Connor, M., eds. London: J. & A. Churchill, pp. 143–167.

———. 1966. *Higher Cortical Functions in Man.* New York: Basic Books.

Meyer, V. 1961. Psychological effects of brain damage. In *Handbook of Abnormal Psychology*, Eysenck, W., ed. New York: Basic Books, pp. 529–565.

Millikan, C. H., and Darley, F. L., eds. 1967. *Brain Mechanisms Underlying Speech and Language.* New York: Grune & Stratton.

Milner, B., Branch, C., and Rasmussen, T. 1964. Observations on cerebral dominance. In *Disorders of Language*, DeReuck, A., and O'Connor, M., eds. London: J. & A. Churchill, pp. 200–222.

Mountcastle, V. B., ed. 1962. *Interhemispheric Relations and Cerebral Dominance.* Baltimore: Johns Hopkins Press.

Nielsen, J. 1941. *A Textbook of Clinical Neurology.* New York: Paul Hoeber.

———. 1947. *Agnosia, Apraxia, Aphasia*, 2nd ed. New York: Paul Hoeber.

Osgood, C., and Miron, M., eds. 1963. *Approaches to the Study of Aphasia.* Urbana: University of Illinois Press.

Penfield, W., and Roberts, L. 1959. *Speech and Brain Mechanisms.* Princeton, N. J.: Princeton University Press.

Pribram, K. H. 1971. *Languages of the Brain.* Englewood Cliffs, N. J.: Prentice-Hall, Inc.

Reitan, R. 1955. Certain differential effects of left and right cerebral lesions in human adults. *Journal of Comparative Physiology and Psychology*, 6, 474–477.

———. 1966. Problems and prospects in studying the psychological correlates of brain lesions. *Cortex*, 2:1, 127–154.

Russell, W., and Espir, M. 1961. *Traumatic Aphasia.* London: Oxford University Press.

Shankweiler, D., and Studdert-Kennedy, M. 1967. Identification of consonants and vowels presented to left and right ears. *Quarterly Journal of Experimental Psychology*, 19, 59–63.

Sperry, R. W. 1970. Perception in the absence of neocortical commisures. In *Perception and Its Disorders*. Research Publication. A.R.N.M.D. 48, 123–138.

Subirana, A. 1964. The relationship between handedness and language function. *International Journal of Neurology*, 4, 215–234.

Teuber, H. 1962. Effects of brain wounds implicating right or left hemispheres in man. In *Interhemispheric Relations and Cerebral Dominance*, Mountcastle, V., ed. Baltimore: Johns Hopkins Press, pp. 131–157.

Von Bonin, G. 1962. Anatomical asymmetries of the cerebral hemisphere. In *Interhemispheric Relations and Cerebral Dominance*, Mountcastle, V., ed. Baltimore: Johns Hopkins Press, pp. 1–6.

Weinstein, S. 1962. Differences in effects of brain wounds implicating right or left hemisphere. In *Interhemispheric Relations and Cerebral Dominance*, Mountcastle, V., ed. Baltimore: Johns Hopkins Press, pp. 159–176.

———. 1964. Deficits common with aphasia or lesions of either cerebral hemisphere. *Cortex*, 1:2, 154–169.

Weisenburg, T., and McBride, K. 1935. *Aphasia.* New York: Commonwealth Fund.

Wernicke, C. 1874. The symptom-complex of aphasia. In *Diseases of the Nervous System*, Church, A., ed. New York: Appleton, 1908, pp. 265–324.

3

Correlates of Aphasia I: Intellectual Functioning

If we observe the aphasic patient during the course of his involvement there is little question that we are dealing with an individual who is experiencing rapid and ongoing behavioral changes. For some patients the changes are a direct and immediate reaction to their motor, sensory, and linguistic impairments. For other patients, who have only minimal residual motor and sensory deficits, their linguistic disruptions, their aphasic involvements *per se*, are the fundamental problem to which they must make continuing adjustments during the course of their recovery.

In this chapter and the next we shall review the psychological correlates, the intellectual modifications and behavioral aspects, and the changes in personality that become manifest following brain injury which are often associated with aphasic involvements. Implications for therapy of these concomitants or correlates will also be considered. For many of the factors, the implications will be readily apparent. Later, in Chapter 12, some of the implications will again be reviewed and considered with regard to problems of vocational adjustment.

Intelligence and Intellectual Functioning

Pierre Marie (1906) insisted that persons who incur brain damage associated with aphasia always showed some degree of impairment in language comprehension as well as some degree of intellectual impairment associated with their language deficits. There has been considerable research as well as sophisticated clinical observation since Marie's pronouncement. As of the present time, the key questions are not whether persons with aphasic involvements, taken as a total population, differ from non-brain-damaged peers and from their premorbid selves with regard to intellectual functioning.[1] The key questions, we believe, are related to the implications of brain damage *per se* resulting in the person's need for reorganization of intellectual functioning with a markedly reduced number of cortical cells, and the relationship of the expression of intelligence when language, the usual medium for thought, is impaired. Another related aspect is that brain damage is likely to result in a modification of personality and drive which further impairs the individual's expression of thought and so of functioning, practically, on a level in keeping with his intellectual potential. We believe that this notion of the relationship between intellectual functioning and aphasia was held by Hughlings Jackson, who viewed aphasia as a breakdown of propositional thinking. Jackson (1879) referred to the aphasic patient as being "lame in thinking" but not necessarily on that account deficient in intelligence.

In his view of aphasia as an impairment of symbolic formulation and expression, Henry Head (1926; 1963, p. 211) implies that the aphasic person is deficient in his functional intellectual activity:

By symbolic formulation and expression I understand a mode of behaviour, in which some verbal or other symbol plays a part between the initiation and execution of the act. This comprises many procedures, not usually included under the heading of the use of language, and the functions to be placed within this category must be determined empirically; no definition can be framed to cover all forms of action which may be disturbed at one time or another according to the nature and severity of the case. If clinical experience shows that some particular aspect of behaviour is affected in association with these speech defects, it must be included, although it is not logically implied, in the purely descriptive term "symbolic formulation and expression."

Head elaborated his concept of aphasia as an impairment of symbolic formulation and its implications for practical intellectual functioning as follows (1926; 1963, p. 211):

It is not the "general intellectual capacity" which is primarily affected, but the mechanism by which certain aspects of mental activity are brought into play. Behaviour suffers in a specific manner; an action can be carried out in one way, but not in another. In so far as these processes are necessary for the perfect exercise of mental aptitudes, "general intelligence" undoubtedly suffers. For a

---

[1] By using the term *intellectual functioning* rather than intelligence we are avoiding the implication of intellectual impairment as a nonreversible associate of brain damage. We prefer to take the position that changes in intellectual functioning can be demonstrated but that *under optimal conditions*, however infrequently such conditions may prevail, some individuals can function on a level close to their preaphasic-involvement potential. Experimental investigations and the usual stresses of psychodiagnostic evaluations do not represent optimal conditions for most persons, and certainly do not for persons who have incurred brain damage and associated aphasic involvements.

man who, in the course of general conversation, is unable to express his thoughts, or comprehend the full signficance of words and phrases, cannot move freely in the general field of ideas. If in addition he cannot manipulate numbers with ease, or find his way from one place to another, he will certainly appear to be more stupid than his fellows. Moreover, it must not be forgotten that the intellectual life of civilised man is so greatly dependent on speaking, reading and writing, that any restriction of these powers throws him back upon himself; he shuns company and cannot occupy himself with the newspaper or social intercourse. This inevitably leads to a diminished field of thought and many aphasics gradually deteriorate in mental capacity. Yet closer observation shows that this "want of intelligence" is based primarily on some distinctive defect in a definite form of behaviour.

Weisenburg and McBride (1935) are credited with being the first, and were certainly among the first, to employ standardized tests of intelligence and educational achievement tests to assess aphasic patients for intellectual functioning.[2] The essential findings from the point of view of our present discussion is that the overall performance of some of the aphasic subjects was not significantly distinguishable from that of the non-brain-damaged subjects. However, most of the aphasic subjects did show significant decrements in intellectual functioning on the nonlanguage items of the test battery. Thus, we accept Zangwill's observation (1964, p. 264) with regard to the Weisenburg and McBride findings that "it is noteworthy that most of their patients showed some degree of deterioration in nonlanguage as well as in language performance, suggesting that such intellectual defects as may have been present were not wholly restricted to the linguistic sphere. Indeed, one must assume either that these patients did have a mild degree of overall intellectual loss or else that a number of more specialized intellectual defects may coexist in aphasic states."

In his discussion of intelligence in aphasia, Zangwill (1964) points out that Head's position as to the relationship of aphasia to functional intelligence becomes particularly apparent in his treatment of semantic aphasia. Head (1926; 1963, p. 257) used the term *semantic aphasia* to indicate impairments in the comprehension of words and phrases as a whole. More broadly, Head stated: "I am dealing here mainly with a loss of power to comprehend the full significance of words and phrases together with a want of capacity to employ such modes of expression as a whole. . . .

"We can only understand the peculiar nature of this disorder of symbolic formulation if we bear in mind that the fault is essentially a want of relative significance and intention. Everything tends to be appreciated in detail, but the general significance is lacking."

It is important to appreciate that, for Head, semantic aphasia was not limited to the impairments in the "full comprehension" of linguistic content. Head

---

[2] The aphasic subjects in the Weisenburg and McBride study included 37 vascular, 15 tumor, and 8 traumatic patients all under age 60 and free of psychosis and evidence of advanced arteriosclerosis. The comparison subjects were 85 normal adults who were in treatment on surgical and orthopedic wards. An additional comparison group consisted of 38 subjects with unilateral brain lesions but without evidence of aphasic involvements.

(1926; 1963, p. 258) cites cases where patients are unable to explain the significance of pictures. Typically, he explains, the patient may look at a picture and point out one detail after another but " ... asked what the picture means, he may be entirely at a loss and either gives up altogether or invents some preposterous explanation."

Head may have anticipated Kurt Goldstein in his position that aphasia involves a defect of intellectual functioning that underlies language behavior but is more general and more impairing in its implications. Goldstein, we recall, emphasized that brain damage associated with aphasia produced a general defect or impairment in *abstract attitude*. Goldstein (1948) viewed the aphasic individual as one whose behavior was modified in the direction of a change from his ability to employ an abstract attitude (a nonconcrete strategy)—to perceive generalizations and to deal with concepts or categories and to separate and project himself from immediate demands of a stimulus situation—toward one of concretism and ego orientation. Thus, a patient who cannot evoke the appropriate name for an object may in fact be expressing his failure to appreciate the proper class or category for the object. Presumably, the name or term the aphasic evokes, and more generally the patient's thinking and acting, are directed and determined by the immediate claims that one particular aspect of the object or situation makes at the moment a reaction is required. Goldstein is aware that the "instrumentalities of speech" which do not necessarily involve higher mental processes are also impaired in aphasia. However, the underlying impairment that is central to aphasia is the patient's reduced ability for conceptualization and abstraction.

Our own impression is that many aphasic persons do indeed manifest a reduction in the employment of an abstract attitude, but that this is not as universal a characteristic or change as Goldstein found. Often, we believe, what the patient manifests is better viewed as a disinclination toward the abstract which may become aggravated as a result of his difficulty in evoking an appropriate class or categorical term for an event.

Zangwill (1964, p. 273), based on his own assessment of aphasic patients with a variety of defects, concluded that "there is no good evidence that abstraction in the sense of Goldstein is differentially affected in aphasia." Zangwill used the Progressive Matrices Test as his instrument for assessment. He found that performance on the test was not grossly impaired for patients with motor aphasia, jargon aphasia, or those with amnesic disturbances. Performance was found to be defective only when the aphasic disturbances were associated with constructional apraxia.

The position of Bay (1962, 1964) lies along much the same lines as those we have highlighted for Head and Goldstein and is reminiscent of Hughlings Jackson. According to Bay (1964): "The aphasic patient is impaired in conceptual thinking and in the actualization of concepts; for this reason he is unable to make a statement or to name objects." Bay uses a battery of his own performance tests that include picture completion and modeling objects with plastic material "from memory." Bay observes (1964): "So far we have not met an aphasic who is able to draw in the missing item unless he is able to name it as well." In modeling from memory of such common objects as a coffee cup, an egg, a snake, a crocodile, a lizard, and a giraffe, Bay finds that "aphasic patients have concepts, but these are of inferior quality and their actualization is impaired." Although the models produced by the aphasics suggested the stimulus model, essential features are often missed; for example, a coffee cup may look more like a dish with an "ear" on one side than a cup; an egg may lack the ovoid shape and be produced as a sphere. In general, Bay holds that performance requiring conceptual thinking—whether it be propositional statements or visual representational products—is likely to be impaired regardless of whether the "statements" are made in articulated speech, in gestures, in drawing, in modeling, or in any other nonverbal way.

Bay observes that the impairment in conceptual thinking tends to improve as the patient shows general improvement. He recommends that: "Therapeutic efforts must aim to occupy and to strengthen his conceptual thinking and his concept formation."

Bay's observations are based on his clinical impressions. They represent a position which, as we have indicated, is a continuation of one first enunciated by Hughlings Jackson that an aphasic is "lame in his thinking" and incorporates the psychophilosophy of Goldstein that the essential defect in aphasia is the patient's impairment in his abstract attitude and his categorical behavior.

Weinstein (1964) reported a study in which he compared the test results of 62 men with brain wounds on the Army General Classification Test (AGCT) with the scores of the same men on induction into the army. He found that the post-test, taken approximately 10 years after injury, revealed a significant decline in score for almost all men with left parieto-temporal lesions. Interestingly, comparable defects were shown by patients whose temporo-parietal lesions were not associated with aphasia. Weinstein concluded: "Thus, aphasia, *per se*, although frequently sufficient, is not necessary to produce intellectual impairment as we measured it."

Weinstein (1964) also reported on several other studies in which he was the investigator or coinvestigator that produced findings of significance relative to cognitive, sensory, and motor functions for aphasic patients. "Studies of aphasic and nonaphasic brain-injured subjects revealed impairment specific to aphasia for tests involving: knowledgy of the body (body schema), ability to locate embedded geometrical figures (hidden figures), complex visual problem-solving ability (conditional reaction), and map-reading with pathfindings (spatial orientation)."

Orgass and Poeck (1969) employed a battery of standardized tests to discriminate aphasic from nonaphasic brain-damaged patients. The tests included a German adaptation of the Wechsler Adult Intelligence Scale, the Token Test (De Renzi and Vignolo), a German adaptation of the Benton Test for Visual Retention, and a paired-associate test for verbal learning. In addition, tests for copying a short paragraph, writing to dictation, arithmetic calculation, and the

Hand-Eye-Ear Test (Henry Head) were used. The investigators found that all of the tests were correlated to a high degree with the total Intelligence Quotient. They therefore concluded that "the differences in the performance of aphasics and of nonaphasic subjects may depend, at least in part, on more severe mental deterioration in the aphasic patients."[3]

There are many other studies that are, directly or indirectly, pertinent to our discussion of the relationship and modification of intellectual functioning in brain-damaged persons as a special population, and in aphasics as a subgroup of this population. Some of the studies are concerned with correlations between hemispheres site of lesion and particular functions; others are concerned with specific site of lesion and impaired function. Still other studies, as Reitan (1966) points out, have been directed toward an evaluation of the comparative effects of different types of lesions in the same location and to be associated with behavioral changes over time. Such studies are reviewed by Reitan and by several contributors in the symposium on interhemispheric relations and cerebral dominance (Mountcastle, 1962).

At this point, the matter of changes in intellectual functioning in aphasics taken as a special population may be summarized by Critchley's (1970, p. 166) observation:

General intelligence suffers in aphasiacs, first as a straightforward epiphenom-enon of an extensive destruction of cerebral tissue independent of the loss of speech. In the second place mentation is altered qualitatively in aphasiacs, in that conceptual thinking and behaviour are generally considered to be difficult if not impossible, being replaced, it is claimed, by a far more concrete attitude. And thirdly, general intelligence suffers in so far as the appropriate mental operations demand the use of verbal symbols. Clearly the total impairment will depend partly upon the premorbid personality of the victim, including his habitual type of imagery, as well as his former habits and usages of speech. It will also directly depend upon the number of available verbal symbols. An aphasiac with a solitary recurrent utterance can be looked upon as being very nearly speechless, having only a single verbal symbol available for exterioriza-tion.

Critchley's observation is probably too pessimistic as a tentative closing note on the intellectual modifications associated with aphasic involvements. Again, we need to remember that persons who make rapid, spontaneous recoveries are not as likely to be included in investigations as are those who are hospitalized or in rehabilitation settings for therapy. Beyond this, our impression is that language recovery is often accompanied by improvement in general intellectual functioning. For some persons such functioning may be so close to their

---

[3] We need to be mindful that investigations such as those of Orgass and Poeck are usually conducted with available hospitalized patients, or those who are in rehabilitation agencies. Individuals who make speedy and good recoveries are not likely to be included in any considerable number in the subject population. Moreover, despite the trends that are found, some subjects show a relatively high performance. We must be careful, therefore, to reserve our conclusions as far as any individual is concerned.

precerebral insult level as to make no practical difference. For others, as we have indicated, high-level intellectual functioning is related to optimal environmental conditions. On an optimistic note, Wepman (1951, p. 75) observed: " . . . data indicate that the aphasic adult tends to make lower scores on standard intelligence tests after his injury than he did before it. They also show that, with recovery of his language processes, the aphasic patient tends to show a recovery of ability on intelligence tests that approximates his pretraumatic ability."

Performance on Cognitive, Nonverbal Tasks

Numerous studies are reported in the literature in which aphasic subjects are compared with nonaphasics on cognitive tasks which presumably do not call upon language, internalized or externalized, for appropriate performance.[4] The results of the studies are highly variable, possibly because of differences in the experimental subject populations and differences in specifics of the experimental designs. A number of these studies are reviewed by Archibald, Wepman, and Jones (1967). In their own study, Archibald *et al.* compared a group of left-brain-damaged aphasic patients with a group of left- and right-brain-damaged nonaphasic patients on four nonverbal tests of cognitive functioning. The subjects of the study were 39 left-brain-damaged and 22 right-brain-damaged patients with lesions in most cases a result of cerebrovascular accident. All were native English speaking and all had incurred their lesions more than three months prior to the time of testing. The subjects ranged in age from 27 to 70 years and in education from 4 to 20 years. There were no statistically significant differences in age or education either between the aphasic and nonaphasic groups or among the aphasic groups. Patients were rejected if they were uncooperative or if they had visual problems.

The tests used in the Archibald *et al.* study were the Language Modalities Test for Aphasia (LMTA) constructed by Wepman and Jones and four nonverbal cognitive tests: the Ravens Coloured Matrices, the Shure-Wepman Concept Shift Test, the Grassi Block Design Test, and the Elithorn Mazes. These tests were selected because they all tap cognitive functions which may be impaired in organic patients. To make it possible to explore the limits of the patients' performance, very generous (but fixed) time allowances were made before a given test item was discontinued.

The Ravens Coloured Matrices Test was designed as a test of reasoning employing visual materials. The task requires the subject to manipulate colored patterns "with some regard for their logical spatial position."

---

[4] Cognitive tasks may be broadly defined as any activity which involves thinking in contrast to tasks which are of a more specific sensory or perceptual nature such as sensory discrimination, e.g., size or weight judgments, maze problems, etc. Presumably such tasks can be performed without language mediation.

The Shure-Wepman Concept Shift Test is a modification of Weigl's Color-Form Sorting Test. This test is designed to assess whether a patient can sort materials according to simple concepts or classes and whether he can shift his basis of classification from one concept, such as color, to another, such as form. Other attributes that provide a basis for concept categorization are thickness and weight.

The Grassi Block Design Test is a modification of the Goldstein Cube Test. It is designed (1) to assess the subject's powers of analysis and synthesis in copying three-dimensional designs, and (2) to determine visual scanning and "planning ahead."

The Elithorn Mazes when used by Archibald *et al.* in their study had no standardized or published norms. They were, however, considered by the investigators to be promising in terms of differentiating brain-damaged from normal patients.

The results of the study showed that in general the more severe aphasic patients were impaired in nonverbal cognitive performances compared with less severe aphasic patients and brain-damaged nonaphasic patients. The greatest differences were found in the Ravens Matrices and the Shure-Wepman tests. An interesting additional finding was that right-brain-damaged patients obtained much lower scores on the Elithorn Mazes than testable aphasic patients, "thus supporting evidence in the literature that right-brain-damaged subjects have a central visual-spatial impairment" (Archibald *et al.*, 1967, p. 293).

In contrast with the Archibald *et al.* study, and specific to findings on the Ravens Matrices Test, De Renzi and Faglioni (1965, p. 429) report: "In the comparison of aphasic versus left nonaphasic and left-sided versus right-sided patients there were no differences in the performances on Ravens Matrices." De Renzi and Faglioni raise a question pertinent to their experimental population.[5]

"Why is the performance on Ravens Matrices of right-sided patients, who have more severe lesions, not worse than that of left-brain-damaged patients?" Their conjectual response to this question is as follows: "It is suggested . . . that this may be due to the fact that the left hemisphrere is crucial for all intellectual tasks, verbal as well as nonverbal."

New Learning

Another approach to the objective assessment and understanding of the intellectual functioning of aphasic persons is through investigations of performance on new learning tasks. A review of the literature reveals considerably more consensus in the results of such investigations than in studies of nonverbal

[5] This population included 58 left-brain-damaged aphasics (42 vascular, 7 neoplastic, 5 traumatic, and 4 abscess), 40 left-brain-damaged nonaphasics (16 vascular, 20 neoplastic, 2 traumatic, 1 abscess, and 1 "other"), and 68 right-brain-damaged nonaphasics (40 vascular, 22 neoplastic, 3 traumatic, 2 abscess, and 1 "other").

cognitive performances. We shall review a few studies that are representative of the literature on the learning characteristics of recovering aphasic patients.

Carson, Carson, and Tikofsky (1968) compared the performance of 64 aphasics and 64 normal adults in four experimental studies that involved (1) stimulus uncertainty and response time, (2) rote serial learning, (3) repeated digit symbol tasks, and (4) rule learning tasks. In general, the studies were directed toward determining if aphasic patients are able to learn and to acquire specific new materials rapidly or to relearn specific old materials. The findings revealed the following. (1) Aphasics as a total population showed significant regularities in their ability to learn new tasks and to retain their skill over passage of time, and they were able to handle a wide range of complexity for a variety of stimulus material. (2) Characteristics which distinguished aphasics from normals were slower speed and frequently a lower level of attainment. (3) Aphasics did not distinguish themselves as a group from normals by an absence of ability to perform on any of the relatively difficult experimental tasks. (4) Consistent improvement was manifested by (a) decreased times in the Response Time experiment, (b) an increased number of correct anticipations in the Rote Serial Learning Experiment, and (c) faster rates of responding in the Digit Symbol experiment.

In comparison with normals, aphasic subjects revealed (a) a greater effect of increasing uncertainty in the Response Time experiment, (b) less facility in using serial associations in the Rote Serial Learning experiment, and (c) a greater interference from repeated stimuli in the Rule Learning experiment (Carson et al., 1968, p. 110).

Carson et al. (1968, p. 110) also observed that although aphasics as a group demonstrated limited retention and transfer in learning, nevertheless, on an individual basis almost all of the aphasics improved with practice in a specific stimulus-response situation. However, although they might have called upon old learning in a specific routine task, they appeared to treat the task as totally new. Nevertheless, when given sufficient practice, aphasics were able to approach normal levels of performance. Finally, although aphasics showed greater variability among themselves than did the normals, individual variability was reduced with practice.

In an earlier study, Tikofsky and Reynolds (1963) employed the Wisconsin Card Sorting Test to determine the effects of varying the order of presentation of three sorting concepts or strategies (problems) on (1) the overall task-learning rate, (2) the percentage of error responses, and (3) the percentage of perseverative errors.[6] Tikofsky and Reynolds found that the aphasic subjects who could complete the card sorting tasks showed improvement even when the strategy for the task was not explained to them. (The number of subjects varied from 11 through 23 out of an initial population of 50.) The improvement resulted from a reduction in nonperseverative errors "without concomitant change in the

---

[6] The Wisconsin Card Sorting Test calls for arranging (sorting) cards on the basis of color, form, and number of items on a stimulus card.

amount of perseveration." The investigators conjecture that "improvement might have occurred sooner had the subjects been trained to differentiate between perseverative and nonperseverative errors."

It should be noted that Tikofsky and Reynolds were studying the learning characteristics of adult aphasics and were not, in this investigation, concerned with comparing aphasic and normal persons.

In more recently reported studies, Tikofsky (1971) employed serial learning tasks to assess learning in adult aphasics who were compared with nonaphasics. Serial verbal learning was examined in two experimental conditions. In one condition, a ten word list was constructed in which there was a high degree of association between adjacent words. In the second condition, the set of words was rearranged so that there was a minimal degree of association between adjacent words.

Tikofsky hypothesized that the aphasic subjects would differ markedly from nonaphasics in terms of learning rate and the amount of learning that could be achieved. Further, Tikofsky predicted that the overall patterns of performance as determined by the learning and serial position curves for the two groups of Ss would be relatively parallel. This prediction asserts that aphasic learning patterns on verbal tasks would closely parallel those of the nonaphasics. The investigator also hypothesized that aphasics would show a greater proportion of perseverative and out-of-list errors than would the nonaphasics. Further, he expected that "prior practice with the list having high intra-item association would have a deleterious effect on learning the low intra-item association list." On the other hand, Tikofsky predicted the reverse effect for subjects who were given initial training with low intra-item association lists.

The results of two pilot studies indicated that nonaphasics perform considerably better than the aphasics. However, despite the differences in performance the learning curves generated by the aphasics were found to be similar to those of the nonaphasics. The aphasic subjects also demonstrated fairly good retention of the material they had learned. The studies also revealed that initial experience with the high-associates list has a deleterious effect on learning the low-associates lists. In contrast, initial experience with the low-associates list enhanced performance on the high-associates list.

Tikofsky interpreted the results of the pilot experiments as supportive of the assumption that aphasics as a group demonstrate performance characteristics which reflect a reduction in both the rate and amount of material that they can acquire in a given verbal learning task. Also of interest is the finding that while aphasics performed at a level well below that of the nonaphasics, their performance patterns were found to be quite similar.

INEFFICIENCY

In our discussion of nonverbal, cognitive tasks there was considerable evidence of inefficiency in the learning of aphasics. Brookshire (1968) compared nine aphasic and eight nonaphasic hospital patients on a discrimination learning problem. The learning task called for establishing differential motor responses to visual stimuli. Specifically,

In the first portion of the session (training), the subject received a chip each time he pressed the red right hand button in the presence of the red light, which was on the right, or when he pressed the green left hand button in the presence of the green light, which was on the left. More than one reinforced response could occur during each light presentation. As soon as the subject's response rate and pattern stabilized the contingencies were changed and the subject received chips for pressing the red button in the presence of the green light and for pressing the green button in the presence of the red light (reversal). The change in contingencies was made from the control room and was not signaled to the subject. The only indication of the change was the change in the relationships between the stimulus lights and which responses were reinforced.

Brookshire found that the aphasic subjects, taken as a group, had more difficulty in learning the nonspeech discriminating task than did the nonaphasic subjects. The performance of the aphasics showed considerable intersubject variability. The most severely impaired aphasic patients "tended to adopt primitive strategies; the less severely involved patients used more sophisticated strategies." Brookshire (1968, p. 691), commenting on the clinical implications of his findings, says:

Differences in performance by aphasic subjects in this study were pronounced, even though the discrimination task was a relatively simple one. The differences observed were not a simple division of subjects into learners and non-learners, but were differences arising from the strategies with which subjects attempted to solve the problem presented to them. Most of the aphasic subjects failed to solve one or more parts of the problem. Simply classifying these subjects as non-learners would be a serious mistake for the clinician who is concerned with retraining speech and language functions. The clinician evidently cannot accept simple "can do-cannot do" classifications; he must be more analytical, he must determine the reason or reasons why a subject cannot do a task. Knowing why the subject does not solve a problem will dictate the modifications that must be made in order to help the patient acquire the needed problem-solving ability.

In summarizing the results of studies on new learning in aphasics, we find that common characteristics include poor planning, failure to adopt appropriate strategies, or to shift strategies according to the demands of a new situation. Aphasics require more time to make responses and to shift responses than do nonaphasics of like age and education. Perseveration behavior errors are frequent. However, we must again recall that most of the investigations included subjects who were still "in training." Moreover, despite their learning ineffi-ciencies, the overall pattern tends to parallel that of nonaphasics. Aphasics, then, can and do learn, both nonverbal and verbal tasks. They require more controlled and individually more optimal conditions for learning than do non-brain-damaged peers.

References

Archibald, Y. M., Wepman, J. M., and Jones, L. V. 1967. Nonverbal cognitive performance in aphasic and nonaphasic brain damaged persons. *Cortex*, 3:3, 275–294.

Bay, E. 1962. Aphasia and nonverbal disorders of language. *Brain*, 85, 411–426.

———. 1964. Present concepts of aphasia. *Geriatrics*, 19, 319–331.

Brookshire, R. H. 1968. Visual discrimination and response learning by aphasic patients. *Journal of Speech and Hearing Research*, 11:4, 677–692.

Carson, D. H., Carson, F. E., and Tikofsky, R. S. 1968. On learning characteristics of the adult aphasic. *Cortex*, 4:1, 92–112.

Critchley, M. 1970. *Aphasiology*. London: Edward Arnold.

De Renzi, E., and Faglioni, P. 1965. The comparative efficiency of intelligence and vigilance tests in detecting hemispheric cerebral damage. *Cortex*, 1:4, 410–433.

Goldstein, K. 1948. *Language and Language Disturbances*. New York: Grune & Stratton.

Head, H. 1926. *Aphasia and Kindred Disorders of Speech*. New York: Cambridge University Press and Macmillan. Reprinted by Hafner Publishing Co., New York, 1963.

Jackson, J. H. 1879. On affectation of speech from diseases of the brain. *Brain*, 1, 304–330.

Marie, P. 1906. Revision de la question de l'aphasie. *Semaine Medicale Paris*, 26, 241–247.

Mountcastle, V., ed. 1962. *Interhemispheric Relations and Cerebral Dominance*. Baltimore: John Hopkins Press.

Orgass, B., and Poeck, K. 1969. Assessment of aphasia by psychometric methods. *Cortex*, 5:4, 317–330.

Reitan, R. M. 1966. Problems and prospects in studying the psychological correlates of brain lesions. *Cortex*, 2:1, 127–154.

Tikofsky, R. S. 1971. Two studies of verbal learning by adult aphasics. *Cortex*, 7:1, 105–125.

Tikofsky, R. S., and Reynolds, G. L. 1963. Further studies of nonverbal learning and aphasia. *Journal of Speech and Hearing Research*, 6:4, 329–337.

Weinstein, S. 1964. Deficits common with aphasia or lesions of either cerebral hemisphere. *Cortex*, 1:2, 154–169.

Weisenburg, T. H., and McBride, K. E. 1935. *Aphasia: A Clinical and Psychological Study*. New York: Commonwealth Fund.

Wepman, J. M. 1951. *Recovery from Aphasia*. New York: Ronald Press.

Zangwill, O. L. 1964. Intelligence in aphasia. In *Disorders of Language*, DeReuck, A., and O'Connor, M., eds. London: J. & A. Churchill, pp. 261–284.

4

Correlates of Aphasia II: Personality and Behavioral Modifications

Personality Changes

We would consider it surprising that an individual who has incurred cerebral insult and associated aphasic disturbances would not undergo consequent changes in personality. Certainly, impairments in language directly affect the instrumentalities of expression, and thus the usual manner in which personalities are manifest. Critchley, in his concluding remarks at the symposium on disorders of language (1964, p. 340 and pp. 344–345), suggested some of the relationships between an individual's use of language and his personality in states of health as well as disease:

We have heard little or nothing, however, about the patient's pre-morbid personality and his pre-morbid verbal equipment and literary attainment, as factors which may go some way, perhaps a long way, in determining the eventual aphasic picture. Jackson's "four factors of the insanities" need to be remembered. Questions of natural eloquence, verbosity, size of vocabulary, literacy, plurilingualism, style, aesthetic delight in words for their own sake; and the sound, shape and colour of words; the choosing, matching and combining of words in euphonious and pleasing patterns—however obsessional—these are surely most important when it comes to understanding the eventual picture of the victim who finds himself crippled in a linguistic sense. . . .
   Language in other words is not merely communicative. It is an integral part of one's personality; it is a behavioural pattern and as such it subtly differs from one individual to another just as facial appearances differ despite an overall similarity.

Language—whether regarded as a communicative system or as a pattern of behavior—is so fundamental that it transcends widely the use of words. Non-verbal communicative systems and systems of self-expression therefore merit close attention, in health and in disease states.

In our discussion of personality modifications we shall include some observations from the published professional literature and many more from publications of recovered aphasics that indicate awarenesses and insights about their own "new forms" of behavior. We shall begin by making references to broad changes in behavior which have been observed as sequalae of brain damage.

Goldstein (1942, p. 69) observed:

The characteristic difference between the older and the more recent orientation in psychopathology is that the former regarded the observable symptoms simply as manifestations of changes in different functions or structures, whereas in the new approach many symptoms are seen as expressions of the change which the patient's personality as a whole undergoes as a result of disease, and also as expressions of the struggle of the changed personality to cope with the defect and with demands it can no longer meet. We must distinguish various groups of symptoms, therefore, which must be evaluated differently, and which confront us with respectively different tasks in our attempt to improve the patient's behavior.

One group of symptoms is *not* a direct result of damage to a part of the brain. It is the expression of the struggle of the changed organism to cope with the defect, and to meet the demands of a milieu with which it is no longer equipped to deal.

The attempt of the organism to find a new adjustment gives rise to two kinds of symptoms: the first kind reveals the struggle; the second reflects the tendency to build up substitute performances which allow it to escape this struggle and to come to terms with the demands of the outer world in the best possible way under the given conditions.

COPING AND DEFENSE MECHANISMS

Galanter, Miller, and Pribram (1960, p. 116) consider what may happen if a person's established ways of behaving are no longer possible to him, or the behavior is no longer adequate to meet a situation. They point out that "plans may well form a part of the clinical picture of hysteria and, when very marked, of catatonia. Both hysteria and catatonia are characterized by ritualistic patterns of behavior that substitute for the development of new useful plans." Further, they say, "For whatever reasons, whether it be a threat to a person's image or intrinsic to the wholesale abandonment of large segments of plans, the more or less sudden realization that an enduring plan must be changed at a strategic level is accompanied by a great deal of emotional excitation. When this excitation can find no focus in either the image or in action, the person experiences 'anxiety.' The patient may then develop plans to cope with anxiety (defense mechanism) instead of developing new plans to cope with reality."

We suggest that Goldstein and Galanter *et al.* are probably referring to the same phenomenon. The persons (patients) they are describing have suffered disruption in their capacity for planning. One of the consequences is to develop defenses against the need to cope and to strive to arrive at appropriate plans for ongoing situations. Interestingly, Jenkins and Schuell (1968) observed that in the course of examination, aphasic patients showed significant and marked acquiescence response bias on all tests. "The results clearly indicate that the aphasic patients show an appreciable bias toward responding in the positive direction (agreeing with a sentence or saying that it is correct) as opposed to distributing their errors randomly. . . . Aphasics adopt a strategy of agreement when dealing with materials they do not completely understand."

Many clinicians, we are certain, have found patients who adopt a negative rather than a positive strategy. The point, however, is that a strategy is adopted, a plan used, that permits a kind of coping with situations in which the patient probably feels inadequate.

Friedman (1961) describes the behavior, verbal and nonverbal, of aphasic patients in group therapy in a Veterans' Administration Hospital.

From the comments of the various group members, it was readily apparent that language impairment had made a profound emotional impression. Although intensity of reaction varied from patient to patient, near unanimity was expressed as regards the felt loss of both biological and psychological integrity. While the patients' expressions of fear, loneliness, lowered self-esteem, and defensive concern with the thoughts of others confirm the findings of previous observers, they also serve to emphasize the regressive aspects of aphasia. In this connection it is of interest to note that few, if any, of these patients were able to free themselves from the misconception (or distorted perception) that non-aphasics were not really interested in them. Deeply rooted was the feeling that in some way or other, above and beyond their organic impairments, they were different from other people. Their rarely relaxed behavior with group peers attested to a wariness of extended close contact even with patients who suffered similar difficulty. Indeed, several commented on a desire to be on a ward with "normals" rather than with other aphasics.

The various mechanisms used by these patients in coping with the problems of group interaction are similarly revealing. Close scrutiny of their behavior indicated the need of the aphasics to employ a wide variety of defenses to mediate the trauma of group activity devoid of ancillary or supportive means. Both withdrawal and projection were apparent as each patient acted in isolation and yet complained of this characteristic in the others. The defensive use of impairment was evidenced in the need to maximize the extent of memory loss in failing to remember emotionally charged material from one session to the next. Such maximation of impairment was also the basis for the aphasics' complaint that the group leader was expecting them to talk without considering that they were really not able to do so. Yet, at other times when threatened by dealing with personal reactions to their illness, they denied the significance of this very same language impairment. Under such conditions the strategy was to minimize their language handicaps and to emphasize other organic impairments. Finally, there was the defensive use of dependence as manifested in a recurring demand that they be given more help by the therapist and preferably in smaller groups where individualized attention would be provided.

CONCRETISM AND IMPAIRMENT OF ABSTRACT ATTITUDE

In our discussion in Chapter 3 of intelligence and intellectual functioning we viewed concretism and impairment of abstract attitude as intellectual modification. It should be apparent that such changes, when they occur and become dominant characteristics of intellectual functioning, should necessarily also be regarded as personality changes. Our clinical impression is strong that many aphasics who become predominantly concrete and ego-oriented in their behavior were premorbidly so inclined. However, the influences of their environment did not always permit them to yield to such inclination. Thus, their behavior—their thinking and their language—had to conform to environmental expectations even though often the effort *did not come easily.*

It is our view that many chronic aphasics are persons who premorbidly were inclined to be as ego-oriented and concrete minded as they patently become as aphasics. Thus, as we have observed (Eisenson, 1963), the chronic aphasic is a person who, because of his premorbid inclinations, becomes unequal to the extreme demands for reorganization of behavior patterns, including verbal behavior, brought about by the disruptions consequent to the cerebral insult. Cerebral lesion produces disruption and loss of control. Recovery is primarily a process of reorganization and resumption of control and of adjustment to some losses and impairments, both physical and intellectual.

It is not too surprising that some aphasics, even though their physical status has become "stabilized," are nevertheless unable or unwilling to make all the adjustments necessary to overcome the forces of disruption. In the absence of ongoing organic pathology, the aphasics who do not make appreciable improvement with ordinary motivation are those who are trying to accomplish reorganization through ego-orientation. *Their* inclination, *their* needs, *their* interpretations, rather than those of their cultural environment, become the dominant ones. Thus, verbal expressions have limited meanings and restricted significance. This ego-oriented approach to reorganization of behavior may be contrasted with persons who accomplish considerable recovery within a few months of the onset of their cerebral insults. The ones who make good recoveries are those who adjust to the behavior of the others in their environment, including the ways of people with words as well as the ways of words with persons who use them.

This observation is not intended as an indictment of chronic aphasics, but rather as an explanation as to the relatively severe language impairments that are maintained by some persons who, based on prognostic criteria for recovery, should have been able to make fair to good recoveries. Perhaps the recovery that they could not make was from their premorbid inclinations.

It might help us to understand some of the dynamics that underlie ego-oriented and concrete behavior by presenting several examples from the author's examination files.

A 53-year-old male with damage to the left temporo-parietal area, presented with a multiple-choice item for the recall of the name of a bird chose the name *Jackie*, which was correct. He explained his choice by saying "I accept Jackie because I am Jackie."

In answer to the question, "What do birds move when they fly?" He answered, "They start with their feet. I can't remember the other name."

For items calling for *pretended action* his response to "Show me how to drink from a glass" was "Sorry, I can't show you. I don't have a glass." (The patient performed correctly when given an empty glass.) When directed to "Show me how to comb your hair," the patient suited the action to the words by saying and performing "I push my hair to the front, and then to the side."

In answer to word-finding items the following were elicited:

Question: On what do you sleep?

Answer: Bed number 40.

Question: On what do you cook?

Answer: I don't do no cooking.

Question: What do you use for cutting meat?

Answer: They give me soft meat. I don't have to cut it.

EGO INVOLVEMENT

The person without sense of self, without awareness of how he as an individual thinks and feels in ways which relate him to others in his environment, is likely to be considered, at least in Western cultures, as emotionally ill. Thus, ego involvement is not a negative characteristic as an aspect of mental health. However, the person with excessive ego involvement, whose concerns with what he was or might have been get in the way of making adjustments to acquired disabilities, presents a special therapeutic problem. One patient who, less than two years after the onset of his aphasic involvement, had made an excellent linguistic recovery as well as an overall emotional adjustment, had the following interchange with the author:

"What was your problem at the beginning? Can you tell me so that I can tell others about it?"

The patient responded with: "Let me draw you a picture of my problem." He drew a picture of himself coming to his first therapy session. The picture depicted him as being weighted down by two handbags. One, considerably larger than the other, was marked EGO. The smaller one was marked RESOURCES. The drawing showed him sweating and leaning towards the ground in the direction of the heavily loaded EGO bag. The ex-patient said: "You see, this is how I was at the beginning. Loaded down by my ego and unable to use my resources. As you see, I was literally being dragged to the ground."

"How is it now?" I asked, "Will you draw a picture of how you see yourself today?"

He drew a second picture. Surprisingly, the EGO handbag was still as big as in the first drawing, but now the RESOURCES bag was of equal size.

Although the figure holding the bag was not sweating, there was a slight lean in the direction of the EGO bag. I asked for an explanation and was informed: "You know, out of habit, I still walk this way."

Behavioral Changes

The separation of personality from behavior is, of course, an arbitrary one. Behavior is dictated by and is an expression of the personality. Behavior is what we observe. In keeping with this perhaps simplistic distinction, we shall discuss several of the more frequent behavioral manifestations that are associated with brain lesion and aphasia.

VARIABILITY OF RESPONSE

Aphasic patients show great variability and inconsistency of response in the early stages of their involvement when they are neurophysiologically still unstable. However, many aphasic persons continue to show considerable variability in their response patterns even after they have presumably stabilized in their neurophysiological condition. Anxiety, stress, fatigue, and conditions that generally may be conducive to variability of response in non-brain-damaged persons are likely to increase variability in the brain-damaged. Schuell, Jenkins, and Jiminez-Pabon (1964, p. 161) sum up the conditions which are associated with variability and inconsistency and conversely, with relatively good performance.

The speech of aphasic patients varies under different conditions in reasonable ways. In general aphasic patients talk more readily when they are rested and relaxed than when they are tired or tense. It is easier for most aphasic patients to talk to one person at a time than to enter into a group conversation. Like most of us, aphasic patients find some people easier to talk to than others. It is difficult for aphasic patients to talk to anyone who seems busy or hurried. The patient knows it takes him longer than most people to say what he wants to say and that, if he reacts to real or imagined impatience on the part of the listener, his speech may break down altogether.

Aphasic patients differ also in individual reactions to situations, probably much as they differed before they were aphasic. One patient with a good deal of speech hesitates to talk to anyone because he is afraid he will make a mistake. Another, with a repertory of three or four stereotyped phrases, grins and greets everyone he encounters with "How are you doing, pretty good?"

Most aphasic patients, understandably, do not talk as easily in medical conferences as they do on the hospital ward or in the clinic. Some patients, however, are stimulated by a friendly audience and almost forget they are aphasic. However, even in such circumstances, differences are in total verbal output and not in altered speech or language patterns.

We consider variability and inconsistence of response to be aspects of intellectual inefficiency. The conditions are associated with impaired attention and memory deficits. For most aphasic patients, variability and inconsistency are reduced as improvement in general takes place. However, performance may suffer significantly if the expected letter from a wife (husband) or girl friend (boy friend) did not arrive, or carried news that was upsetting, or if the aphasic was otherwise disturbed by his relations with a friend, relative, or another patient. Generally, as we have indicated, the aphasic is more vulnerable to the effects of the unexpected or the undesired than are non-brain-damaged persons.[1]

EMOTIONAL LABILITY

Almost all patients display emotional lability, and many have insights about this aspect of their problem. All too often, unfortunately, the problem becomes aggravated by well-intentioned persons who are overly solicitous and who "talk down" to the patient. Douglas Ritchie (1961, pp. 26–28) describes some of his emotional reactions in the early stage of his recovery from aphasic involvements.

At this time, too, I began to fly into sudden rages. The nurses were the chief target, and one of these, a middle-aged woman whose heart was overflowing with love and kindness toward me, I could not bear in the room, even for a moment. In the first days in the nursing home I was grateful to her for her constant waiting on me. But she got into the habit of talking baby talk to me. I think that was the beginning of it. Every time there was a knock on the door, her head peeped sideways in and she would say "Peep-bo" or something like that. If I left a tray of food with some cakes on it or a plate of tapioca—which to me has a disgusting taste and a more repulsive appearance—she said: "Naughty boy! He must finish up his tapioca. It's good for him." Once she even tried to make me eat some custard, holding the spoon. My sickly smile refused to come on my face on this occasion, and she said: "Temper, temper!"

I burst into laughter as soon as the nurse had left the room, and my wife joined in, in relief at seeing me laugh for the first time since I had been in the nursing home. I was choking with laughter when I realized I had lost control of myself. I do not think my wife was aware of it, but I think that it was from that moment that I began to feel that I had a serious illness. My paralysis and my inability to speak had not touched me—in a little while I would recover from these disabilities—but the loss of control of myself seemed to me a matter of the brain. Laughing was all very well, and the relief of it after the passion of rage which the innocent nurse had conjured up was quite understandable, but this laughter was sobbing and uncontrollable. However, my control was soon on again and I told myself it was nothing.

[1] Schuell et al. (1964, p. 161) point out that "in contrast to fluctuating environmental conditions, testing is a controlled situation. If the patient is neurologically stable, and if a relationship of confidence is established, maximal responses can usually be obtained. It is a maxim of psychometric testing that while scores may be depressed for many reasons, it is not possible for a subject to perform better than he can. Aphasic patients are highly motivated to perform well, and experienced examiners rarely have trouble finding out what the patient is able to do."

PERSEVERATION

In their discussion of fundamental disorders in aphasia, Kreindler and Fradis (1968, p. 79) observe that failure of a patient to evoke a proper response—for instance, to repeat a word as directed—may be a result of one or more factors. One of these is "impaired mobility of nervous processes, the patient fixing himself upon, or becoming 'intoxicated' with a stimulus or previous reaction because he has lost his capacity to pass with normal readiness to another reaction." Another factor is "a state of fatigability, the whole verbal system being in a state of inhibition."[2]

If we generalize from the Kreindler and Fradis explanation of the possible underlying dynamics for a given verbal failure to performance failures, verbal or nonverbal, we are then dealing with the phenomenon of *perseveration*, a behavioral characteristic common to persons with brain damage.

Perseveration may be defined as the abnormal persistence of a response when the stimulus which initially elicited it is no longer present and another response to a subsequent stimulus has been presented. Perseveration may be manifest either in obvious repetition or in blocking. Sometimes perseveration produces a partial interference which carries over from one response to another, as when a patient identifies a series of objects such as *key, button, spoon, fork*, by calling them *key, cutty, skoon, sfork*. Perseveration may be observed in errors in spelling which often parallel those in naming, in motor acts in drawing figures or forms such as in Bender Gestalt drawings, and even in maintenance of such acts as block tapping when a patient continues his repetitive performance "indefinitely" in response to a direction to tap a given number of times. Luria (1966, pp. 181–186) discusses the phenomenon and the neurodynamics of perseveration. In experimental situations he observes (p. 437ff) that perseveration represents difficulties associated with inertia of a previously formed dynamic structure that continue to be manifest during the performance of intellectual operations. Luria believes that perseveration is associated with lesion of the frontal lobes, especially when there is evidence of "disturbance of the complex hierarchic structure of activity, responsible for the creation of preliminary programs of behavior and for subordinating the further course of the processes to those preliminarily created programs" (Luria, 1966, p. 466).

Following are some examples of perseverative errors in writing and figure drawing (copying).

---

[2] The other factors indicated by Kreindler and Fradis (pp. 78–79) are "blockage within the word functional system interrupting the connection between the heard word and the corresponding articulatory pattern" and "impossibility to perceive the stimuli because they have not been delivered in the optimal sequence; decrease in reaction speed which delays the reaction though it is still possible; performance variability with a momentary incapacity to fulfill the task; impaired sequence of nervous processes involved in correct pronunciation of the word."

Copying

 I am 58 years old. **presented material**

 copied product

Bender-Gestalt Drawings

Attempts at copying card A of Bender gestalt. In previous interview patient spelled (or attempted to spell) whenever he was asked to name objects or complete sentences. (Figures presented for copying are on the right.)

Trial 1

Trial 2

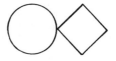

Trial 3

Card 1

Card 2

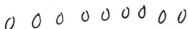

Figure 4–1. Examples of perseverative errors. The patient, a 58-year-old high school graduate, had incurred a left posterior vascular lesion. (Figures in column on right from Bender, Lauretta, *Visual Motor Gestalt Test and Its Clinical Use.* Copyright, the American Orthopsychiatric Association, Inc. Reproduced by permission.)

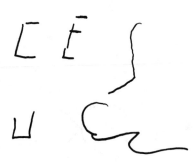

Figure 4–1 *(continued)*

Card 6

Repeated drawing on own initiative.

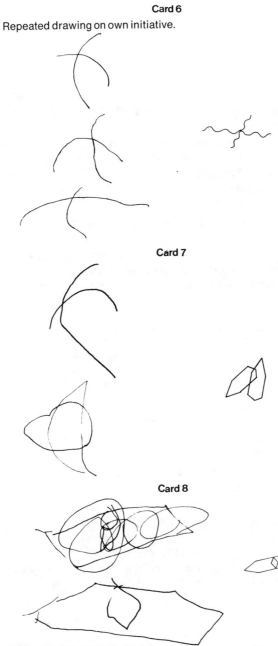

Card 7

Card 8

Patient said, "It's a little better"

Figure 4–1 *(continued)*

EUPHORIA AS SELF-DEFENSE

The maintenance of a feeling of well-being inconsistent with "truth or reality" may be regarded as a form of self-defense. A clinical interpretation of euphoria is that the person (patient) is incapable or unwilling to face reality because of the disastrous effects it may produce in him. Objectively, the patient appears to display a lack or absence of self-criticism associated with an exaggerated feeling of well-being. Bay believes that euphoria is a characteristic of patients with sensory aphasia, probably as a more general aspect of organic brain lesion. Bay (1964, p. 134) says: "This euphoric lack of self-criticism is a common feature of many organic brain lesions, for instance of general paralysis. It is a disorder of behaviour independent of language and appropriate examination clearly reveals the fact that it is not confined to the linguistic sphere (as a kind of anosognosia) but becomes manifest in every achievement, for instance in non-verbal performance tests which are equally impaired in aphasic patients."

However, there is some evidence that patients, at least in retrospect, may have some awareness of their euphoria as well as of thy psychodynamics related to it. Douglas Ritchie, a stroke patient with aphasia, recalls (1961, pp. 35–36):

I had become insulated. I heeded only the most obviously optimistic things that were said to me and for the rest I did not hear them or came to the conclusion that they were wrong. If I had allowed myself to be given a glimpse of the truth, I believe I would have gone out of my mind. So, unconsciously, I let myself down gently, until some two years later I reached the floor of the truth, or, at any rate, the floor of *my* truth. (I began to write this book when my feet were safely on the ground, that is to say, nearly two years after the stroke.)

DEPRESSION

Depression is a recurrent theme in the diaries of persons who have made good recoveries from aphasia. McKenzie Buck (1968, p. 21) emphasizes that "the dysphasic's greatest enemy is depression." Buck also notes that extreme swings in affect may resemble or be a transient aspect of changes that accompany brain damage—part of the "syndrome of organicity." Specifically, Buck notes (1968, p. 42): "Some of the behavioral patterns shown by dysphasics are truly symptoms of an organic psychosis manifested by chronic states of unwavering depression or extremes of unrealistic cheerfulness."

GUILT

Feelings of guilt are part of the problem faced by persons recovering from aphasia. McKenzie Buck, in discussing emotional reactions, emphasizes the need to appreciate the patient's feelings of guilt and its immediate consequences. Buck says (1968, p. 23): "It seems most humane at first to consider our patient's emotional reactions. He cannot avoid some feelings of guilt. In observing tensions of the immediate family, the patient is apt to sense that he has altered many living patterns of the persons for whom he has the highest regard. This basic concern, in combination with the multitude of personal reductions, very often results in a persistent desire for complete social withdrawal."

Douglas Ritchie, in his diary of his own recovery from aphasia, also discusses his feelings of guilt. Ritchie touches on his awareness of behavioral changes that preceded the actual stroke and his aphasic involvements, and his impression that his visitors may have had some awareness of his guilt (Ritchie, 1961, p. 38):

I felt guilty. I do not know why I felt guilty, but something told me that I was. The illness had been brought on by something. There had been a certain slackness about my work. For instance, I had begun to linger over my luncheon for an hour and a half or more; a half-filled diary pleased me better than a full one. Sitting at my desk, I used to let my thoughts wander at will instead of vigorously driving them where they belonged. Then, there was the drinking. A large gin and french just before luncheon, and two or three before dinner. I needed it, but it spoiled my concentration, and it was much too expensive. Whatever it was, and the illness must have been due, I considered, to all these things, the feeling of guilt remained, and I thought that all the visitors who came to see me knew, or suspected, my guilt, though they did not utter a word, and were moved by a sense of pathos as well as sympathy. I welcomed their sympathy but I felt uneasy.

Summary Impressions

The reader, in reflecting on the materials presented in this chapter, might well have observed, "There, but for the grace of God, go I." Aphasic involvements happen to persons who as individuals have had a variety of strategies to meet problems, who have had developed personalities and traits including some that those who make judgments in our culture considered undesirable. Rarely, if ever, does brain damage improve a persons's behavior in ways generally accepted by our society. Generally, the effect is to aggravate those traits which are on the debit side of a personality. However, with the possible exception of concretism in some instances, we do not find new traits but rather manifestations in an intensified form of old traits. Unfortunately, with language and the ordinary instrumentalities of expression impaired, the degree of intensification of old traits may be so great as to appear new, at least in the sense that they cannot be ignored by persons having close and frequent contact with the aphasic. Fortunately, the picture tends to change for the better for those persons who recover from their aphasic involvements. Under pressure, however, the tendency to "regress" to "newly acquired" nonverbal behavior to cope with difficult situations may be difficult to control.

Buck (1968, Chaps. 2, 3, and 4) presents an intimate exposition of the adjustment problems of the aphasic patient. The exposition is based on his personal experiences as a recovering and recovered aphasic as well as his experiences as a practicing speech pathologist. Buck's book and the one by Ritchie (1961) are *must* readings for clinicians who have therapeutic contacts with aphasic patients.

References

Bay, E. 1964. In *Disorders of Language*, DeReuck, A., and O'Connor, M., eds. London: J. & A. Churchill, pp. 122–139.

Buck, M. 1968. *Dysphasia.* Englewood Cliffs, N. J.: Prentice-Hall, Inc.

Critchley, M. 1964. Concluding remarks. In *Disorders of Language*, DeReuck, A., and O'Connor, M., eds. London: J. & A. Churchill, pp. 339–345.

Eisenson, J. 1963. Aphasic language modifications as a disruption of cultural verbal habits. *Asha*, 5:2, 503–506.

Friedman, M. H. 1961. On the nature of regression in aphasia. *Archives of General Psychiatry*, 5, 252–256.

Galanter, E., Miller, G. A., and Pribram, K. H. 1960. *Plans and Structure of Behavior.* New York: Holt, Rinehart and Winston.

Goldstein, K. 1942. *Aftereffects of Brain Injuries in War.* New York: Grune & Stratton.

Jenkins, J. J., and Schuell, H. 1968. Acquiescence response set in aphasics. *Journal of Abnormal Psychology*, 70, 111–113.

Kreindler, A., and Fradis, A., 1968. *Performance in Aphasia.* Paris: Gauthier-Villars.

Luria, A. R. 1966. *Human Brain and Psychological Processes.* New York: Harper & Row.

Ritchie, D. 1961. *Stroke: A Study of Recovery.* Garden City, N. Y.: Doubleday.

Schuell, H., Jenkins, J. J., and Jiminez-Pabon, E. 1964. *Aphasia in Adults.* New York: Harper & Row.

5

Classification of Disorders

Basic Questions Relative to Classification

The monograph *Human Communication and Its Disorders* (NINDS, 1970, p. 138) presents some questions relative to classification of aphasic disorders that, despite attempts going back to Broca, still remain unresolved. A key question asked is "Can linguistic encoding functions be separated from those of decoding?" Historically, and often despite protestations to the contrary, linguistic impairments presented by the aphasic patient have been dichotomized into intake and output disturbances. Terms, we may note, have changed with the times. The terms include sensory and motor aphasia; receptive and expressive, evaluative and productive, and, at the present time, decoding and encoding. To be sure, aphasiologists are not naive and make no either/or assumption with regard to an aphasic's presenting manifestations. It takes little clinical experience to appreciate that no aphasic whose linguistic productions (encodings) are impaired does not also have some difficulty in decoding language. The possibility remains that for most aphasics, expressive involvements are surface manifestations of an underlying impairment for intake. Schuell, in the monograph referred to above, suggests an approach for understanding as well as classifying aphasic language disturbances. Schuell asks, "Has the aphasic patient lost language competence, in the sense that Chomsky uses this term, or has he merely incurred impairment of some of the performance aspects of language? In other words, has the aphasic patient lost the knowledge of his language that is common to all of

81

its users, or has he merely incurred impairment of some of the mechanisms involved, such as retrieval, short-term memory span, feedback control, *et cetera*?" (NINDS, 1970, p. 112).

As we shall note in our review of classification "systems," the questions raised by Schuell represent a contemporary restatement of ones which, in one form or another, aphasiologists since Hughlings Jackson's time have tried to answer. Our brief historical review will be prefaced by observations relative to the present "state of the art" with regard to classification.

In approaching the problems of classification and assessment of aphasic impairments, even when the impairments are restricted to those of language, we are confronted with the classifiers' and examiners' concept of aphasia. Even a limited amount of clinical observation leads to the conclusion that Aphasic A is different from Aphasic B, who is different from Aphasic C, and so on. Despite differences and variability from patient to patient, and for the individual patient as he progresses in his recovery from his initial trauma, we can accept the observation of Spreen and Wachal (1970, p. 13) that, taken as a total population, "aphasics produce significantly more vocal gestures, mispronounced words, neologisms, dependent and independent units, unrecognizable sounds, pause fillers, paralogisms and parasyntactic words." Spreen and Wachal also observe that "an inspection of the data for individual subjects indicates that some aphasics produced a large number of these 'oddments' while others had none or very few. Our conclusion at this time is that specific types of distinct differences in the degree of aphasia are suggested by these findings and that an analysis for types and degree . . . will be fruitful."[1]

Pribram (1971, p. 358) presents his views of the apparent contemporary division of thinking with regard to aphasic disturbances. He says:

The proponents of the unitary view base their interpretations on the communicative aspects of language—language as a system of signs and symbols by which an organism can communicate his conceptions of the world and his feelings about himself. The proponents of the multiple view, on the other hand, are interested not only in the communicative use of language but also in linguistic structure and the *varieties* of uses to which language is put. . . . The examiner of the unitary view tries, as a rule, to find out how well the patient understands what is going on around him and whether the examiner understands what the patient is trying to tell him. The examiner with the multiple view approaches the patient to find out whether the *form* of linguistic use is disturbed, not whether the disturbed form is still useful.

We shall return to contemporary classification approaches later in this chapter. For the present, we shall summarize a broad position on classification based on site of lesion from a statement by Pribram (1971, pp. 358–359):

---

[1] Spreen and Wachal are developing procedures for the recording, transcription, and coding of free speech samples of adult aphasic patients which will be compared with the speech production of adult normal speakers. They will analyze the data with regard to measures of lexical diversity, morphological complexity, and grammatical form-class usage, generative-syntactic complexity, sentence length, abnormal productions and of paralinguistic features (rate of speech, pauses, pause fillers, vocal gestures, etc.).

All investigators agree that damage to the posterior superior temporal cortex of the dominant hemisphere results in a communicative disability in the use of language. When the lesion extends anteriorly from this locus, the disability tends to be more expressive; when the lesion extends posteriorly, the disability is more profound, i.e., the patient appears not only to have difficulty in expressing himself but also appears to be confused as to what is to be expressed. Further differences in sensory and motor modality depend on the direction of extension of the lesion. A posterior inferior extension will likely damage the visual mode to produce reading difficulties (alexia); a posterior superior extension into the parietal cortex will likely impair semantic relationships in language, especially those which involve the somatic mode such as pointing, touching, pushing, and pulling. An anterior superior lesion will likely result in agraphia because of involvement of the hand representation of the motor cortex; an anterior inferior lesion will likely result in dysarthria because of involvement of the tongue representation. But the important consideration is that this "language field" of the brain is a fairly large area of cortex, fed by the middle cerebral artery, in which the representations of the ear, throat, tongue, and mouth overlap. Within this cortical field a great deal of the machinery of human verbal communication becomes represented and therefore malfunction resulting from partial damage produces disability in such communication.

Classification: A Brief Historical Survey

P. Broca was among the first to classify language disorders associated with cerebral pathologies. Henry Head (1926; 1963, p. 27) presents his evaluation of a presentation by Broca in 1868 to the British Association for the Advancement of Science[2]:

He came near to defining the different forms that might be assumed by affections of speech. He rejects first of all those due to gross intellectual changes, and those produced by some defect of function of the organs of articulation. He then divides disorders of speech, due to a central lesion, into two main groups, "aphémie" and "amnésie verbale" and lays down clearly the difference between them. The aphemic patient has a profoundly reduced vocabulary and may be speechless except for some monosyllables, oaths or words that do not seem to belong to any language. His ideas are intact, as shown by gestures, and he can understand what is said to him, and recognise words and phrases which he cannot pronounce or even repeat. On the other hand, the amnesic patient no longer recognises the conventional associations established between ideas and words. He can pronounce them, but they do not seem to have any bearing on the ideas he wishes to express; he is able to show by gestures that he has not lost all kinds of memory; it is the special memory, not only of spoken but of written words, that he has lost.

Henry Head (1926; 1963, pp. 428—429) classified aphasic language disturbances (impairments of symbolic formulation and expression) into four broad

---

[2] As a historical note, credit for being "among the first" to recognize the importance of the left cerebral hemisphere for control (dominance) of language functions should go to Dr. Marc Dax on the basis of a paper written in 1936. For a review of the Dax-Broca controversy, see Critchley (1970, pp. 63—66).

categories. Because of their historic significance, we shall review them briefly at this time:

1. "*Verbal aphasia* consists of a difficulty in forming words for external or internal speech." The patient's ability to comprehend spoken or written content is usually considerably greater than is his ability for utterance or writing. "The disorder affects mainly verbal structure and words as integral parts of a phrase; their nominal value and significance remain relatively intact."

2. "*Syntactical aphasia* is essentially a disorder of balance and rhythm; syntax suffers greatly. . . the patient has plenty of words, but their arrangement into coordinated phrases is defective. . . . Comprehension of the meaning of words, however, is always in excess of power to employ them in discourse."

3. "*Nominal aphasia* comprises loss of power to use names and want of comprehension of the significant value of words and other symbols . . . patients read with extreme difficulty, writing is grossly affected, and they suffer from defective appreciation of single numbers or letters."

4. "*Semantic aphasia* consists in a want of recognition of the full significance of words and phrases apart from their direct verbal meaning . . . the patient may understand a word or a short phrase, but its ultimate significance escapes him and he fails to comprehend the final intention of some command imposed on him orally or in print."

Head's categories represented an attempt to avoid classification according to an intake-output dichotomy. In addition, they reveal Head's bias against the notion of discrete or single (pure) aphasic disorders. The categories were, however, too broad to differentiate clinically among aphasic patients. Too many subdifficulties are included under each category, and there is considerable overlap between categories. Despite these limitations, Head's classification system did influence the thinking of students of aphasia. The influence appears to be reflected clearly in the classification system of Weisenburg and McBride.

Weisenburg and *McBride* (1935), like Henry Head, developed a classification system that avoided a clear commitment to the intake-output dichotomy for aphasic disorders as well as the notion of pure or isolated language defects. They used the following classifications for aphasic linguistic disturbances:

Predominantly receptive—The greatest amount of disturbance is in the individual's ability to comprehend spoken or written symbols.

Predominantly expressive—The greatest amount of disturbance is in the individual's ability to express ideas in speech or in writing.

Amnesic—The patient's chief difficulty is in the evocation of appropriate words as names for objects, conditions, relationships, qualities, and so on. Amnesic disturbances are in effect a subtype of expressive disturbance.

Expressive-receptive—Both receptive and expressive language functions are extremely disturbed. In early stages of aphasic involvements, this is likely to be true of a great many patients. Only a comparatively few patients continue to manifest equally severe disturbances of both reception and expression. Usually, receptive functions improve spontaneously to a greater degree than do expressive functions.

Essentially the same criticism we noted for the Head classifications may be directed to the Weisenburg and McBride categories. They are too broad, cover too many impairments under a single grouping, and do not serve to differentiate aphasic patients according to syndromes of impairment. The classifications probably represent a reaction against overclassification according to isolated linguistic symptoms and to discrete localization of cerebral pathology based on specific impairments. Despite the limitations of the Weisenburg and McBride classifications, they have served as a model for the development of aphasic inventories, such as *Examining for Aphasia* (Eisenson, 1954), which indicate awareness of the broad categories but which have provided subcategories for differentiating aphasic disorders.

A. R. Luria (1964, 1966), a Russian neuropsychologist and aphasiologist, provides us with a classification system that has its basis in Pavlovian neurophysiology. Luria's system classifies aphasic impairments according to their underlying or primary disturbed function and the related defect in speech and language. The basic classifications follow:

1. *Sensory aphasia*: a disturbance in the analysis and synthesis of speech sounds (primary defect) resulting in defects in the comprehension of speech, defects in word production, and in writing which parallel those of speech.

2. *Acoustic-amnestic aphasia*: a disturbance, often transitory, in the retention of audio-speech traces resulting in impairment that increases as the content—the amount of information the patient is required to process—is increased. Thus, a patient may be able to repeat or write a single word or a digit on direction, but have difficulty with a nonfixed series of verbal items. Patients often "find significant difficulty in developed speech and speech thought, which is greatly disturbed because of the instability of verbal traces" (Luria, 1964, p. 151).

3. *Afferent (kinesthetic) motor aphasia*: the basic disturbance is in the kinesthetic analysis of speech movements. "If the necessary afferent synthesis is impaired, the differential directional impulses, necessary for speech muscles, become impossible." The result of such underlying impairment is a disturbance in the production of the fundamental units of speech, the *articulemes*. In its most severe form, the patient may show a complete apraxia for articulation. In less severe form, the patient may repeat isolated sounds, or confuse sounds which are made by action of the lips (b, p, m) or by action of the tongue tip (l, d, n). Basically, the patient shows deficiency in using afferent stimulation as a control for articulatory production.

4. *Efferent (kinetic) motor aphasia*: the basic impairment is in the kinetic analysis for a *sequence or succession of speech movements*. The patient does not have difficulty with the production of the individual sound (articuleme) but with the sequential order of articulation required in oral linguistic production. Parallel defects are found in writing, so that patients may transpose letters, or repeat letters in their written effort, though they may have no difficulty in the correct writing of a single letter.

5. *Semantic aphasia*: the primary disturbance is in the simultaneous organization of the components of speech, the special significance a unit of language has by virtue of its context or verbal connections. This impairment is manifest in the patient's difficulty for the appreciation of the meaning of a verbal formulation, of the "logico-grammatical structure of speech" (Luria, 1964, p. 156).

6. *Dynamic aphasia*: "Fundamental to this dynamic aphasia is probably a disturbance of *inner speech* which ... has a shortened structure, a predicative function, and serves as a fundamental means for the transformation of a fore-shortened idea into developed outer speech and for the change of developed speech into a fore-shortened scheme of thought" (Luria, 1964, pp. 159–160). Although Luria does not appear to be as certain of the nature of the primary impairment for dynamic aphasia as he is for his other types, the patient's basic difficulty seems to be in a failure to transform self-talk into talk for others (to encode his thinking into verbal propositions) or transform (decode) another's propositions into self-thinking or "inner speech." The apparent defect is active propositionizing.

It is obvious that Luria's system of classification rejects any notion of dichotomy between intake and output defects, or of any discrete or pure aphasic disturbances. An underlying disorder (*primary defect*) as for phonemic analysis (sensory aphasia) may produce a variety of aphasic symptoms which include comprehension of speech, of naming, reading, and writing. How the individual learned language functions will in part determine his impairments. Thus a person who learned to read by "sounding out" will have more difficulty in reading in the event of sensory aphasia than will one who learned to read by the "whole word" or "word-picture" method and bypassed any sounding out of the visual (letter) representations.

R. Jakobson approaches the classification of aphasic language disorders from the position of a linguist on the premise that "the most striking symptoms of aphasia cannot be found without the guiding and vigilant assistance of linguistics" (1964, p. 21). Aphasic involvements, Jakobson believes, can be classified with two broad basic categories: *similarity disorders* and *contiguity disorders*. Similarity (selection) disorders are basic to errors in decoding; contiguity or combination disorders are basic to errors in encoding.

Jakobson reconciles his two broad categories with Luria's six types of aphasia. "Three types of aphasia—the so-called efferent, dynamic and afferent types are characterized by *contiguity* disorders with a deterioration of the context; whereas the three other types— . . . the sensory, semantic and amnestic—display *similarity* disorders with damage to the code. The same two groups, viewed in terms of verbal behavior, are opposed to each other as *encoding* and *decoding* disturbances (Jakobson, 1964, pp. 35–36).

Jakobson's emphasis on a dichotomy between decoding and encoding impairments seems to be moving in a direction away from Luria. We agree with Jakobson that the term *predominantly* should be the assumed prefix before each of the categories "since impairments in one of the two coding processes generally affect the opposite process also" (Jakobson, 1964, p. 26).

Figure 5-1 indicates the linguistic dimensions that, according to Jakobson, underlie the six types of aphasia.

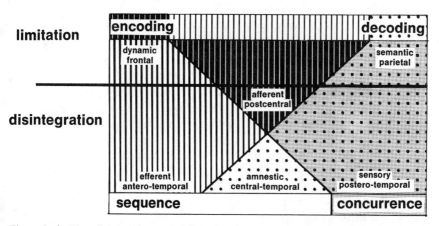

Figure 5–1. The dichotomies underlying the six types of aphasic impairments. (From Jakobson, Roman, Toward a linguistic typology of aphasic impairments. In DeReuck, A. and O'Connor, M., eds., *Disorders of Language*. London: The Ciba Foundation, 1964, p. 35.)

J. Wepman and *L. Jones*, in discussing their Language Modalities Test for Aphasia (1961 and 1966), present a fivefold classification for aphasic language disturbances. Three of the classifications, the pragmatic, semantic, and syntactic, follow the model of the linguist, Charles Morris (1938), in his view of the language process. The Wepman and Jones classifications follow:

1. *Pragmatic aphasia*—defined as a disorder of symbol formulation in which the patient's impairment is in conceptualizing from a given stimulus. "In pragmatic aphasia there appears to be a disruption of the ability to obtain meaning from a stimulus and to use it as a basis for orderly symbol formulation" (Wepman and Jones, 1966, pp. 146–

147). Patients so classified present the following defects in their speech: (a) their utterances convey little meaning to a listener; (b) their verbal output features high-frequency words and repetitive neologisms in place of substantive words (nouns, verbs, adjectives); (c) they use inappropriate substantive words; and (d) they show a lack of awareness of their errors.

On the positive side, pragmatic aphasics tend to maintain appropriate pitch and intonation and, despite their restricted vocabularies, present a normal distribution of the various parts of speech.

2. *Semantic aphasia*—a disorder of symbol formulation in which the patient has difficulty in recalling and evoking an appropriate and meaningful verbal sign of a previously acquired concept. Patients with semantic aphasia present the following defects: (a) except for very high-frequency generalized terms, the semantic aphasic has great difficulty in evoking once well-known proper names and substantive words; and (b) circumlocutions and gestures may be substituted for words which cannot be recalled.[3]

Positive attributes of the semantic aphasic include the maintenance of appropriate grammatical forms and intonation and the high-frequency substantive words, as well as the function words (articles, prepositions, demonstratives, and pronouns).

3. *Syntactic aphasia*—defined as a disorder of symbol formulation characterized by impairment in the individual's previously established grammatical structure. Syntactic aphasic patients present the following defects: (a) omission or misuse of function words and grammatical markers (inflectional endings) to indicate tense and numbers; (b) except for automatic "set" phrases and sentences, such as "go away," there is a marked inability for producing conventional sentences; utterances become "telegraphic," consisting essentially of single substantive words; and (c) the pitch and intonation are absent, although appropriate inflection may be used for single-word utterances.

4. *Jargon aphasia*—characterized by unintelligible sound combinations but by recognizable intonation. Significantly, although the utterances convey no meaning to a listener, the sounds and sound combinations used are consistent with the phonemic patterns of the patient's linguistic system.

We regard jargon aphasia as a transitory stage and not as a true aphasic classification.

5. *Global aphasia*—characterized by severe impairment in the production, and presumably in the comprehension of language. A patient's output may be limited to a single automatized word, phrase, or a neologism.

---

[3] We recognize, of course, that the Wepman-Jones classification of semantic aphasia fits into the traditional concept of *anomia*.

The patient, if he attempts communication at all, is likely to do so by employing primitive gestures.

We regard global aphasia as a severe early state of disorder. If it is maintained, it is probably accompanied or is at least indistinguishable from intellectual deterioration. Wepman and Jones (1966, p. 146) regard the *pragmatic, semantic,* and *syntactic* aphasias as impairments of three specific linguistic processes which suggest that aphasia might be viewed "as a regressive psycholinguistic process phenomenon."[4]

H. Schuell's (1964) classification systems differs from the others that we have discussed in that she is primarily concerned with the diagnostic and prognostic implications of the patients more than she is with categorizing the specific disturbances they present. Schuell rejects systems based on receptive-expressive dichotomies because she believes "no such dichotomy exists." She considers that the classical categories, such as amnesic and syntactic aphasia, offer no meaningful basis for classification because they are not mutually exclusive.

On the basis of her concept of aphasia as "a general language deficit that crosses all language modalities and may or may not be complicated by other sequelae of brain damage, . . . the language deficit itself is characterized by reduction of available vocabulary, impaired verbal retention span, and impaired perception and production of messages, perhaps secondary to impairment of the first two dimensions" (Schuell, Jenkins, and Jiminez-Pabon, 1964, p. 113). Schuell emphasizes that the aphasic's language impairment *is not modality specific*.

Schuell believes that almost all aphasic patients will fall into one of five major categories or groups (1964, pp. 190–191):

Group 1: Simple aphasia—the patient's functional language is characterized by decrements in all language modalities; the patient presents no specific perceptual, sensorimotor, or dysarthric components.

Group 2: The patient's aphasia is complicated by "central involvement of visual processes."

Group 3: The patient manifests "severe reduction of language in all modalities complicated by sensorimotor involvement."

Group 4: The patient has "aphasia with some residual language preserved, and scattered findings that usually include both visual involvement and dysarthria."

Group 5: The patient has "an irreversible aphasic syndrome characterized by almost complete loss of language skills."

The Schuell categories differ essentially in degree of severity of language disturbance and related central sensory or motor impairments.

[4] Wepman presents a more detailed exposition of his classification system in his contribution on "Approaches to the Analysis of Aphasia" in the NINDS Monograph (1970) *Human Communication and Its Disorders*, pp. 127–138.

Summary of Classifications of Aphasia

There is little point in presenting or elaborating on other classification systems at this time. We shall, however, consider several different approaches to classification in the next chapter, which deals with assessment procedures. Classifications depend on how the individual aphasiologist, whether he is a clinician or a theoretician, views aphasic disturbances. Despite the apparent diversity of viewpoints, we believe it is significant that over the past century, from Wernicke (1874) to the present, and despite differences in terminology, several basic common characteristics have been observed in linguistic behavior of aphasic

TABLE 5-1
Nomenclature of the Aphasias[a]

Classical	Wepman	Jakobson	Head
Broca's Motor, Expressive, Anterior	Syntactic	Contiguity	Verbal
Posterior Wernicke's sensory	Pragmatic	Similarity	Syntactic
Anomic Amnesic Amnestic	Semantic	Similarity	Nominal

[a]Dr. Norman Geschwind's tabulation, indicating essential similarities.

patients. These were summarized succinctly by the neurologist Geschwind (1966) and are presented in Table 5-1. Our own position is that the terminology included in Chapter 1 includes an adequate basis for the classification of aphasic disorders as well as of disorders frequently associated with aphasia.

References

Critchley, M. 1970. *Aphasiology and Other Aspects of Language.* London: Edward Arnold.

DeReuck, A., and O'Connor, M., eds. 1964. *Disorders of Language.* London: J. & A. Churchill.

Eisenson, J. 1954. *Examining for Aphasia*, rev. ed. New York: Psychological Corporation.

Geschwind, N. 1966. In *Speech, Language, and Communication.* Vol. 3 in *Brain Function,* Carterette, E. C., ed. Los Angeles: University of California Press, pp. 1–16.

Head, H. 1926. *Aphasia and Kindred Disorders of Speech.* New York: Cambridge University Press and Macmillan. Reprinted by Hafner Publishing Co., New York, 1963.

Jakobson, R. 1964. Toward a linguistic typology of aphasic impairments. In *Disorders of Language,* DeReuck, A., and O'Connor, M., eds. London: J. & A. Churchill, pp. 21–46.

Luria, A. 1964. Factors and forms of aphasia. In *Disorders of Language,* DeReuck, A., and O'Connor, M., eds. London: J. & A. Churchill, pp. 143–167.

_____. 1966. *Higher Cortical Functions in Man.* New York: Basic Books.

Morris, C. 1938. Foundations of the theory of signs. In *International Encyclopedia of Unified Science.* Chicago: University of Chicago Press.

NINDS Monograph No. 10. 1970. *Human Communication and Its Disorders.* Washington, D. C., U. S. Department of Health, Education and Welfare, National Institutes of Health.

Pribram, K. 1971. *Languages of the Brain.* Englewood Cliffs, N. J.: Prentice-Hall, Inc.

Schuell, H., Jenkins, J. J., and Jimenez-Pabon, E. 1964. *Aphasia in Adults.* New York: Harper & Row, pp. 188–210.

Spreen, O., and Wachal, R. S. 1970. Psycholinguistic analysis of aphasic language. *Research Monograph* No. 18. Victoria, B. C.: University of Victoria.

Weisenburg, T., and McBride, K. 1935. *Aphasia.* New York: Commonwealth Fund.

Wepman, J., and Jones, L. 1961. *Studies in Aphasia: An Approach to Testing.* Chicago: University of Chicago: Education-Industry Service.

_____. 1966. In *Speech, Language, and Communication.* Vol. 3 in *Brain Function,* Carterette, E. C., ed. Los Angeles: University of California Press, pp. 141–172.

6

Assessment of Aphasic Disorders

Views of Aphasia and Approaches to Assessment

There is considerably more to the assessment of aphasic persons than we shall attempt to consider in this chapter. In earlier chapters we discussed intellectual and behavioral modifications associated with aphasia and considered some of the procedures and tests employed in studies along that line. There are, however, other areas of study which, although important for the student concerned in general with the implications of acquired brain damage, and which are without doubt of significance in understanding all that may happen to an aphasic individual, are beyond the immediate scope of this chapter.[1]

What to include in assessing an aphasic person is, of course, related to how the assessor views aphasia and what he considers to be of such importance that omission would make the inventory inadequate except possibly as a screening device. In his proposal for an international standardization and unification of neuropsychological examination methods, Weigl (1966) summarized his recom-

[1] The student interested in these related areas of study may consult The Information Center for Hearing, Speech, and Disorders of Human Communication, *A Bibliography of Adult Aphasia Tests*, Baltimore: Johns Hopkins Medical Institutions, 1968. This bibliography includes 86 references to studies, tests, and procedures for assessing perception of space, auditory perception, brain scanning approaches for localization of lesions, evoked potential studies, modifications of intellectual function, as well as published inventories for language impairments *per se*.

Another relevant bibliography is Wepman, J., *A Selected Bibliography on Brain Impairment, Aphasia, and Organic Psychodiagnosis*, Chicago: Language Research Associates, 1961.

mendations for minimal items to be included in an inventory of aphasic and agnostic disturbances. These items are incorporated in Table 6–1.

As we indicated earlier, the approach to testing of aphasic patients, and specific procedures consistent with the approach, depend on the examiner's philosophy of the overall nature and implications of aphasic disturbances. If the individual's philosophy is one which looks upon the aphasic as a person who, because of brain damage, has undergone permanent intellectual changes and has evolved a "new" personality, then the testing should seek to evaluate the changes so that a therapeutic program consistent with the changes can be undertaken. For example, for the clinician who accepts the point of view of Kurt Goldstein (1948, Chap. 4) that the various dysfunctions of aphasia are the manifestations of a single basic disorder—the loss of ability to grasp the essential nature of a process—the approach should be one for determining the extent of the basic disorder. Assessment then would employ psychological techniques such as are used by Goldstein and Scheerer (1941) in their test for abstract and concrete behavior, or by Weigl (1966). An aphasiologist such as Schuell (1965), who views aphasia as a unitary language disorder that "crosses all language modalities," approaches assessment differently from one such as Wepman (1961), who considers aphasic disturbances to be modality-bound and therefore differentially classifiable. We shall review several of the published tests available and in current use in English-speaking countries as well as test inventories presently being developed.[2] The problems inherent in test construction, as Benton (1967) observes, vary not only with how the author of the inventory views aphasia, but also with how he may view language or intelligence. We recommend the Benton (1967) essay on "Problems of Test Construction in the Field of Aphasia" as required reading for students of aphasia who are interested in problems and approaches in assessment.

Examination Procedures

Two assessment procedures—Henry Head's Serial Tests and Weisenburg and McBride's tests—are important landmarks in any consideration of examinations for aphasia.

HEAD'S SERIAL TESTS

Head's tests (1926; 1963, Vol. I, pp. 142–165) represent a systematic *procedure for assessing aphasic impairments*.[3] The underlying philosophic principle of

---

[2] Space limitations do not permit the inclusion of all currently published procedures and tests in English for assessing aphasic disorders. No slight is intended to authors of inventories not included in this chapter.

[3] In any contemporary sense, Head's Serial Tests are not standardized but represent, instead, a systematic procedure for administering his inventory. Head used 26 subjects of

TABLE 6–1 Standard-Minimum for the Examination of Aphasic and Agnosic Disturbances (Syndromes)

Input	Output						
	Verbal Examination			Nonverbal Examination			
				Through Selection of Sounds, Objects, or Words from Several Offered			
	Oral	Graphic	Gnoso-practic				
Recognition of Objects							
Visual	Naming	Spontaneous writing	Description through gestures	Sounds	Objects (for tactile perception)	Words (written)	Words (spoken by examiner)
Tactile	Naming	Spontaneous writing	Description through gestures	Sounds	Objects (for visual perception)	Words (written)	Words (spoken by examiner)
Auditory	Naming	Spontaneous writing	Description through gestures	Objects (for tactile perception)	Objects (for visual perception)	Words (written)	Words (spoken by examiner)
Understanding of words							
Visual (reading)	Reading aloud	Copying	Description through gestures	Sounds	Objects (for visual perception)	Objects (for visual perception)	Words (spoken by examiner)
Auditory (hearing)	Repeating	Writing from dictation	Description through gestures	Sounds	Objects (for tactile perception)	Objects (for visual perception)	Words (offered in writing)

From Weigl, E., "On the Construction of Standard Psychological Tests in Cases of Brain Damage," *Journal of Neurological Sciences*, 1966, 3, 123–127.

Head's test is revealed in his statement, "An inconsistent response is one of the most striking results produced by a lesion of the cerebral cortex" (Head, 1926; 1963, p. 145). Accordingly, Head decided that adequate assessment must include testing and retesting of a function in graduated sequences and in several different ways (through different modalities). To quote Head (1926; 1963, Vol. I, pp. 145–46):

Not only is it necessary to arrange the tests in sequence, but each set must be placed before the patient in several different ways. For example, six common objects are laid on the table in front of him, and he is asked to point to the one which corresponds to a duplicate placed in his hand out of sight. This is repeated for eighteen or twenty-four observations, so that the choice of any one object recurs three or four times in the course of the series. He next gives names to the various objects one by one, indicates each one in turn as it is named by the examiner and makes his selection in answer to printed words set before him on a card. Finally, he writes down the names without saying anything aloud. The order in which each single test follows another in the series remains the same throughout the various methods of examination; this alone makes it possible to draw any conclusion from the inconstant responses which are so disconcerting, unless the answers are recorded in this manner. Moreover, this method enables us to learn how the patient responds to the same sequence of tests presented to him in different ways.

It is also important to graduate the severity of the task before concluding to what extent the patient can speak, read or write. For instance, he may be able to touch his eye or his ear correctly to oral or printed commands, although he fails entirely to do so if the right or left hand is specified. Similarly, a man can write his own name and address, but not that of his mother with whom he lives, and the hands of the clock may be set to an order given in figures, but not when it is expressed in words.

Head's Serial Tests included the following:
1. *Naming and recognition of common objects*: "Six objects of daily use, such as a pencil, a key, a penny, a match-box, a pair of scissors, and a knife." *Recognition* was determined visually by matching to sample and tactually by having a duplicate object placed in the subject's hand. *Naming* included oral naming for each object indicated, naming to printed command, repetition of word, writing of the name of the object, and copying name from print.
2. *Naming and recognition of colors*: The "objects" named are eight strips of colored silk.
3. *The man, cat, and dog tests*: The patient is asked to read aloud, write from dictation, write by seeing pictures, repeat, and copy sentences and picture equivalents such as the cat and the man, the dog and cat, the man and the dog, and so on.

---

varying age and etiology, including 19 World War I veterans with gunshot or sharpnel wounds. He administered his tests over a period of years to the same patient population and made detailed notes of his observations, which he reported in Volume II of his *Aphasia and Kindred Disorders of Speech* (1926).

4. *Clock Tests*: Two clocks are used, with various times set on one. The other is given to the patient and "he is asked to place the hands in an exactly similar position to that of the other one, set by the observer." The test calls for direct imitation, telling the time, setting hands of the clock to oral commands and to printed commands (by ordinary nomenclature and by railway time; e.g., twenty to one and 12:40).

5. *The coin bowl tests*: The patient is required to place a coin—a penny—into one of four bowls "according to a series of numerical commands." These commands include one spoken by the examiner, by a printed command read silently by the patient, and one given by the patient's reading the direction (command) aloud so as "to carry out the action demanded under the influence of words spoken by himself." (Head, 1926; 1963, p. 156).

6. *The hand, eye, and ear tests*: "First of all the patient, seated opposite the observer, attempts to imitate a series of movements which consists in touching an eye or an ear with one or the other hand (p. 157)." Subsequent tasks include executing the action reflected in a mirror, executing the command according to a pictorial representation (direction), pictorial commands reflected in a mirror, oral command, written (silent reading) command, and oral reading. In addition the patient is asked to write down the movements made by the examiner, and to write down the movements reflected in a mirror or of the examiner sitting opposite to him.

Other tests included by Head were *reciting and writing the alphabet* in sequence and arranging the letters in sequence from 26 cards, each with a different letter. Similarly, patients were examined with *days of the week* and *months of the year. Comprehension of reading* was ascertained by having the patient read a paragraph from a newspaper or a book and paraphrase the contents. Picture interpretation might be included by placing a picture before the patient and asking him to describe, orally and/or in writing, what he sees. *Oral and written counting* up to a hundred, as well as arithmetic computation of two sets of three-figure numbers, with and without "carrying," were included. Additional tests included *coin naming* (oral and written), *drawing* from a model and from memory, and drawing of an animal—an elephant. Head observed (p. 164) that "the salient features of an elephant, especially its trunk and tusks, are so obvious that their omission from the drawing clearly indicates defective powers of formulation." Other drawing tasks included "anything that comes into mind, unprompted" and producing a sketch of a ground plan of some familiar room.

It is apparent that Head's tests were taxing of patient time and interest. Many of the procedures were confusing as well as boring. However, they represent what Head considered relevant to determining the presence and degree of symbolic formulation and expression as manifest in speaking, reading, writing, and gesture. Weisenburg and McBride (1935, p. 91), in commenting on Head's tests, say: "As to their value in differentiating the aphasic from the normal, the simpler tests are satisfactory while the more difficult tests are not, for the latter require complex performances in which many normal persons are not altogether successful. These more difficult tests cannot be used satisfactorily with aphasic patients without knowledge of normal performances, both qualitative and quantitative, which Head did not obtain."

Several brief examinations employing Head's procedure relative to type of task—for example, use of common objects and multiple means of eliciting responses—were published and attained fairly wide use in the United States during the period immediately preceding and following World War II. These include Chesher's *Test for Clinical Examination in Aphasia* (1937), *The Wells-Ruesch Examination* (1945), and the *Halstead-Wepman Screening Test for Aphasia* (1949).

All three of the cited examinations are screening instruments intended for determining obvious areas of impairment or of relative strengths in brain-damaged persons who might be expected to have aphasic involvements. Slight or subtle deficiencies are not likely to be picked up by the results of the examinations unless the examiner is a sophisticated clinician who is able to observe and note time delays in responses and the quality of a patient's response in the light of his premorbid vocational and educational background and assumed (correlated) level of intellectual potential.

THE GOLDSTEIN-SCHEERER TESTS OF ABSTRACT AND CONCRETE THINKING

The Goldstein-Scheerer Tests (1941) constitute an inventory of psychological procedures intended to assess quantitative and qualitative changes in intellectual functioning in brain-damaged persons with specific reference to abstract and concrete reasoning. According to Goldstein and Scheerer (1941, p. 9),

Organic pathology in patients with brain disease disintegrates human behavior in such a way that the capacity for abstract behavior is impaired to a greater or lesser degree in the patient. Thus, he becomes more or less reduced to a level of concreteness of situational thinking and acting so that he can perform only those tasks which can be fulfilled in a concrete manner.

In order to avoid misunderstanding, we have to emphasize that the process of disintegration toward the concrete does not abolish the arousal of ideas and of thoughts as such. What the deterioration affects and modifies is the *way of manipulating and operating with ideas and thoughts*. Thoughts do, however, arise but can become effective only in a concrete way. Just as the patient cannot deal with outerworld objects in an abstract manner, he has to deal with ideas simply as "things." With respect to the outerworld we may say that concepts or categories, meanings other than situational or means-end relations are not within the patient's scope. This lack of abstract frame of reference holds also for the patient's inner experiences; it manifests itself in his inability to arouse and organize, to direct and hold in check ideas or feelings by conscious volition. He cannot detach his ego from his inner experiences; therefore he is rather a passive subject to instead of an active master of them (e.g., obsession, compulsion, in functional disturbances—rigidity, etc.). In patients with cortical damage, voluntary arousal or recall of images, events, or sentences, etc., is impaired and only takes place if the patient is brought into the concrete situation to which that content belongs.

The battery of tests in the Goldstein-Scheerer inventory includes block designs, color form sorting, a stick test, and one for object sorting.

We view the Goldstein-Scheerer tests as a procedure for assessing a brain-damaged person's change of inclination away from the abstract and toward the concrete rather than an assessment of absolute and irreversible modifications. As such, the tests may reveal problems that the aphasiologist needs to understand in a therapeutic program for an aphasic person.[4]

WEISENBURG AND MCBRIDE'S TESTS

The assessment procedures of Weisenburg and McBride (1935) come considerably closer to a standardized examination than did those of Henry Head. The aphasic population to which the Weisenburg and McBride battery of psychological and educational achievement tests were administered included 60 hospitalized aphasic patients (8 traumatic, 15 tumor, and 37 with vascular lesions), all English speaking and all under 60 years of age, who were "cleared" for evidence of psychosis or advanced arteriosclerosis. Two comparison groups were used. One of the groups—the "controls"—consisted of 85 adults, presumably free of psychosis and evidence of brain damage, who were patients on surgical and orthopedic wards. The second comparison group included 38 patients with unilateral brain lesions but without evidence of aphasic involvement.[5]

Weisenburg and McBride did not produce a new test or inventory for assessing aphasic patients. Instead, they "constructed" a test battery, chosen, as we have indicated, from published and standardized psychological and educational tests. The tests were selected to meet the following criteria: (1) to cover all the

[4] As a footnote to the point on the aphasic's disinclination toward the abstract attitude rather than an "irreversible" loss, we should like to point out that our own experience indicates that many patients can be motivated to a higher and more abstract level of performance than their new "norm" of functioning. We have found this to be so with traumatic (head-penetrating wound) military patients during World War II and the Korean War, as well as with vascular civilian patients treated more recently. During World War II we invited Dr. Kurt Goldstein to reexamine some strongly motivated military patients who had been tested with the Goldstein-Scheerer inventory. These selected patients did not show any significant impairment in abstract attitude. After doing his own evaluation Dr. Goldstein observed, somewhat perplexed, "Americans, they are different!"

[5] Schuell, Jenkins, and Jiminez-Pabon (1964, p. 41) indicate both their appreciation and reservations about the findings obtained by Weisenburg and McBride. The chief criticism is that despite their general sophistication of procedures, Weisenburg and McBride used subjects who were not neurologically stable and incorporated the findings on these patients along with others who were neurologically stable. This group included 22 subjects with right-cerebral lesions and without aphasia. Weisenburg and McBride's findings indicate that the performance of this subgroup was essentially like that of normal adults on tests of language but inferior to normals on nonlanguage tests. This finding is consistent with subsequent studies (see Reitan and others) reported in the more recent literature on intellectual modifications associated with brain damage.

performance which may be affected by brain lesion, (2) to provide for further testing (in depth) for a detailed study of particular disturbances, and (3) to make it possible to arrive at "a qualitative analysis of the performance, enabling the examiner to study the relative importance of the specific speech defect and other changes, the patient's method of work, and so forth" (Weisenburg and McBride, 1935, p. 139).

The Weisenburg and McBride battery took an average of 19 hours for each patient. Such an amount of time may be fruitfully invested in an experimental investigation, but is obviously not practical for routine patient examination. Two shorter battery of tests, one intended for patients with severe disorders and one intended for cases with slight disorders, are included in Appendix II of the Weisenburg and McBride text. The estimated time for administration of these batteries is given as from two to three hours.

The principal tests used by Weisenburg and McBride are presented in Table 6–2.

TABLE 6–2
Principal Tests in Weisenburg and McBride Battery

Speaking

Records of spontaneous speech and reactive responses
Automatic word series: saying days of week and months of year; saying the alphabet; reciting a prayer or poem

Naming

Naming of standard objects, colors, and line drawings

Repeating

Words containing all English sounds, and short familiar phrases and sentences

Understanding Spoken Language

Response to everyday questions and comments
Comprehension of words and sentences, as shown by response to Gates Word, Phrase, and Sentence Reading Test, read aloud to the patient
Response to Test of Following Directions
Response to tests involving the comprehension of spatial terms and relationships, including Head's Hand, Ear, and Eye Test and the Abelson Geometrical Figures Test

Reading

Oral: Gates Word Pronunciation Test
Gray Oral Reading Paragraphs
Reading comprehension: Gates Primary Reading Tests
Chapman Unspeeded Reading-Comprehension Test
Thorndike McCall Reading Scale

Writing

Records of spontaneous writing
Writing to dictation
  Word dictation: Morrison McCall Spelling Scale
  Sentence dictation: Stanford Achievement Dictation Test
Oral spelling: List of words from Gates
Copying: Standard paragraph

Arithmetic

Computations: Stanford Achievement Arithmetic Computation Test
Problems: Stanford Achievement Arithmetic Reasoning Test

Language Intelligence Tests

Controlled association tests
  Opposites
  Mixed analogies
Sentence-completion test: Kelley Trabue Completion Exercises
Absurdities
Vocabulary
  Oral: Stanford Binet Vocabulary Test
  Printed: Thorndike Test of Word Knowledge

Reproduction of Verbal Material

Reproduction of digit and letter sequences, series of nonsense syllables, disconnected words, sentences, and a short story

Nonlanguage Tests

Formboards, imitation tests, digit-symbol substitution tests, drawing and picture completions and reconstructions: Pintner Paterson Performance Scale and Pintner Non-Language Mental Test
Drawing
  Figures reproduced immediately after presentation
  From model: drawing of a chair
  Drawing of a man scored on the Goodenough Scale

From Weisenburg, T. E., and McBride, K., *Aphasia: A Clinical and Psychological Study.* New York: The Commonwealth Fund, 1935, pp. 135–136.

EXAMINING FOR APHASIA (J. EISENSON, 1954)

Eisenson's inventory was devised as a clinical instrument to provide the examiner with a guided judgment for assessing the variety of language disturbances and disturbances related to language functions (agnosias and apraxias) which are considered to be common features of aphasic patients. It is avowedly a clinical instrument intended to provide a protocol of type and degree of severity of language and related deficits. Developmentally, the instrument and the general approach follows the lines of Weisenburg and McBride (1935). The various test items, some of which are taken directly or adapted from standardized educational achievement tests, are selected to reveal both the assets and liabilities of the patient at the time of testing. Much of the material is graded, so that a level of ability within a given area of language function can be estimated. Although most of the items are scored on a pass-fail basis in terms of the actual examination stimulus material, the clinician is advised to consider any correct or near-correct responses offered by the patient. There are, in addition, open-ended test items intended to elicit responses which require individual evaluation. Test items are arranged to permit assessment for primarily receptive (evaluative) functions and for manifestly productive (expressive) functions. Receptive-evaluative items include visual, auditory, and tactile agnosias, auditory (verbal) aphasia, and silent reading (alexia). The manifestly productive (expressive) disturbances include nonverbal and verbal apraxias, subpropositional (automatic) speech, spelling, writing, naming (identification), word finding, and arithmetic processes. Two paragraphs for oral reading provide a basis for assessing paraphasic defects for nonspeaker-formulated content and an opportunity for comparing such content with the patient's spontaneous language.

Examining for Aphasia includes a manual of directions and a record entry form. The manual describes administrative procedures and scoring. It includes illustrative material used in the examination. A check sheet permits the clinician to make a profile of the patient's tested abilities.

The author has found the inventory useful as an initial examination for estimating the areas and approximate levels of linguistic abilities as well as a retest instrument for measuring patient improvement.

The entire examination takes from 30 to 90 minutes to administer, depending on the severity of the patient's impairments and the effective rate at which he can work. *Examining for Aphasia* may be used for rapid screening by administering the first and last items of each subtest. The scope of the examination is indicated in Table 6–3.

TABLE 6–3
Examining for Aphasia: Summary[a]

Primarily Evaluative and Receptive Disturbances

Place letter of item in appropriate column.

	Complete	Severe	Moderate	Little	None
A. Agnosias					
1. Visual agnosia					
a. Objects					
b. Pictures					
c. Colors					
d. Forms					
e. Reduced-size pictures					
f. Numbers					
g. Letters					
h. Words					
i. Sentences					

2. Auditory agnosia
  a. Sounds
  b. Words
	Complete	Severe	Moderate	Little	None

3. Tactile agnosia a. Object identification	Complete	Severe	Moderate	Little	None

B. Aphasias

1. Auditory verbal
   comprehension
  a. Sentences
  b. Paragraphs
	Complete	Severe	Moderate	Little	None

2. Silent reading
   comprehension
  a. Sentences
  b. Paragraphs
	Complete	Severe	Moderate	Little	None

Notes:

Predominantly Productive and Expressive Disturbances

Place letter of item in appropriate column.

A. Apraxias

1. Nonverbal apraxia
  a. Body parts
  b. Simple skills
  c. Pretended action
	Complete	Severe	Moderate	Little	None

2. Verbal apraxia
  a. Numbers
  b. Words
  c. Sentences
	Complete	Severe	Moderate	Little	None

B. Aphasias

1. Automatic speech
  a. Counting to 20
  b. Recitation of alphabet
  c. Recitation of days of
    week
  d. Recitation of months
    of year
  e. Singing
	Complete	Severe	Moderate	Little	None

2. Writing numbers and
   letters
  a. Numbers
  b. Letters
	Complete	Severe	Moderate	Little	None

3. Spelling	Complete	Severe	Moderate	Little	None

4. Writing from dictation	Complete	Severe	Moderate	Little	None
5. Naming	Complete	Severe	Moderate	Little	None
6. Word finding	Complete	Severe	Moderate	Little	None

7. Arithmetic processes
   a. Computations
   b. Problems
	Complete	Severe	Moderate	Little	None

8. Clock setting	Complete	Severe	Moderate	Little	None
9. Oral reading	Complete	Severe	Moderate	Little	None

Notes:

THE LANGUAGE MODALITIES TEST FOR APHASIA (J. WEPMAN AND L. JONES, 1961)

Wepman and Jones view their test as an instrument to provide a psycholinguistic analysis for an aphasic's language production. To highlight the difference between the Language Modalities Test and other inventories in current use, Wepman and Jones (1966, p. 142) observe (1) that useful distinctions need to be made between responses to visual and auditory material, (2) that considerable information is obscured by testing according to a pass or fail dichotomy, and (3) often real differences become apparent in many patients in their comparative ability to respond to specific stimuli and their ability to communicate in relatively unstructured situations. As a result of these observations, Wepman and Jones developed a "differential psycholinguistic" method for the scoring of an examinee's responses to specific items related to input modality and an evaluation of the patient's free speech. Essentially, the Modalities Test assesses a patient's comprehension and functional use of language according to standardized procedures.

The overall content of the examination covers essentially the same areas as do older as well as other contemporary inventories. Test items which differ from those of the Eisenson inventory include the copying of geometric figures and the opportunity to produce "free speech" by a stimulus picture about which the patient is to make up a "story."

The basic psycholinguistic classifications arrived at by Wepman and Jones in their protocal analysis were discussed in Chapter 5. Their scoring system is summarized in Table 6–4.

TABLE 6–4

Language Modalities Test for Aphasia Scoring Summary (Wepman and Jones)

Scale value (s.v.)[a]	Visual Stimuli												Auditory Stimuli											
	Oral Responses						Graphic Responses						Oral Responses						Graphic Responses					
	1	2	3	4	5	6	1	2	3	4	5	6	1	2	3	4	5	6	1	2	3	4	5	6
Stimulus type																								
Pictures				3	1	2				2	3	1	3				1	2						
Words				3	3								1			4	1		2	1		3		
Numbers	4			2											2	1		3						
Sentences	1		2	3																				

[a]Scoring categories (s.v.) for all oral and graphic responses:

1. correct response
2. phonemic or orthographic response
3. syntactic errors
4. semantic errors
5. jargon or illegible
6. no response

From Carterette, E. C., ed., *Brain Function*, Vol. III: Speech, Language, and Communication, Los Angeles: University of California Press, 1966, p. 143.

MINNESOTA TEST FOR DIFFERENTIAL DIAGNOSIS OF APHASIAS
(H. SCHUELL, 1965)

Schuell says that her test inventory was "designed to permit the examiner to observe the level at which language performance breaks down in each of the principal language modalities, since this is what there is to observe in aphasia... the Minnesota Test looks at the language behavior of aphasic patients, and then proceeds to ask questions about the nature of the disruptions that occur" (Schuell, 1965, p. 3). Although Schuell's inventory assesses aphasia in the principal modalities, she nevertheless emphasizes that *aphasic disturbances cross all language modalities*. However, "the over-all pattern of involvement varies from patient to patient, and this variation makes differential diagnosis possible."

Schuell's major classifications of aphasia, based on an analysis of data derived from her inventory, were discussed in Chapter 5. Schuell views differential diagnosis as the basis for both description of the status of the patient and for prognosis relative to recovery from aphasia. "Careful description of aphasic impairment provides a guide for treatment, since therapy must deal with the disabilities that are present" (1965, p. 5).

The Minnesota Test is a long inventory that in depth and scope enables an examiner to assess the parameters of language and related sensory and motor involvements of aphasic persons. The major areas for assessment include (1) auditory disturbances (items ranging from word recognition, discrimination to sentence and paragraph comprehension), (2) visual and reading disturbances (items include matching of forms to reading comprehension of paragraphs as well as oral reading of sentences), (3) speech and language disturbances (items include testing for articulatory movement to naming, word defining, picture description, and paragraph retelling), (4) visuomotor and writing disturbances (items include copying of forms and letters to writing to dictation and written sentence formulation), and (5) disturbances of numerical relationships and arithmetic processes (items include making change, clock setting, simple numerical combinations, and written problems).

The Minnesota Test for Differential Diagnosis requires considerably more time to administer in full than the two inventories we have just considered. A short version of the test, intended primarily as a screening device, is available (Schuell, 1957).

PORCH INDEX OF COMMUNICATIVE ABILITY (PICA)

Porch (1967) suggested that the two major requirements of an aphasia test are high reliability and a scoring system which specifies the nature of the patient's response in terms of multiple dimensions. He developed a test battery, the Porch Index of Communicative Ability (PICA), in order to satisfy the clinical needs.

A multidimensional scoring system was designed for use with the PICA which describes a response in terms of several dimensions rather than limiting the description to the plus-minus dichotomy which ignores so much important information. This system includes the following dimensions:

Accuracy—the degree of correctness or rightness of a response.

Responsiveness—the ease with which the response is elicited, especially in terms of how much information the patient requires in order to complete the task.

Completeness—the degree to which the patient carries out the task in its entirety.

Promptness—the presence or absence of significant delay in making a response.

Efficiency—the degree of facility the patient demonstrates in performing the motoric aspects of the response.

The procedure for using the multidimensional scale is similar to that for using any rating scale. When the patient responds to a given test item, the scorer decides which of the 16 categories best describes the response and then records the score for that category.

The test battery is made up of 18 subtests, sampling gestural, verbal, and graphic abilities at various levels of difficulties. Each task revolves around ten common objects placed before the patient, a method similar to the one suggested by Head (1926) in his serial tests. This method enables the tester to make some comparisons of results across modalities.

The PICA results are interpreted through the use of an Overall Score which is the mean response level for all test items, a mean response level for each modality, and a mean for each subtest. Additional test interpretation is provided by the use of profiles of subtest means plotted on graphs. These profiles, when compared with percentile contours based on aphasic patient norms, are useful in planning treatment and predicting degrees and rates of potential change in the patient's performance.

The scope of the PICA is indicated in Table 6–5.

Since the publication of the PICA, Porch has refined his scoring procedures. The procedures are described in detail in an article on "Multidimensional Scoring in Aphasia Testing" (Porch, 1971).

THE BOSTON DIAGNOSTIC APHASIA TEST
(H. GOODGLASS AND E. KAPLAN, 1972)

The Boston Diagnostic Aphasia Test was developed in the tradition of approaching the aphasia examination on the one hand as a psychological analysis and measurement of language-related skills and on the other hand as a problem in relating particular configurations of symptoms with their neuropathological correlates. The goal of the authors was to devise an instrument that was

TABLE 6–5
Outline of Test Tasks[a]
Porch Index of Communicative Ability

Test	Output	Task
I	Verbal	To discuss each test object, differentiating its primary characteristics
II	Gestural	To demonstrate the function of each object
III	Gestural	To demonstrate the function of each object as it is handed to subject
IV	Verbal	To name each object
V	Gestural	To read each of ten cards and place it according to printed instructions near the object whose function is stated on the card
VI	Gestural	To point to each object whose function is given verbally by the examiner
VII	Gestural	To read each of ten cards and place it according to printed instructions near the object whose name is stated on the card
VIII	Gestural	To match a picture of each object with the appropriate object
IX	Verbal	To say the name of each object which completes a sentence about the object's function
X	Gestural	To point to each object as it is named by the examiner
XI	Gestural	To match identical objects with each object
XII	Verbal	To imitate the name of each object
A	Graphic	To write a sentence about the function of each object
B	Graphic	To write the name of each object
C	Graphic	To write each object's name spoken by the examiner
D	Graphic	To write each object's name spelled by the examiner
E	Graphic	To copy each object's name
F	Graphic	To copy geometric forms

[a]The test objects were selected according to the following criteria: (a) common to the experience of adults of both sexes, (2) capable of being demonstrated gesturally, and (3) approximately equal in difficulty across all tests. The objects used in the present test are listed here in standard order, i.e., the order in which they are presented to the patient:

1. Toothbrush   3. Pen   5. Fork   7. Pencil   9. Key
2. Cigarette   4. Knife   6. Quarter 8. Matches 10. Comb

sufficiently comprehensive in its exploration of the various facets of language to serve as the basis for a careful case study. At the same time they wished to provide materials with a sufficiently wide range of difficulty and a large enough sampling within subtests to make for reliable quantitative scores over the usual range of severity of patients. A third consideration relative to scoring is that inventories that use pass-fail subtests are likely to miss those features of aphasia which are the principal bases for neurological diagnosis and cerebral localization—the more subtle linguistic features which are hard to quantify—namely, the quality of articulatory errors, grammatical facility, types of paraphasia, and the availability of substantive words in comparison to fluency of output.

Patient's Name_____ Date of rating_____

Rated by_____

Aphasia Severity Rating Scale

0. No usable speech or auditory comprehension.

1. All communication is through fragmentary expression; great need for inference, questioning, and guessing by the listener. The range of information which can be exchanged is limited, and the listener carries the burden of communication.

2. Conversation about familiar subjects is possible with help from the listener. There are frequent failures to convey the idea, but patient shares the burden of communication with the examiner.

3. The patient can discuss *almost all everyday problems* with little or no assistance. However, production of speech and/or comprehension makes conversation about certain material difficult or impossible.

4. Some obvious loss of fluency in speech or facility of comprehension, without significant limitation on ideas expressed or form of expression.

5. Minimal discernible speech handicaps; patient may have subjective difficulties which are not apparent to listener.

Rating Scale Profile of Speech Characteristics

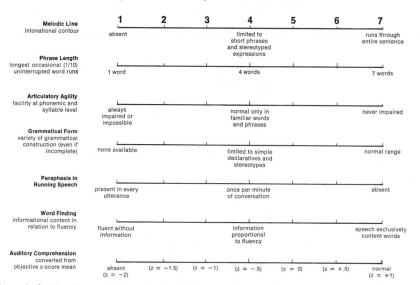

Figure 6–1. The Boston Diagnostic Aphasia Test. (From Goodgalss, H., and Kaplan, E., *Assessment of Aphasia and Related Disorders*. Philadelphia: Lea & Febiger, 1972.)

In common with most aphasia inventories, the Boston Diagnostic Aphasia Test includes subtests in all the modalities of input and output, grouped by modality, and scaled for difficulty within subtests, so that a test may be discontinued at the point the patient fails. The subtests are also arranged in a sequence beginning with elementary matching, and automatized performances to tasks that make a high propositional demand. The selection of tests and the arrangement of items are aimed at making the examiner aware of special features of the aphasia, for example, which if any semantic word categories (numbers, body parts, etc.) are selectively disturbed, and whether comprehension of word category and connotation is spared when word identity is lost. The comparison among subtests on a summary profile sheet is facilitated by their conversion to Z-scores.

A unique feature of the test is a requirement for the careful rating of prosody, fluency, articulation, grammatical level, paraphasia, and word-finding difficulty from a tape-recorded sample of free conversation plus narrative description of a picture situation, with which the examination starts. These are the features which cannot yet be adequately quantified by scored subtests. The Rating Scale Profile of Speech Characteristics along with the Z-Score-Summary Profile can then be compared with samples representing the various localizable aphasic syndromes provided in the manual.

The Aphasia Test proper does not go beyond language to the examination of apractic movement disorders, calculation, and visuo-spatial abilities. However, the accompanying manual, *Assessment of Aphasia and Related Disorders*, provides tests and norms for these functions as well as suggestions for further exploration of language skills. The parameters of functions assessed and the procedure for rating severity of disturbance are indicated in Figure 6-1.

INTERNATIONAL TEST FOR APHASIA

Benton, Spreen, De Renzi, and Vignolo, a team of psychologists and neurologists, are engaged in the construction of a test battery for aphasia that they hope will be adaptable to languages throughout the world. English and Italian versions are being developed at centers in the United States and Italy (Benton, 1967). The preliminary battery is based on the theoretic assumption that "the traditional associationist approach still possessed sufficient validity to warrant formulation of certain test procedures along these lines." The test battery includes the following (Benton, 1967, pp. 42—44):

1. *Visual naming* of common objects (10—40).
2. *Description of use*—the patient is directed to tell the use of 10—20 objects from the basic set of 40.

3—4. *Tactile naming*—on the basis of feeling alone, first with the right and then with the left hand, the patient is directed to name 10—20 objects of the basic set of 40.

5. *Sentence repetition*—the patient is instructed to repeat tape-recorded sentences.

6. *Digit repetitions*—the patient is instructed to repeat tape-recorded series of digits ranging in length from 3 to 9.

7. *Digit reversal*—the patient is instructed to repeat tape-recorded digit series ranging in length from 2—7.

8. *Word fluency*—the patient is instructed to say all the words he can recall beginning with a specific letter; three one-minute trials for three different letters (F, A, S).

9. *Sentence construction*—the patient is instructed to make up sentences from five sets of two or three words.

10. *Object identification by name*—the patient is directed to point to objects named by the examiner. The objects are from the basic 40 used in the inventory.

11. *Identification by sentence*—the patient's comprehension of language is assessed by observing disability to execute (perform) commands of progressively increasing complexity.

12. *Reading names orally*—the patient reads aloud the names of objects from the basic set of 40.

13. *Oral reading*—the patient is instructed to read 12 of the command sentences used in test 11.

14. *Silent reading of names*—the patient reads the written name of an object in a display of ten objects used in the test series.

15. *Reading sentence for meaning*—the patient is instructed to execute 12 written commands used in test 11.

16. *Visual-graphic naming*—the patient is required to write the names of ten objects presented visually. (In this subtest, performance is scored on ability (appropriateness) of naming and not for correctness of spelling.)

17. *Writing names*—essentially, a second scoring of test 16, this time for correctness of spelling. If a patient is not able to write the name of the object presented to him, he is told the name and asked to write it.

18. *Writing to dictation*—the patient is required to write two sentences presented to him orally. Performance is scored on the basis of spelling, punctuation, omissions, and duplications.

19. *Copying sentences*—the patient is presented with two short sentences and is instructed to copy them. Performance is scored as in test 18.

20. *Articulation*—the patient is instructed to repeat 30 meaningful and eight nonsense words presented from a tape recording. Performance is scored on the basis of the number of correctly articulated consonant sound and sound blends.

Benton and his collaborators do not consider that their test battery will provide in-depth protocols of aphasic patients. They view their inventory as an instrument to provide useful clinical information and which will serve as a valid research technique.

Through the uniform application of a standard examination Benton hopes that aphasiologists may establish an *operational understanding* for scientific communication in the field of aphasia. Specific aims for the international (multilingual) battery include (1) the development of standards for an examination that will assess quantitative and qualitative aspects of aphasic disorders, and (2) language performance that can be related to the nature of involvement, prognosis, and clinical procedures.

In the final form, the International Test for Aphasia will be reduced to no more than ten subtests that may be administered in an examination period not to exceed 50 minutes.

THE TOKEN TEST FOR RECEPTIVE DISTURBANCES IN APHASIA

E. De Renzi and L. A. Vignolo (1962) have developed a special test which they consider to be especially sensitive for the detection of receptive disturbances so slight that they are ordinarily overlooked during the course of a clinical evaluation. The test requires the patient to execute (perform) commands based on directions that involve an arrangement of tokens (forms) of two different shapes, two different sizes, and five different colors. The patient is given a series of oral commands which constitute progressively complex and nonredundant messages. In response to each command message, the examinee is required to execute a simple manual act such as picking up, touching, or moving one or more of the token forms.

The Token Test is incorporated in the International Test for Aphasia. De Renzi and Vignolo view their test as "a practical clinical tool, endowed of great sensitivity and contaminated as little as possible by intellectual difficulties." They have, in fact, found that their inventory does detect receptive disturbances which, as already indicated, are not apparent in the usual clinical examination or in conversation with a patient. We consider the Token Test to be an important clinical instrument for the assessment of verbal comprehension through nonverbal simple performance behavior. It is, therefore, as De Renzi and Vignolo indicate, a sensitive instrument for evaluating receptive verbal impairment which would not otherwise become apparent to clinicians. The sentence directions translated by the authors from the original Italian follow:

1. Put the red circle on the green rectangle.
2. Put the white rectangle behind the yellow circle.
3. Touch the blue circle with the red rectangle.
4. Touch—with the blue circle—the red rectangle.
5. Touch the blue circle and the red rectangle.
6. Pick up the blue circle or the red rectangle.
7. Put the green rectangle away from the yellow rectangle.

8. Put the white circle before the blue rectangle.
9. If there is a black circle, pick up the red rectangle. (N.B. There is no black circle.)
10. Pick up the rectangles, except the yellow one.
11. When I touch the green circle, you take the white rectangle. (N.B. Wait a few seconds before touching the green circle.)
12. Put the green rectangle beside the red circle.
13. Touch the rectangles, slowly, and the circles, quickly.
14. Put the red circle between the yellow rectangle and the green rectangle.
15. Except for the green one, touch the circles.
16. Pick the red circle—no!—the white rectangle.
17. Instead of the white rectangle, take the yellow circle.
18. Together with the yellow circle, take the blue circle.
19. After picking up the green rectangle, touch the white rectangle.
20. Put the blue circle under the white rectangle.
21. Before touching the yellow circle, pick up the red rectangle.[6]

The forms (tokens) used in the Token Test are presented in Figure 6—2.

BAY'S TESTS

The German neurologist *E. Bay* (1962) describes a series of tests for the evaluation of both verbal and nonverbal disorders of language. Bay is particularly concerned with making differential distinctions between the impairments of the purely motor aspects of speech—apraxias and dysarthrias—and the true aphasic involvements. Bay, like Goldstein, stresses the importance of evaluating aphasic patients for impairments in level of conceptual thinking. Bay believes that aphasics, as a total population, and those who have naming difficulties in particular, are inclined to impaired conceptual thinking.

Bay uses drawing of pictures from memory and modeling with plastic clay as his procedure for making clinical evaluations as to the patient's ability in conceptualization. For modeling, Bay employs objects such as an egg, a cup, a crocodile, a snake, and a giraffe, or objects chosen by the patient.

Bay draws an analogy between the impairments in the drawings and modeling of aphasic patients and impairments revealed in verbal functioning. He observes that (1962, p. 425):

besides their lack of distinctness, the concepts of aphasics are impaired as to their variability necessary for the adaptation of their actual contents to the shifting demands of the context or situation. This becomes evident in the failure

---

[6] "It should be noted that the test was originally designed for and applied to Italian patients. The orders presented here are the same, translated into English as accurately as possible; therefore, they should be considered merely as a demonstration of the degree of difficulty of the different items. It would be convenient, perhaps, to substitute or modify some of them so as to make them convey, in English, differences of meaning comparable to those involved in the original Italian text" (De Renzi, E., and Vignolo, L. A., *Brain*, 1962, 85, 671).

of aphasics to realize metaphorical meanings or to appreciate jokes and comics, the effect of which depends on an unexpected change in connexion and meanings of concepts. This applies to verbally or pictorially represented comics equally. Such disorders of concept formation become evident in all aphasic patients in all appropriate examinations. Clear conceptual thinking, however, is an absolute prerequisite of human language. Disorders of conceptual thinking of this kind necessarily must produce disorders of language as they appear in aphasia.

The Token Test

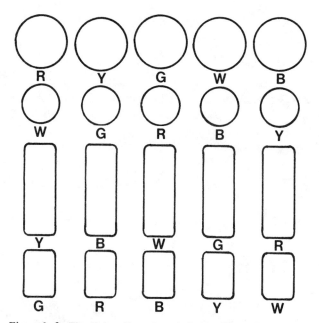

Figure 6–2. The Token Test. R=red, B=blue, G=green, Y=yellow, W=white. Colors are distributed entirely at random. (From De Renzi, E. and Vignolo, L. A., 1962. The Token Test: A sensitive test to detect receptive disturbances in aphasics. *Brain*, 85, 670–672.)

Bay's "tests" of drawing and modeling are clinical procedures which permit a sophisticated clinician to arrive at a judgment about an aspect of intellectual functioning in aphasic patients. The tests are not in any sense to be considered standardized instruments which yield data for objective evaluation. Figure 6–3 includes photographs of models produced by an aphasic patient.

OTHER TEST INVENTORIES AND APPROACHES TO ASSESSMENT

As we indicated earlier in this chapter, we have not attempted to describe or evaluate the numerous test inventories in current use for the assessment of

egg   **pot**

pot   **snake**

crocodile   **giraffe**

Figure 6–3. Examples of plastic objects produced by aphasic patients from models. (From Bay, E., 1962. Aphasia and non-verbal disorders of language., *Brain*, 85, 411–426.)

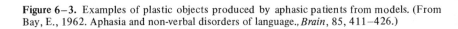

aphasic disorders. We are aware that many agencies engaged in diagnoses, research, and/or therapy with aphasic patients have their own inventories that serve them according to their special purpose. Some of these, such as the Sklar Aphasia Scale (Sklar, 1966), are published instruments. In our selection of inventories, which we hope is representative, we have concentrated on tests and procedures that illustrate differing points of view on the nature of aphasic involvements and philosophies of assessment. Additional approaches that emphasize the use of standardized tests of intelligence, conceptual functioning, and language achievement are described in the literature and may be found in the writings of Weisenburg and McBride (1935), Goldstein (1942 and 1948), and Goldstein and Scheerer (1941). More recent approaches may be found in the writings of Zangwill (1964), Weigl (1966), Bay (1962, 1964), and Luria (1964, 1966a, and 1970). This selection of references is by no means intended to be exhaustive or even fully representative. At best, the references suggest the differences of philosophy and approaches to the assessment of impairments of language and of modifications of intellect that are associated with cerebral pathology and aphasia.

References

Bay, E. 1962. Aphasia and non-verbal disorders of language. *Brain*, 85, 411–426.

_____. 1964. Principles of classification and their influence on our concepts of aphasia. In *Disorders of Language*, DeReuck, A., and O'Connor, M., eds. London: J. & A. Churchill, pp. 122–142.

Benton, A. 1967. Problems in test construction in the field of aphasia. *Cortex*, 1, 32–58.

Chesher, E. C. 1937. Technique for clinical examination in aphasia. *Bulletin of the Neurological Institute of New York*, 6, 134–144.

De Renzi, E., and Vignolo, L. A. 1962. The token test: A sensitive test to detect receptive disturbances in aphasics. *Brain*, 85, 665–678.

Eisenson, J. 1954. *Examining for Aphasia.* New York: Psychological Corporation.

Goldstein, K. 1948. *Language and Language Disturbances.* New York: Grune & Stratton.

_____. 1942. *After effects of Brain Injuries in War.* New York: Grune & Stratton.

Goldstein, K., and Scheerer, M. 1941. Abstract and concrete behavior. *Psychological Monographs*, 53, 2.

Goodglass, H., and Kaplan, E. 1972. *The Boston Diagnostic Aphasia Test.* Washington: Lea & Febiger.

Halstead, W. C., and Wepman, J. 1949. The Halstead-Wepman aphasia screening test. *Journal of Speech and Hearing Disorders*, 14, 9–15.

Head, H. 1926. *Aphasia and Kindred Disorders of Speech.* New York: Cambridge University Press and Macmillan. Reprinted by Hafner Publishing Co., New York, 1963.

Information Center for Hearing, Speech, and Disorders of Human Communication. 1968. *A Bibliography of Adult Aphasia Tests.* Baltimore: Johns Hopkins Medical Institutions.

Luria, A. R. 1964. Factors and forms of aphasia. In *Disorders of Language*, DeReuck, A., and O'Connor, M., eds. London: J. & A. Churchill, pp. 143–167.

_____. 1966a. *Higher Cortical Functions in Man.* New York: Basic Books.

_____. 1966b. *Human Brain and Psychological Processes.* New York: Harper & Row.

_____. 1970. *Traumatic Aphasia.* The Hague: Mouton, Chaps. 9–14.

Porch, B. 1967. *Porch Index of Communicative Ability.* Palo Alto, Calif.: Consulting Psychologists Press.

_____. 1971. Multidimensional scoring in aphasia testing. *Journal of Speech and Hearing Research*, 14:4, 776–792.

Schuell, H. 1957. A short examination for aphasia. *Neurology*, 7, 625–634.

_____. 1965. *Differential Diagnosis of Aphasia with the Minnesota Test.* Minneapolis: University of Minnesota Press.

Schuell, H., Jenkins, J., and Jiminez-Pabon, E. 1964. *Aphasia in Adults.* New York: Harper & Row.

Sklar, M. 1966. *Sklar Aphasia Scale.* Beverley Hills, Calif.: Western Psychological Services.

Weigl, E. 1966. On the construction of standard psychological tests in cases of brain damage. *Journal of Neurological Science*, 3, 123–127.

Weisenburg, T., and McBride, K. 1935. *Aphasia: A Clinical and Psychological Study.* New York: Commonwealth Fund.

Wells, F. L., and Ruesch, J. 1945. *Mental Examiners Handbook*, 2nd ed. New York: Psychological Corporation, pp. 48–50.

Wepman, J. 1961. *A Selected Bibliography on Brain Impairment, Aphasia, and Organic Psychodiagnosis.* Chicago: Language Research Associates.

Wepman, J., and Jones, L. 1961. *Studies in Aphasia: An Approach to Testing.* Chicago: University of Chicago Education-Industry Service.

_____. 1966. In *Speech, Language, and Communication.* Vol. 3 in *Brain Function*, Carterette, E. C., ed. Los Angeles: University of California Press, pp. 141–172.

Zangwill, O. L. 1964. Intelligence in aphasia. In *Disorders of Language*, DeReuck, A., and O'Connor, M., eds. London: J. & A. Churchill, pp. 261–274.

II

The Recovery Process

7

Prognostic Factors and the Value of Therapy

Prognostic Factors and Some Problems Related to Prognosis

An underlying danger in applying the observations from studies on prognostic factors for recovery is that an individual may suffer from the generalizations. The author's clinical experience dictates caution because of his numerous "exceptional" cases, ones for whom most of the criteria which we shall later present strongly suggested a poor outlook for recovery, but who nevertheless recovered sufficiently well to return at least on a modified basis to their vocations and professions. Another danger is that a poor prognosis, if made known to the family of a patient or if discouragingly accepted by a therapist, may become self-fulfilling. The aphasic patient may sense the discouragement and, unless he is particularly "stubborn and aggressive," may not become wholeheartedly involved in his recovery. If he does not become involved, either through his own efforts (spontaneous recovery?) or through the establishment of a therapeutic relationship with another person, he may not make any significant improvement, and so fulfill the prediction.

What we have said is not intended to suggest that all patients have an equal chance in their recovery from aphasia, but rather that each should be given an unbegrudging chance. Unless a patient is suffering from an ongoing and progressive cerebral pathology or has incurred diffuse bilateral cerebral damage, the outlook for some degree of recovery is not hopeless. Occasionally, as we shall report later, recovery may be quite good.

119

Before presenting the findings, clinical and those generated from specific studies, we shall consider some problems related to the reports in the literature.

INTERRELATIONSHIP OF FACTORS

Although cerebrovascular accidents can happen to anybody regardless of age, aphasias associated with cerebrovascular pathology are more likely to occur in persons who are past middle age than in younger persons. On the other hand, younger persons are more likely to incur head-penetrating wounds than are older ones. Up to the middle or late twenties, and in some instances to the early thirties, education and age are related factors. With important individual exceptions, intelligence is also related to educational level and socioeconomic status.

TERMINOLOGY

Other problems arise out of classification systems—the types of aphasic involvements and differences in definitions of the involvements. Thus, we cannot be sure that the same terms have the same meanings and therefore the same implications in the reported studies.

Darley (1972), in an article which included a survey of the literature on aphasia therapy, reminds us: "Some investigations of aphasic patients have involved patients who may or may not have been aphasic, their productive symptoms being the articulatory disorder more correctly defined as apraxia of speech. Speech pathologists cannot rely on terminology alone. . . ."

Nevertheless, and despite these stated reservations, there are predictive (prognostic) factors about which most aphasiologists are in common agreement for aphasics taken as a total population.

PROGNOSTIC FACTORS: A BRIEF SURVEY OF THE LITERATURE

Eisenson (1949) summarized his clinical observations of more than 100 aphasic patients ranging in age from 18 to above 60 years. "Prognosis would seem good for young aphasic patients whose disturbances are associated with traumatic causes, who have or had outgoing personalities, for whom a training program is started early, and who have a modest aspiration level. Prognosis appears less hopeful for older patients, for those for whom training is delayed, for those who have persistent euphoria, for patients whose personality picture reveals rigidity or psychopathic tendencies, and for those patients who develop great dependency on their clinicians." We believe that the evidence since these observations were made tends to support the impressions.

Similar observations were made by Wepman (1951, pp. 68–82). Longerich and Bordeaux (1954, p. 90) believe that expressive aphasics are more likely to recover than receptive aphasics. Vignolo (1964) observes that "there are hints that anarthria has a significant retarding effect on recovery from aphasia." Schuell, Jenkins, and Jiminez–Pabon's (1964, Chap. 9) prognostic factors are related to their test findings and are the basis for their classification of aphasic patients. Essentially, the findings indicate that the aphasic who does not have related perceptual, sensorimotor, or dysarthric components has a better outlook for recovery than one with such complications.

One prognostic factor that most clinicians accept as hopeful is the patient's ability for self-correction. A negative implication is a patient's persistent failure to become aware of errors, or to correct an error when attention is directed to it.

The value of language training for the most severe (global) aphasics seems doubtful. Sarno, Silverman, and Sands (1970) report that neither programmed nor nonprogrammed speech therapy enhanced or made a significant difference in language recovery compared with no specific effort at training for a group of severe receptive-expressive patients who had incurred cerebrovascular insults. This report agrees with that of Schuell who found, as we have indicated, that patients characterized by almost complete loss of functional language skills presented an irreversible aphasic syndrome. Schuell *et al.* (1964, p. 199) observed, "We are therefore forced to the conclusion that there is a degree of cerebral damage that is incompatible with recovery of language skills."

We should note for the record that both Sarno *et al.* and Schuell *et al.* were limiting their observations to *recovery of language skills*. In fact, Sarno *et al.* emphasize that the rehabilitation efforts for the severe expressive-receptive aphasic should be social and psychological in thrust.

We feel it important to add a precautionary note with regard to severe (global) aphasics. A conclusion that a patient has no functional speech should not be made on the basis of a single assessment or when the patient is severely ill. Judgment should be withheld for a period of two or three months after onset and then be made on the basis of two or more separate assessments at least a week apart and after a two- or three-month effort at training.

The observations and reports we have just considered did not isolate factors such as age, education, intelligence, nature of pathology, handedness, and initiation of therapy after onset of aphasia as prognostic factors. Although, as we indicated earlier, the factors are often interrelated, we shall make some attempt to "tease out" the implications of each as a separate prognostic factor.

Etiology and Site of Lesion. Based on a survey of the literature, Darley (1972, p. 16) observes: "Patients with aphasia of different causes—that is, vascular, traumatic, infectious, or neoplastic—probably recover from aphasia at different rates." Butfield and Zangwill (1946), on the basis of oral speech recovery following instruction, reported considerable improvement in 21 of 35 traumatic cases while the speech condition remained unchanged in only two cases. In the vascular and neoplastic groups, on the other hand, speech was unimproved in approximately a third of the cases. Our own observations (Eisenson, 1964) indicate that patients with head-penetrating wounds show greater improvement than do those with cerebrovascular lesions or those with neoplasms. Luria (1963, p. 5) compared patients with head-penetrating wounds and those with nonpenetrating head injuries relative to recovery from aphasic disorders within three to four months after time of injury. Luria reports the number of cases of recovery (aphasic disorders disappear completely) to be twice as great for the nonpenetrating wound cases than for those who had incurred penetrating wounds.

With regard to site and extent of lesion, we have observed (Eisenson, 1964) that patients with single lesions in an area other than the temporo-parietal region have a better prognosis than those with such lesions, and patients with single-episode lesions do better than those with recurrent episodes. In general, the more widespread the lesions, the greater the number of aphasic involvements, and the poorer the likelihood for recovery.[1] Russell and Espir (1961, p. 141) also noted in their population of traumatic aphasics (head-penetrating, war-incurred injuries) that "when the right side of the brain remains undamaged, remarkable recoveries may occur in these young men. . . . However, when both parietal regions are damaged, the possibilities for recovery are greatly reduced."

Age. Evidence on the factor of age indicates a consensus that younger patients have a better prognosis than older ones. Eisenson (1949) reported on a population of war-injury cases who had several months of therapy. The patients who made good progress ranged in age between 20 and 32 years, with a mean age of 24; those who made little progress ranged in age between 22 and 47 years, with a mean of 31. For a similar population, Wepman (1951, p. 51) reported that patients in the age range 19 to 38 (mean 25.8) showed good progress while in therapy. The patients who made poor progress (global aphasics) ranged in age from 23 to 38, with a mean of 29.5 years. However, the members of this group showed the greatest divergence after training.

Among older patients, age continues to be an important factor related to recovery. Sands, Sarno, and Shankweiler (1969) report on a long-term study on a population of 30 patients, "middle age and elderly" (age range 38–70, average age 56.5 years), who had suffered stroke. The patients received daily speech therapy for periods ranging from two weeks to two years and eight months (medial length of 7.5 months). Improvement was assessed by the Functional Communication Profile (FCP), Taylor (1965). The group was followed and reevaluated from four months to twelve months after treatment was terminated. The findings revealed a gain of ten percentage points in language function as measured by the FCP on the completion of therapy, and an additional five percentage points between discharge from therapy and reevaluation (median time interval 13 months). "Examining the upper and lower sixths of the total

[1] An extensive lesion is likely to be associated with both sensory and motor defects. Thus, we may accept the observation of Russell and Espir (1961, pp. 170–171): "The scaffolding on which speech is developed is built up in relation to hearing, vision, and the sensorimotor skill in uttering words. Injury to the central part of this structure disrupts all aspects of speech, but small wounds at the periphery of the scaffolding may lead to a special disorder of one or other speech functions, such as motor aphasia, agraphia, or alexia." The more widespread the lesion, or lesions, the greater the likelihood that the "central part" of the structure may be involved.

group, we find that those who improved most achieved an average gain of 36 percent whereas those who experienced the least change gained an average of 4 percent on the FCP. Of the total group of 30 patients, 27 showed some measured improvement whereas 3 remained the same or regressed." Sands *et al.* state: "Age appeared to be the most potent variable influencing recovery . . . when we considered the sixth which showed the greatest improvement, we found those patients to be the youngest in our series, having an average age of only 47. Whereas those . . . who recovered least averaged 61 years." Although a population of only 30 patients is a small group on which to base generalizations, the results are consistent with other findings, including those of Smith (1971) and Vignolo (1964). Vignolo concluded: "Improvement appears to be much less frequent in old people than in young people." (Young people were below 40 years of age; middle-age people were in the 40–60 year age range; old people were above 60 years.) However, Vignolo also observed that those above 60 years of age included two patients who met the criterion for improvement in that they reached a communication level of proficiency. Thus, despite the general negative prognostic implication of age, Vignolo says, "These cases suggest that prognosis of aphasia in patients over sixty need not be pessimistic if, at the time of the examination, less than 2 months have elapsed from onset."

Time Between Onset of Aphasic Involvements and Initiation of Therapy. Reports are consistent that the time between the onset of aphasia and the initiation of therapy is a significant factor for recovery. The findings of Butfield and Zangwill (1946), Wepman (1951), Vignolo (1964), and Sands *et al.* (1969) all permit the conclusion that patients for whom training was initiated before six months after onset showed significantly more improvement than patients who did not begin therapy until after six months. Vignolo, as we noted above, recommends that training be initiated less than two months after onset. This recommendation is consistent with Culton's (1969) finding that significant spontaneous improvement is not evident during the second month after onset of aphasia. Thus, to conclude with an observation from Vignolo, "Time elapsed from onset is a very important prognostic factor. Moreover, it suggests that the end of the second month represents a turning point in the course of the disturbance."

Intelligence and Educational Level. The studies on premorbid level of intelligence and improvement suggest that there is a positive relationship between intelligence and improvement. Wepman (1951) found a positive relationship between premorbid level of intelligence and educational achivement. Tentatively, we may accept Darley's (1972) conclusion that "the higher the original IQ, the greater the gains in therapy."

Educational level is so highly correlated with intelligence that it is difficult to isolate this factor (education) for its prognostic implication. Our own data would indicate that in a population that included older persons (50–60 years) with advanced academic degrees, about as many achieved excellent recoveries as those who made little improvement. Smith (1971), in his study of 78 stroke patients with chronic aphasia, found a higher proportion of global aphasics in his low-education group (mean of 9.4 years of formal schooling) than in his high-education group (mean of 14.3 years of schooling). Smith also found that the severity of comprehension defects *decreased* in relation to the amount of premorbid education. However, residual language defects were somewhat greater in the high-education group than in the low-education group. Thus, tentatively, we may conclude that highly educated persons have more to lose and therefore have more residual defects than do persons who have less formal education. On the whole, however, prognosis for recovery is more favorable for persons at the upper end of the intelligence scale and for the highly educated than for those at the low end of the scale.

Handedness. In our review of cerebral dominance, handedness, and aphasia (see pp. 35—40) it was evident that (1) left-handed persons were more likely to have some aphasic involvements following cerebral insult than right-handed persons, and (2) left-handed persons made better recoveries than those who were right-handed. Smith (1971, p. 188) notes that his population of 78 chronic aphasics included only one who was left-handed. In general, we may conclude that left-handed persons have a better prognosis than do the right-handed. This observation is supported by the findings of Zangwill (1960), Luria (1970), Subirana (1958), and others cited in our discussion of cerebral dominance.

Severity and Predominant Nature of Aphasic Involvements. The severity of aphasia appears to be related to the degree of recovery. Sands *et al.* (1969), in their study of 30 patients, observed: "It is generally agreed that there is a negative correlation between severity of aphasia in the early recovery period and the amount of improvement which occurs during the recovery process whether or not speech therapy is given. . . . Thus, the severity of language impairment at initial evaluation is a moderately good predictor of the amount of recovery that may be expected."

Schuell *et al.* (1964) found that the most severely impaired group made the least recovery. Butfield and Zangwill (1946) found a negative relationship between severity of aphasic disorders and amount of improvement. However, it should be noted that although 34 percent of the severe cases showed no improvement, marked improvement in speech was shown in 40 percent of their cases. This compared with 56 percent for those rated moderate and 58 percent for those rated mild.

Differences may be found based on the predominant characteristics of the aphasia. Smith (1971) found that in chronic aphasics, "with only rare exceptions, comparisons of spoken and written responses reflected significantly greater impairment in writing in almost all cases." Smith also found that the severity of comprehension defects could be used as a general indicator of the severity of overall language impairment. Culton (1968), in his study of spontaneous recovery from aphasia, found that overall recovery of language was poor when, on initial evaluation, the patient was not able to point to pictures of named objects. This observation is consistent with Schuell's (1953), who regarded the inability to point to pictures of named objects as a poor prognostic sign. Culton also found that the inability to write words to dictation a few weeks after onset of aphasia was a negative prognostic indicator.

In general, we may conclude that severe impairments in comprehension and in writing are poor prognostic factors. Conversely, ability to comprehend, even though it is assessed only by the ability to point to a named object or picture, may be considered a favorable prognostic indicator. Similarly, early recovery of the ability to write to dictation is a favorable sign.

Other Prognostic Factors. *Self-correction.* There are several other factors which we consider to be significant prognostic factors. One of these is the awareness of error and the ability of the patient to correct himself, or at least to move in the direction of the "target" utterance. Vignolo (1964) considers the patient's ability to come closer to the word he is looking for in his "word-finding" efforts to be a favorable prognostic sign. This, we believe, indicates awareness of error and is an expression of the ability for self-correction. Wepman (1958) also considers the ability to self-correct to be a favorable prognostic sign.

Associated Sensory and Motor Defects. Vignolo (1964) considers the presence of severe articulatory impairment (anarthria and oral apraxia) to be an unfavorable prognostic factor. Schuell *et al.* (1964) identify the poorest recovery group as having associated sensory and motor defects. We may assume that these patients also have fairly widespread brain damage. The failure to recover from sensory and motor impairments may be considered to have serious negative prognostic implications.

Psychological Adjustment. In Chapter 4 we discussed psychological factors and their implications for recovery from aphasia. We consider (Eisenson, 1964) persistent euphoria, marked introversion, premorbid indications of concretism and rigidity, and the persistence of extreme dependency to be negative prognostic indicators. The converse of these factors are positive prognostic indicators.

The Value of Therapy

Although there are still skeptics who question the value of therapeutic efforts with aphasic patients, and who maintain a position that aphasics recover language spontaneously if they recover at all, we are certainly not to be identified with this view. This is not to suggest that all persons with cerebral insults who became aphasic have the same outlook for recovery, or to question that many aphasics do make excellent spontaneous recoveries. Despite the skeptics, we believe that there is presently a sufficient accumulation of evidence relative to prognostic criteria for recovery, and relative to the efficacy of therapeutic intervention to be positive in our own position that therapy makes a difference in favor of most aphasic patients. We are not by any means able to take a firm position as to whether an aphasic person reacquires or retrieves language as a direct result of the particulars of a therapeutic program, or whether stimulation, if on an appropriate level, results in progress and improvement. We are confident that, whether it be the specifics or the effects of stimulation and facilitation, most aphasics are more likely to progress in their language recovery if they are involved in a therapeutic relationship identified with language content than if left alone for "spontaneous" recovery.

In his article, "The Efficacy of Language Rehabilitation in Aphasia," Darley (1972) raises three fundamental questions of serious concern to aphasiologists, aphasic patients, and their relatives. The questions, which have both ethical and economic implications, are as follows:

1. "Does therapy have a decisive influence in the course of recovery and the ultimate outcome?
2. "Are the language gains attributable to therapy worth the necessary investment of time, effort, and money?
3. "What are the relative degrees of effectiveness of various modes of treatment of aphasia?"

Darley, after surveying the literature, admittedly sparse, reports several studies, covering a 50-year period (1920–1970) in England, the United States, and Russia, which clearly indicate that language therapy does have a decisive influence on the course of recovery and on the ultimate outcome for the patient. One report (Sarno *et al.* 1970) found little gain, and no significant difference in gain for a group of 31 "older" stroke patients, all of whom were described as having severe receptive and expressive impairments. Most of these patients were essentially without productive language and had very little understanding of speech at the outset of treatment. The patients were assigned to one of three comparison groups. One of the groups received programmed instruction, a second received nonprogrammed instruction, and the third no formal therapy. Reevaluation, after completion of treatment and a month following, revealed only small gains which were similar for the three groups. However, Sarno *et al.* (1970, p. 621) state: "The fact that speech therapy, of either type, did not affect language recovery in this study is no doubt related to the severity of their aphasia."

The second question raised by Darley, "Are the language gains attributable to therapy worth the necessary investment of time, effort, and money?" is one to which neither the literature nor this author can provide a responsible answer. How much is even a small amount of gain "attributable to therapy" worth to the family, to society, and to the individual? From the point of view of effort and time, it is certainly worth all the patient has to offer. Recovery, as we continue to emphasize, is the patient's special business. It is how he should invest his time and his effort. Money is a problem for society and the family. If even a small amount of language improvement can be translated into an increased degree of self-care and a decreased amount of dependence, we would hesitate to set a maximum cost or price to pay for the improvement. From the point of view of the clinician, we believe that the ethical question to be answered is, "When does the patient no longer need my service to continue his recovery?" Whenever the clinician, whatever his specialty may be, arrives at a time in response to this question, then he has *his answer to time, effort, and cost.*

In answer to Darley's third question, "What are the relative degrees of effectiveness of various modes of treatment of aphasia?", we accept Darley's summary statement (p. 8) that "more data are needed applying to clearly specified samples of the aphasic population subjected to clearly specified regimens of therapy by clinicians, for clearly specified periods." It may well be that initial forms of training should be different from the training when residual problems are presented by patients. General stimulation may be appropriate in early stages, and particularized content training for others. Preventive training, which we shall consider in Chapter 9, may be in order for "generally traumatized patients." Certainly the thrust or emphasis for patients who make little recovery should be different than for those who make rapid gains in overall aspects of improvement. When more data become available from future studies we may be better able to answer the multifaceted question about the efficacy of therapy and kinds of therapy for aphasic patients.[2]

Spontaneous Recovery

In a provocative paper on "Some Current Trends in Aphasia Rehabilitation," Holland (1969) presents a problem relative to aphasia therapy that we consider realistic. Says Holland: "Tap the mind of a physician and you will probably find the belief that language return, when it happens, is a function of spontaneous recovery. Aphasic patients are usually referred to language services only when the critical period for maximum therapeutic effectiveness—the spontaneous recovery period—is over. A vicious cycle ensues. Even our most creative and skillful work is blunted if it is not applied in time. And because we frequently see patients only when it is too late, we are judged to be, and we feel, somewhat extraneous."

Although we believe Holland's statement to be somewhat severe and possibly an overgeneralized indictment, it deserves respectful consideration. Perhaps we shall better appreciate the significance of the statement in the light of our discussion of *spontaneous recovery* which follows.

[2] We think it important to note that recognition of the value of therapy is represented in the support of studies on forms of therapy rather than on the justification of therapy for aphasic patients. Recent reports include *Psycholinguistic and Behavioral Variables Underlying Recovery from Aphasia*, Rehabilitation Service, Washington, D. C.: U. S. Department of Health, Education and Welfare, 1971 (Audrey L. Holland, Project Director) and *Proceedings of the Conference on Language Retraining for Aphasics*, Social and Rehabilitation Service, Washington, D. C.: U. S. Department of Health, Education and Welfare, 1968, (John W. Black, Project Director).

THE PROCESS OF SPONTANEOUS RECOVERY

In his book *Traumatic Aphasia*, Luria (1970, p. 49) asks the question, "How to explain those few *negative cases* in which *injury of the principal speech zones does not produce speech impairments* or *cases in which severe aphasic disturbances undergo rapid and complete recovery*? How can one explain the fact that in certain cases one finds *great differences in the dynamics of spontaneous recovery*?" Luria presents several possible answers to his question.

It may be that in such cases there only appears to be destruction of brain tissue, whereas in reality the injuries only temporarily depress the function of certain areas. This depression, or diaschisis, may spread to a whole system of functionally related areas, when it has passed, the disturbed function may recover completely. Such a mechanism might explain cases of rapid recovery after slight injuries.

A second mechanism which may account for spontaneous recovery of disturbed function is the *adaptive transfer of a given function* from one area of the brain to others, thus compensating for the functional defect sustained as a result of brain damage.

Such functional transfers, according to Luria, may be of several types. "It varies from 'vicarious' compensation, in which another area of the brain assumes the functions of the damaged area, to more complex *transformations of the function itself*. In the latter case a function comes to be performed by a new process occurring in areas having altogether different functions." Luria is careful to observe, however, that "there are limits to the plasticity of brain function" (1970, p. 50).

Luria suggests that transfer of function may take place by "responsible" structures either at a subcortical level or in symmetrical areas of the right hemisphere. He also suggests that the degree of lateralization of complex function may be different in different individuals and that for some individuals functions usually served by an area (zone) in one hemisphere may be divided between the two hemispheres. This would account for spontaneous recovery in a small percentage of right-handed persons who have incurred left-cerebral lesions and a considerably larger percentage of recovery in left-handed persons. (See the discussion of the relationship of handedness to cerebral dominance, pp. 35–40.)[3]

A third possible explanation for spontaneous recovery offered by Luria is related to the nature of the lesion. "Is it possible that the absence of aphasic symptoms or the rapid recovery after brain injuries may be explained by the fact that only *slight pathological changes of brain tissue were involved*?" (Luria, 1970, p. 51). Luria is confident that the answer to his question is "Yes." It is

[3] See also Smith, A., "Objective Indices of Severity of Chronic Aphasia in Stroke Patients," *Journal of Speech and Hearing Disorders*, 1971, 36:2, 195–199, for a discussion of spontaneous recovery *and* right-hemisphere functions.

important to note that Luria's observations are on patients who incurred head injuries from external sources. However, we believe that the explanations may also account for spontaneous recovery in patients with cerebrovascular and other pathologies that do not produce widespread lesions.

Our closing note on this section may well have been used to open the discussion on spontaneous recovery. What do we really mean by spontaneous recovery of language function? Perhaps the best answer is one offered by Schuell *et al.* (1964, p. 218) who observe, "It is our opinion that dramatic cures result from priming a mechanism when physiological readiness is present." In some instances the patient does his own priming. Even so, he does this with another person in a communicative situation. In some instances, the other person is identified as a therapist, who helps with the priming of the physiologically recovering or recovered mechanism. No clinician who has had the opportunity to work with many aphasic patients can doubt that a fortunate number do recover quickly and at a rate that cannot be attributed directly and solely to the therapy given them. Recovery may, at least in some instances, be attributed to the time at which the mechanism priming was initiated.

Luria (1963), Vignolo (1964), and others suggest that the first six months after onset of aphasia is the period for spontaneous recovery. Culton (1969), basing his conclusion on a test-retest study, indicates that the spontaneous recovery period may not be as long as six months, at least as far as results can be measured by an objective assessment—the Ravens Progressive Matrices Test. Culton found that a group of 11 patients whose onset of aphasia began within 30 days of the initial assessment made significant gains after the first month and smaller gains during the second month on the Ravens Test as well as on a battery of language tests. Culton states: "Rapid spontaneous recovery of language function was noted in the first month following the onset of aphasia. Although an increase in mean score was noted, further significant improvement was not evident during the second month." Culton notes that "this is somewhat incompatible with the predominant notion that significant spontaneous recovery of language function continues to occur three to six months after the onset of aphasia."

SUMMARY STATEMENT RELATIVE TO SPONTANEOUS RECOVERY

Spontaneous recovery is the process of retrieval of language functioning *that may take place* within the first six months, but more likely, and in terms of objectively measured gains, during the first two months after the onset of aphasia. Spontaneous recovery is probably associated with a period of physiological readiness and receptivity for stimulation, even though such stimulation is provided as a product of the patient's "natural" environment rather than by efforts of directed therapy. Not all aphasics show spontaneous recovery. However, although significant spontaneous recovery is a good prognostic indicator, the absence of rapid and significant improvement in the first two months does not rule out the possibility of recovery after this initial period. Recovery is likely to be enhanced if therapy is initiated during the first six months after onset of aphasia, and preferably as early as the second or third month.

References

Butfield, E., and Zangwill, O. 1946. Re-education in aphasia: A review of 70 cases. *Journal of Neurology, Neurosurgery and Psychiatry*, 9, 75–79.

Culton, G. L. 1968. Spontaneous recovery from aphasia. Ph.D. Dissertation, University of Denver.

———. 1969. Spontaneous recovery from aphasia. *Journal of Speech and Hearing Research*, 12, 825–832.

Darley, F. L. 1972. The efficacy of language rehabilitation in aphasia. *Journal of Speech and Hearing Disorders*, 37, 3–21.

Eisenson, J. 1949. Prognostic factors related to language rehabilitation in aphasic patients. *Journal of Speech and Hearing Disorders*, 14, 262–264.

———. 1964. Aphasia: A point of view as to the nature of the disorder and factors that determine prognosis for recovery. *International Journal of Neurology*, 4, 287–295.

Holland, A. 1969. Some current trends in aphasia rehabilitation. *Asha*, 11:1, 3–7.

Longerich, M. C. and Bordeaux, J. 1954. *Aphasia Therapeutics*. New York: Macmillan.

Luria, A. R. 1963. *Restoration of Function after Brain Injury*. New York: Macmillan.

———. 1970. *Traumatic Aphasia*. The Hague: Mouton.

Russell, W. R., and Espir, M. L. E. 1961. *Traumatic Aphasia*. London: Oxford University Press.

Sands, E. S., Sarno, M. T., and Shankweiler, D. P. 1969. Long-term assessment of language function due to stroke. *Archives of Physical Medicine and Rehabilitation*, 50, 202–207.

Sarno, M. T., Silverman, M., and Sands, E. 1970. Speech therapy and language recovery in severe aphasia. *Journal of Speech and Hearing Research*, 13, 607–623.

Schuell, H. 1953 Aphasic difficulties understanding spoken language. *Neurology*, 3, 176–184.

Schuell, H., Jenkins, J., and Jiminez-Pabon, E. 1964. *Aphasia in Adults*. New York: Harper & Row.

Smith, A. 1971. Objective indices of severity of chronic aphasia in stroke patients. *Journal of Speech and Hearing Disorders*, 36, 167–207.

Subirana, A. 1958. The prognosis in aphasia in relation to the factor of cerebral dominance and handedness. *Brain*, 81, 415–425.

Taylor, M. 1965. A measurement of functional communication in aphasia. *Archives of Physical Medicine*, 46, 101–107.

Vignolo, L. A. 1964. Evolution of aphasia and language rehabilitation: A retrospective exploratory study. *Cortex*, 1, 344–367.

Wepman, J. M. 1951. *Recovery from Aphasia.* New York: Ronald Press.

_____. 1958. The relationship between self-correction and recovery from aphasia. *Journal of Speech and Hearing Disorders*, 23, 302–305.

Zangwill, O. L. 1960. *Cerebral Dominance and Its Relation to Psychological Function*, Edinburgh: Oliver & Boyd.

8

Rationale of Therapy for Aphasics

Our discussion in Chapter 7 of prognostic factors for recovery from aphasia permits us to make reasonably good guesses about the outlook for a population of aphasic patients relative to improvement in language functions. However, on an individual basis, we would still be guided by the underlying principle that every aphasic person whose pathology has "stabilized" is deserving of an investment in therapy. We accept Wepman's (1970, p. 128) observation that "too many patients get better and too many fail to do so without our knowing why. If we knew why or even if we know only the stages through which they recovered when they do, perhaps we could begin to understand why others do not get better." Further, Wepman reminds us that "aphasia is not a static condition any more than a brain-injured patient is static in his intellective ability. He changes and so too does his communication ability."[1]

The Recovery Process

Even if we confine ourselves to the language impairments in aphasia, we can at best offer only speculations about what may take place in the individual as he

[1] Implied in Wepman's observations is a plea for initiating research into the process of recovery from aphasia. Perhaps, when we become confident of the essence of aphasic impairment, we can entertain testable hypotheses about therapeutic procedures. What we have to say in this chapter is, for the most part, based on the assumption that there is sufficient evidence to justify direct therapeutic effort for aphasic patients.

regains (improves) in language functioning. By improvement we mean that the individual's abilities to understand what he hears or reads and to respond appropriately approximates more and more his premorbid potential both for the nature of the content and the conditions in which he is engaged in a decoding-encoding (language comprehension-production) situation.

Schuell, Jenkins, and Jiminez-Pabon's observation (1964, p. 338) that "admittedly neither neurophysiology nor cybernetics can yet give us a neural model for recovery from aphasia" still pertains. However, Schuell et al. did present their hypothesis that a process, presumably one that parallels normal language acquisition, may be relevant. "Converging evidence from many lines of research indicates . . . that repeated sensory stimulation is essential for organization, storage, and retrieval of patterns in the brain, and it would be strange if language patterns operated according to some other principle."

Underlying Schuell et al.'s assumption as to the recovery process is one of reorganization. Aphasia, according to our own position, produces disruption and disorganization. The height of disorganization is reached in the early stages when the direct and indirect effects of the cerebral pathology are widespread and the individual is severely impaired in his coping and planning behavior because language, his usual tool and mechanism for these functions, has gone awry both for decoding and encoding. When the immediate effects of the pathology subside, some degree of reorganization takes place. When the neuropathological process becomes stabilized, then the aphasic is involved with the final process of reorganization.

We are aware, of course, that in some instances reorganization and recovery are rapid and "spontaneous,"[2] and within a matter of several weeks or four to six months the person may be considered, at least as far as communicative functioning is concerned, a recovered aphasic and no longer a patient. It is unfortunate that we do not know all the factors that are conducive to spontaneous recovery. It is unfortunate, also, that we can only speculate as to why some persons do not progress according to prognostic criteria for aphasic populations as a whole. One possibility that may account for poor progress despite a good prognosis is that the patient may have suffered a lesion affecting more than one process underlying language functioning. According to Luria, a function disturbed by a lesion essential to a basic process affects and impairs all the hierarchial processes related to it. Thus, Luria (1966, p. 71) emphasizes a fundamental principle: "The higher mental functions may be disturbed by a lesion of one of the many different links of the functional system. . . ." Further, Luria observes (1966, p. 74) that "a lesion of a single, circumscribed area of the cerebral cortex often leads to the development not of an isolated symptom, but of a group of disturbances, apparently far removed from each other." Finally, Luria stresses (p. 76): "The most important fact . . . is *that a*

---

[2] By spontaneous we mean that environmental stimulation rather than any direct attempt at professional therapeutic intervention was associated with the process of recovery.

generalized disturbance in the dynamics of the nervous process must make its effects primarily on those forms of cortical activity with the most complex organization."

Later, we shall consider the therapeutic implications of Luria's postulations.

RETRIEVAL VERSUS NEW LEARNING: THE ROLE OF THE CLINICIAN

We have referred to the recovery process in aphasia as one of reorganization of function, of retrieval *rather than of new learning.*[3] Virtually all aphasiologists accept the premise that whatever it is a clinician may do to help the aphasic to reestablish comprehension of linguistic formulations or to evoke appropriate verbal responses, it is not because the patient has been taught anything he did not already know, but to help him retrieve what he knows more readily than if he were left to his own devices.

The role of the clinician is essentially that of a stimulator or an *agent provocateur.* Except possibly when the clinician directs attention to a strategy for evoking a correct response or inhibiting a possible flow of incorrect responses, the clinician is not a teacher. The clinician's basic task is to control circumstances, to help the aphasic by reducing environmental "noise" through selection and presentation of materials, and through the manner of presentation, to enhance the likelihood of comprehension and production of linguistic behavior. In Chapters 9 and 10 we shall present some principles and techniques for gaining this objective.

Some Assumptions and Questions Relative to Reorganization and Retrieval of Language Functions

It would be comfortable if we could with confidence present a theoretical framework for therapeutic approaches for aphasics. Unhappily, we do not think that the state of the art can at this time be securely supported by any single theoretical postulation. Nevertheless, inherent in the literature of what seems to be of help in facilitating retrieval are several assumptions, not mutually exclusive, that provide a broad base or bases for therapeutic efforts. We shall review some of these basic positions and, where possible, present evidence to support each position.

STIMULATION OF DEFECTIVE SYSTEMS: THE AUDITORY APPROACH

Language is normally acquired "by ear." Should therapeutic efforts employ a basic auditory approach to assist the patient in his retrieval of language?

---

[3] Our reference, of course, is to the linguistic aspects of recovery and not to the physical aspects. The latter are the responsibilities of the medical and paramedical personnel. Some motor functions, such as walking and tool handling for hemiplegic aphasics, may involve what is essentially new learning.

Schuell *et al.* (1964, p. 339) make the broad observation that "auditory processes are always impaired in aphasia. As a result the aphasic patient receives reduced verbal stimulation from his environment, and it is probable that signals that get in are often distorted."

Further, Schuell *et al.* note: "We know that auditory retention span is always reduced in aphasia."

Shewan and Canter (1971) found that aphasic adults had difficulties in comprehension of sentences when compared with normal controls. The parameters assessed were length of sentence, vocabulary difficulty, and syntactic complexity. According to Shewan and Canter:

> The pattern of aphasics' responses indicated that they differed from the normal controls in quantitative performance, but not in qualitative aspects. The aphasic subgroups varied in comprehension ability, with the Wernicke's patients performing the poorest. Syntactic complexity proved to be the most difficult parameter for all subjects. Comprehension of sentences of increased difficulty was significantly poorer than comprehension of easy sentences.

What are the therapeutic implications of these observations relative to impairment for auditory comprehension, which to some degree appears to be shared by most aphasic patients and is particularly severe for Wernicke-type patients? One approach, described by Schuell *et al.* (1964, pp. 353–356) and by Luria (1970, pp. 400–408), will be presented in broad outline.

Recovery of auditory function may in some instances take place through an approach employing direct, controlled auditory stimulation. *Control of stimulation* refers to quantity, complexity, and rate of presentation of the stimulus materials. Complexity suggests proceeding from single words to short phrases to short sentences. In practice, however, it is rare that an auditory stimulus is not associated, at least initially, with a visual event. "Controlled" visual events may include pictures specially drawn or selected for appropriateness to the associated auditory stimulus depicting a nominal word (an identifying name or an action verb, e.g., drink, walk, cut).[4]

RESTORATION OF FUNCTION THROUGH BYPASSING OF IMPAIRED SYSTEMS

This brings us to an alternative assumption relative to the recovery process. It is an approach, or at least a philosophy for an approach, that assumes that a seriously impaired function cannot be restored through direct stimulation of the defective modality. Resumption of function can be accomplished more effectively by bypassing defective systems through the establishment of "new circuitry." Although in some instances direct stimulation of impaired modalities may be effective, often this is not the case. Thus, Luria (1970, p. 381) observes: "This type of recovery is the exception rather than the rule, however, in cases

---

[4] A general principle to be observed for auditory stimulation therapy, and in general for all therapy, is to begin at a level just below where the patient shows a significant amount of impairment and to proceed from that level to more difficult ones.

involving the destruction of cortical tissue. Usually the destruction of a mass of nerve cells results in irreversible functional changes so that recovery of the disturbed functional systems can be achieved only by major reorganization of cortical processes."

Luria is emphatic, at least as far as traumatic aphasic patients are concerned, that elementary functions lost because of cortical lesions are not directly recovered. Consequently, "The only means of compensating for deficits of this type is by transferring the functions to other structures or to other functional systems. Learning to use the other hand when one hand is paralyzed or learning to read Braille when the visual cortex has been destroyed are examples of such 'substitutive compensation' " (Luria, 1970, p. 381).

Luria sums up his position as to the necessary approaches for effective therapy as follows (Luria, 1970, p. 458):

The retraining must be based upon precise knowledge of the nature of the defect and must be directed toward compensation for that defect. The techniques are sometimes directed toward aspects of psychological processes which at first glance, appear to be far removed from the disorder at hand, for in many cases just such factors as these give rise to the major components of the aphasic syndrome. In order to formulate an effective retraining program it is essential that the therapist first performs a painstaking psychological analysis of the inner structure of the defect.

A rehabilitation program grounded in knowledge of the nature of the disturbed function is based largely upon the normal course of development of the function. Auxiliary techniques are often employed which are modifications of the ways in which such functions are normally executed. Never, however, does the retraining of a patient with traumatic aphasia repeat exactly the normal course of development. Usually new processes which previously had no relationship to the disturbed functional system play the major role in reorganization. Sometimes the original function must be broken down into several steps which can be externalized and the psychological process it represents mastered in a new way. This type or retraining rarely culminates in complete automatization of the reorganized function and never results in a function which is identical to that which was lost. A consciously directed systematic course of retraining is the only method of compensating for a defect arising from primary brain damage. By reorganizing the disturbed function it is possible to restore activities which once appeared hopelessly lost.

APHASIA IS IN GENERAL A RETROGRESSIVE DISORDER

Jakobson (1968) and Wepman and Jones (1964) take the position that the aphasic's verbal productions may be considered to be language in dissolution, language that in broad aspects reverses the process of normal language acquisition. To the degree that this may be so for an individual patient, if not for aphasics in general, would it be fruitful to employ a program that seeks to emphasize "key stages" or levels in language acquisition, phonemic, morphemic, and syntactic? In a broad sense, this is what we do when, after assessing an aphasic for his competencies and liabilities, we initiate training *at his level of proficiency.* However, we do not accept the implications of Jakobson's position in a literal strict and restrictive sense. We are more positively inclined to Wepman's cautious version of the concept that in general aphasia may be regarded as a retrogressive disorder. Wepman (1970, p. 127) says:

Thus, a given patient may at one time by his capacity or incapacity to communicate demonstrate a particular level of behavior. As he moves from the presumed causative neural event in time ordinarily his linguistic behavior like his intellective and his physical behavior improves (excepting in those events of increasing neurological debilitation when the changes show a parallel decrease in efficiency and function). In many subjects these changes follow a well worn and previously travelled path thought to be not dissimilar to the stages of development of language in children, . . . but not always and certainly not in every particular. Thus, if one considers only free, spontaneous use of spoken language these stages are frequently seen and easily described. However, in other aspects of language use such as reading, writing and spelling, such changes as occur are often at different rates and seemingly reacquired in a different order and in a different manner than they were originally learned. Too little is really known about the acquisition of language in children to make the parallel meaningful in all of the aspects of communication. It may well be that the parallel which is presently stated purely as a hypothesis will with further study be more apparent than real. Its value lies not in its ultimate truth at the present, however, but in the guidelines it may provide for research, for prognosis and for therapy.

Some Linguistic Questions Relevant to Aphasia

In the monograph, *Human Communication and Its Disorders* (NINDS, 1970, pp. 111–112), Hildred Schuell raised several questions that are of particular concern to linguists who are interested in aphasia as a breakdown of acquired language and what such study may contribute to an understanding of normal language acquisition (see previous discussion of Jakobson on aphasia as a regressive disorder). We believe that the questions raised by Schuell are the proper concern of all aphasiologists and are of particular importance to clinicians who are engaged in therapy with aphasic patients. We shall paraphrase and expand on some of the questions in the hope that the effort may provide a framework and rationale for therapeutic programs for patients with acquired aphasic impairments.

As they acquire language, what do children learn that makes it possible for them to generalize and generate new utterances (ones they have not been taught directly) at as early an age as two? By generation we mean talking creatively, the ability to combine words from a lexical inventory according to some rule or principle the child has not been taught specifically.

What is the order of acquisition for the components of language—speech sounds, morphemes (sounds combined into basic units of meaning), and syntax (rules for arranging words into an utterance, the "grammar" of a linguistic system)? Are there interdependencies to these components as a child normally acquires language? Would a knowledge of such interdependencies help the aphasiologist in developing an appropriate therapeutic program for the individual aphasic patient?

Are there deficiencies in decoding of language that parallel those manifest in encoding and production?

Is it clinically heuristic and therapeutically useful to "separate" aphasic persons into groups primarily identified as (1) those who appear to have impaired language competence, their knowledge about the language or languages they had acquired, and (2) those whose basic difficulties are not obviously in comprehension but in performance, in the application of their knowledge as they encode and produce formulations for response by another person?

Summary Note on a Philosophy and Theory for Aphasia Therapy

As we indicated earlier, the assumptions we presented as to some possible views of the recovery process in aphasia are not mutually exclusive. Many clinicians will not be surprised to discover that in practice they have evolved procedures that can be reconciled with one or even all of the assumptions. As we indicated earlier, when a clinician, on the basis of an initial assessment and by periodic reassessment, begins and proceeds in therapy *where the patient is in regard to a given language function*, he is following the implications related to the assumptions we discussed in the recovery process. Similarly, when the clinician determines how best to stimulate his patient to evoke an appropriate response, he is following one or more of the approaches implied in the assumptions relative to the recovery process in aphasia. This point should be kept in mind in our subsequent discussions of therapeutic approaches and specific techniques for aphasic patients.

References

Jakobson, R. 1968. *Child Language, Aphasia, and Phonological Universals.* The Hague: Mouton.

Luria, A. R. 1966. *Higher Cortical Functions in Man.* New York: Basic Books.

_____. 1970. *Traumatic Aphasia.* The Hague: Mouton.

NINDS Monograph No. 10. 1970. *Human Communication and Its Disorders.* Washington, D. C.: U. S. Department of Health, Education and Welfare, National Institutes of Health.

Schuell, H., Jenkins, J. J., and Jiminez-Pabon, E. 1964. *Aphasia in Adults.* New York: Harper & Row.

Shewan, C. M., and Canter, C. J. 1971. Effects of vocabulary, syntax, and sentence length on auditory comprehension in aphasic patients. *Cortex*, 7, 209–226.

Wepman, J. 1969. Approaches to the analysis of aphasia. In *Human Communication and Its Disorders*, 10. Washington, D. C.: U. S. Department of Health, Education and Welfare, National Institutes of Health.

Wepman, J. M., and Jones, L. V. 1964. Five aphasias: A commentary on aphasia as a regressive linguistic phenomenon. *Research Publications of the Association of Nervous and Mental Diseases*, 42, 190–203.

III

Therapeutic Approaches

9

Therapeutic Problems and Approaches

In the previous chapter we discussed the values of therapy, prognostic criteria for recovery, and the process of spontaneous recovery. In this chapter we shall address ourselves to some problems and approaches related to therapy.

Objectives of Therapy

The objective of therapy for an adult aphasic is to bring him as close as possible to his premorbid status as overall circumstances will permit. The circumstances may include motor and sensory impairments as well as modification in intellect and language. Associated with these circumstances are social and vocational readjustments that often include the patient's family as well as the patient himself. Wepman (1968) refers to the three aspects of aphasia therapy: the neurological, the linguistic, and the social. Wepman reminds us:

Aphasia therapy, like any therapy, is designed to help change behavior. Not in the confines of a therapeutic setting alone, but in life. It must be tailored to the neurological, linguistic, and social needs of the patient. It should not be confused with therapy for the agnosias and apraxias which need to be and can be attacked directly. Recovery from aphasia is a global event; the neurological component adapted to, the linguistic progression enhanced, the social events both inter- and intrapersonal exposed and adjusted to. This overall goal may need to be achieved in small, partial increments, but each aspect must be related to each other and not seen or treated as a separate condition.

For some patients, depending on initial and changing circumstances, one aspect may need to be emphasized considerably more than the others. The aphasic who, despite an all-out effort of a year or more of language therapy, still has little functional communicative ability, may still be able to gain considerably from therapeutic efforts that emphasize psychosocial adjustments. For most patients, however, physical and linguistic recovery are the obvious and more immediate objectives of therapy.

The ultimate goal of therapy is to help the aphasic find a purpose in the life that is ahead for him despite some chronic limitations which he has no choice but to accept. For the more fortunate aphasic, the goal may realistically include a return to his former vocation or profession, as well as to his position in the family and in his social environment. For those who may not be able to improve sufficiently, either physically or linguistically, the objective of restoration to the premorbid level of functioning is not a realistic objective. However, some of these patients may still play some role in their families and in society other than that of completely dependent persons in completely controlled and structured environments. Thus, the emphasis and thrust of therapy for some patients must be on their future roles in life, and the need for persons close to them to accept them as important members of society despite language limitations and the economic implications imposed by the severity of their circumstances.

What we have suggested relative to the aspects and objectives of therapy are not, of course, the sole responsibility of the language clinician. The physician, and often several medical specialists, paramedical personnel, educational and vocational therapists, and sometimes the psychotherapist, may need to be involved in the recovery of the patient. The family plays a key role, and not infrequently the members of the family require counseling so that they can understand the problems and the recovery process of the aphasic. Above all, however, the aphasic must himself become as actively engaged in his recovery as his physical condition permits. Rehabilitation is the professional concern of the individuals identified as therapists. Recovery is the essential occupation of the individual identified as the patient.

The discussions that follow are concerned primarily with the linguistic aspect of recovery.

When to Begin Training

Our answer to the question "When to begin training?" is: "Just as soon as the patient is able to take notice of what is going on about him." Although, as we indicated in Chapter 7 in our discussions of spontaneous recovery and prognostic factors for recovery, many patients improve considerably "on their own" for the first six months after onset of involvement, we also pointed out that the period of two months after onset is crucial in the recovery process. Thus, delay of language therapy until two months after onset may be a disservice to the patient. Even if there were no objective evidence to indicate the desirability of the early initiation of training, the following argument could be made. A delay in training permits aphasic patients to resort to and develop nonlinguistic methods of communication, or to reconcile themselves to being cut off from communication with their environment. For some patients, secondary gains from nonverbal communication might be established. Patients may expect that their needs and wishes will be anticipated, and so reduce their efforts at making their wants known. Once this attitude is established, its modification may be difficult.

Luria (1970, pp. 375–376) discusses the problem of functional inhibition in patients with traumatic aphasia:

The third type of functional inhibition is closely related to the second, or reflex type. A person never reacts passively to injury. If a lesion disrupts an entire functional system he naturally reacts by *actively avoiding* use of the affected system. By shifting as much as possible to other systems he may completely dissociate himself from the disturbed system and fail to show any signs of residual capacity whatever. This phenomenon is seen most commonly with peripheral injuries in the skeletal muscular system where a mental "block" or set may suppress the potential restoration of function for a long time.

Thus, Luria argues, "any rational approach to the rehabilitation of aphasic patients must take into account these dynamic components of functional disturbances. It is essential to free the functional system of inhibition as rapidly as possible. Efforts must be directed toward disinhibiting functions which have been blocked and making use of whatever residual functional capacity exists."

Another approach to the problem is the need to appreciate that, except for physical therapy and reeducation, aphasic patients have little to occupy them. The psychological support afforded the patient by the therapist, the awareness that the patient is having something taking place in which he is an *active participant*, all undoubtedly help to accelerate improvement. We may summarize the arguments for early initiation of therapy by a restatement of Wepman's position (Wepman, 1951, pp. 98–99): "Failure to begin training may result either in the rejection of the patient, or in the patient becoming infantalized; patients who do not receive training may tend to become reconciled to their limitations and to withdraw from social intercourse; and later, they may resist attempts at assistance and evidence irritability or yield readily to catastrophic behavior reaction patterns if frustrated."

Some General Problems Related to Therapy

NEED FOR MOTIVATION

The need for an aphasic patient to improve his linguistic ability is usually so strong that motivation to that end may ordinarily be expected to come from the patient. This is generally so in the period immediately following awareness of the existence of impairment. Unless values become established that make linguistic improvement less worthwhile than the maintenance of these values, motivation for language rehabilitation may be assumed. Occasionally a patient may learn that it is possible to impose tyranny without words where control if not tyranny could not previously be imposed with words. Such a patient may, for a short or an indefinite time, resist or reject reacquisition of verbal behavior and will require external motivation to modify his attitude toward "relearning." As indicated earlier, one of the advantages of early training is that the patient does not have an opportunity to realize that there may be values in being nonverbal, so that self-motivation rather than external motivation can function.

The need for motivation may not be a matter for concern until the patient reaches his first obvious plateau in his retrieval of language. Then, having reacquired some language and having improved to some extent in his comprehension and production of language and in his overall communicative ability, he may require urging to make the necessary effort for further progress. If effort has been great and progress small, the discouraged patient may prefer not to try but to resort instead to wishful thinking that spontaneous improvement will occur, that tomorrow "things will be better." It is also possible that the patient may accept himself with or despite his limitations and feel little need for further improvement. This attitude may in fact be nurtured by members of his family, or by his friends, who may overestimate gains or who may begin to understand his nonlinguistic behavior or to anticipate his wants and so reduce the need for conventional language usage. Another possibility is that family and friends may assume that the plateau represents the end of gains and believe that the patient has done as well as he is likely to do. They may become reconciled, as may the patient, that there is little point in making further effort in language reacquisition.

Degree and Direction of Motivation. Perhaps the most significant problems with regard to motivation are those of how much and toward what objectives. Should the highly educated patient be encouraged to believe that in a short time he may expect to be as linguistically proficient as once he was? Should the engineer, the mathematician, the lawyer, the teacher, or the physician be encouraged to believe that he will again have control of all he once knew and be able to return to his profession? No categorical answer can or should be given to these questions. At the present time we do not know how close a given patient can approximate his premorbid level of verbal and intellectual proficiency. To promise too much may lead to disappointment and frustration. To promise too little may result in a reduction of effort. The approach we recommend is to set up a series of short-term objectives which the patient can recognize, and to raise the sights and objectives as the individual patient's rate and amount of improvement warrant. To the patient's insistent question, "Will I be able to talk and read and write as well as I once could?" the safest and most honest answer is, "We'll see as we go along."

The goals and achievement objectives should be correlated with the overall training program planned for the patient. Questions about the patient's possible vocational training or retraining must be considered and answered. His sensory and motor limitations, if they are likely to be permanent, must necessarily be considered. His past interests, his hobbies, his avocations, must all be evaluated. If a patient, because of permanent motor or sensory disability, cannot possibly resume an occupation even should relatively complete linguistic recovery be possible, the new vocation, if any, should determine in large part the ultimate objective of the rehabilitative program, and so the degree and direction of motivation.

LEVEL OF ASPIRATION

It is understandable that most aphasic patients wish to become restored to a previous level of ability in the shortest possible time. Unfortunately, few if any normal persons ever know their full potential abilities. Normal persons may either underestimate or overestimate ability levels. So also may the aphasic patient. It is likely, however, that the aphasic may not appreciate how long it took him to achieve whatever premorbid level he thinks he had attained, and so he may become impatient to be restored to that functional level. A danger also exists that more often than not the patient will overestimate previously developed abilities and set himself too high an aspiration level for rehabilitation. In language performance this tendency may be expressed in the wish to speak in long sentences and in polysyllabic, low-frequency terminology when short, simple sentences with high-frequency words could do at least as well.

The relationship between motivation and level of aspiration is apparent. The role of the therapist in helping the patient modify or reduce, *as an immediate objective*, a very high level of aspiration should be equally apparent.

Low Aspiration Level. Not infrequently a patient will become apparently satisfied with a relatively low level of achievement. There may be several possible reasons for this tendency. The patient may be one who in his premorbid state never tried particularly hard for any high level of achievement and was easily satisfied with what he could do readily. On the other hand, the patient may be one who reduced his level of aspiration to avoid frustration and repeated experiences of failure. His acceptance of a low-level achievement as an aphasic constitutes a continuation of a preinvolvement attitude and conduct pattern. A third possibility is that the aphasic patient has reevaluated his present assets and liabilities and has reached a decision as to how much language he needs to get along. In arriving at his evaluation, he has included the privileges and exemptions of the physically disabled. His aspiration level is a reflection both of what he expects of himself and what he expects others to do for and about him. Such a patient will require motivation to continue to make new evaluations in terms of amount of improvement. He must have his assets and his potentialities brought to his attention so that his low aspiration level does not become a persistent liability. The clinician should, however, be able to recognize that the patient's acceptance of a low aspiration level may in effect constitute his mechanism for avoiding future failure and frustration. With this awareness the clinician may be able to help the aphasic patient accept occasional failure as a normal aspect of living as well as of the processes of learning and rehabilitation.

CONCRETISM

In Chapters 3 and 4 we considered intellectual and personality inclinations and modifications that have implications for the patient's recovery from aphasic involvements. At this time we shall discuss some of these correlates of aphasia and suggest how they may be managed in therapy.

Concretism, when it exists, is often an expression of the aphasic patient's attitude rather than an inherent aspect of his involvement. There is little question, however, that occasionally a patient does manifest concretism and indicates a strong preference to deal with situations that touch upon his immediate needs and experiences rather than to assume a more difficult, abstract, and outer directed attitude in which the needs and viewpoints of others require consideration. For the therapist, a patient's expression of concretism constitutes an additional challenge. Except with some very old patients, and with patients who regardless of age were premorbidly so inclined, concretism as an attitude and as a mode of behavior can usually be modified in the course of therapy.

We have often been successful in modifying aphasic patients' tendencies and expressions of concretism by directing attention to its manifestations when it becomes apparent. If the patient has no appreciable difficulty in the understanding of speech, a frank discussion of the meaning and implications of concretism may be helpful. The patient can be helped by being given insights into the limitations imposed by concretism in reacquiring verbal behavior and especially in appreciating the intention of speakers as well as the surface meaning of their utterances.

The clinician-therapist should also be aware that concretism may be developed by faulty training techniques. If, for example, a clinician who is working with a patient to build up his vocabulary has the patient learn to identify and name objects such as a black pencil, a crayon pencil, and an automatic pencil, and fails to emphasize that despite the differences, all the objects are *kinds of pencils*, an opportunity to abstract and generalize has been lost. Instead, a patient's tendency to be specific and concrete may be reinforced. In teaching names for objects, situations, or relationships, the clinican should emphasize the generic aspects of the names wherever and whenever the opportunity permits. Thus, a lesson on paper should include different kinds of paper, one on apples should include apples of different sizes, shapes, and colors, and so on. All this need not be accomplished in a single therapeutic session or in a given day. The clinician may confine the teaching to two or three members of a generic family during one learning period, and then begin a second period with a statement such as the following: "Yesterday you identified and named an apple when I showed you a red apple (presenting picture or actual apple). Today we have a green apple. It is shaped like the red one, and is about the same size, but it is green. Some apples are red, some are green, and others are yellow. In fact, apples may have several different colors or shades. Do you know any other kinds of fruit that have different colors or shades?"

In helping the patient to establish naming ability, the clinician should make it a point to provide a variety of related stimulus events for a name category. This requires that the clinician must have a large "bag of tricks," and that the individual items must be changed frequently so that the associations the patient makes will not be limited to a single item under a general category. Specifically, not one ashtray but several of various sizes, shapes, and colors should be included to establish not only the *name* ashtray but the concept as well. So with other objects such as forks, books, brushes, chairs, cups, and so on. To reemphasize a point, the generic term should be taught as well as the specific term. It is the therpapist's task to direct the patient's attention to why, *despite some differences, essential similarities make things belong to the same category and call for their having the same family name.*

Although the discussion above dealt with object naming, the principle is intended for naming in general. Relationships, representations, and, broadly, situations which have either common or proper names can be similarly presented so that specific as well as class names are learned at the earliest possible time. If this is done it is likely that a patient's tendency, if it exists, to be concrete minded will be discouraged. Moreover, the therapist himself will avoid training the patient in a manner which might help to establish a concrete attitude that otherwise might be avoided.

PERSEVERATION

Earlier it was indicated that the perseverating tendency was probably the most frequently found characteristic of persons with organic brain involvement. Perseveration was defined as the tendency for an act of behavior to persist or remount into consciousness spontaneously once it has occurred. We can understand the significance of the perseverating tendency and will be better able to deal with it therapeutically if we have some insight into the dynamics of perseverations.

In general, perseveration may be thought of as a disturbance of volition. Perseveration becomes manifest when the usually potent tendencies for a given performance task are somehow blocked, or diverted in some way by an inhibiting event or idea, or completely overcome by an interfering (previously performed or entertained) act or idea.

Normal persons tend to perseverate when they are fatigued; they also tend to perseverate under conditions which demand more rapid and more frequent change than they can achieve. Epileptic persons increase their frequency of perseveration after seizures. Perseveration, in general, may be the human mechanism's way of reacting to situations which demand adaptations and call for responses which the individual is not capable, momentarily or chronically, of making. If the failure to make the adaptation is momentary, the repetition of a previous act which requires little or no conscious effort affords the individual opportunity to select or to organize a new response which he hopes is appropriate. If, for organic or psychogenic reasons, the inability to make ready adaptations is chronic, the repetition of a response fills a void which would exist if no response were made. The individual, aware that some response is expected, repeats an old response to avoid the embarrassment of failing to make any response. In general, perseveration may be regarded as a manifestation of inadequacy or for coping with a situation on the part of the performer. When the aphasic patient perseverates, he is in effect saying, "I am not able to do what is expected, so I am doing something I have previously done which was appropriate. I hope it is better than doing nothing." Beyond this, however, he is saying something which is of greater significance to the therapist: He is signaling that the therapist's demands, at the given moment in the given situation, are excessive. It becomes the problem of the therapist to discover why the demands are excessive, and to modify them in keeping with the aphasic's present abilities.

The first recommended step for the therapist is to present a situation to the patient for which the perseverated act is appropriate. If, for example, a patient has named one of a series of objects correctly and then, because of inability to name a new object, repeats the name of a previous one, that one should again be presented. The response then becomes appropriate. Then the therapist should review the series up to the point where perseveration occurred. At this point the therapist should himself offer the name and ask for the patient to repeat it. If blocking or perseveration reoccurs, the therapist should again call for a previously successful naming performance and put aside for a later time the learning of the new object. It is then usually wise for the therapist to change the situation and the type of task required so that the patient's inadequacy will not be recalled and so interfere with new learning or relearning. In answer to my question, "What is the significance of perseveration in a learning situation?" a recovered aphasic replied, "It means that the therapist is not aware of what is going on with the patient. Good therapy avoids the need for perseveration. When it occurs, the therapist has failed to do a good job."

Although perseveration cannot always be avoided, awareness on the part of the therapist that his patient is showing signs of fatigue, irritability, or disinterest will go a long way to reducing its incidence. Moderation of pace, or a change of activity, frequently will be all that is needed to eliminate perseveration when it becomes evident, or, even better, to prevent the need for it to become evident.

THE CATASTROPHIC REACTION

The *catastrophic* reaction may be characterized as a "psychobiological breakdown" involving the organism as a whole in a situation where a successful performance does not seem possible. Vascular changes, irritability, evasiveness, or aggressiveness may precede or accompany the catastrophic reaction. An extreme catastrophic reaction may take the form of a loss of consciousness. The dynamics of the catastrophic reaction are comparable to those of perseverating behavior. The patient is revealing inadequacy and a wish to avoid the need to make a response. If a way out is not available and escape from the situation, psychological or physical, is not permitted, the catastrophic reaction may occur. Frequently, it will be preceded by perseverating behavior. Some patients resort to catastrophic behavior more immediately and more frequently than do others. We believe that many of these patients are ones who, prior to brain insult, were likely to resort to psychosomatic symptoms such as headache or fatigue to avoid difficult or demanding situations.

The significance of the catastrophic reaction for the therapist is essentially the same as that of perseveration. If it occurs during the course of therapy, the catastrophic reaction signifies that the therapist's demands, at the given moment, have exceeded the patient's ability to produce an appropriate response. Reduced demand or change of activity is indicated. It is best, of course, to avoid an extreme catastrophic reaction if this can be done. Alertness to signs of irritability, such as apparent disinterest, sweating, or excessive eyeblinking, should serve as cues to the therapist that the patient is finding the situation, or the changing situations, too difficult for his adaptive abilities. A brief recess for a coffee "break" or for casual conversation may be all that is needed to avoid pushing the patient into a catastrophic reaction. Once the catastrophic reaction has been resorted to, a sensitive patient may need considerable time as an ego-saving measure. If he is not sensitive, there is danger that the patient will become consciously aware of a device he may use in the future to avoid difficult situations. To a large measure, the manifestation of the catastrophic reaction, as well as of perseveration, reveals failure on the part of the therapist to recognize the needs and abilities of his patient as well as inadequacy on the part of the patient to meet the needs of his situation.

DEPENDENCY RELATIONSHIPS

Because of the aphasic's communicative, expressive, and frequently associated physical disabilities, there is a strong likelihood that he will quickly become dependent on the first person who understands him and apparently accepts him as he is. Frequently, such a person will be the language therapist. For the welfare of the aphasic patient, and to some degree for the therapist, it is important that dependency be avoided. There is grave danger that the aphasic who finds acceptance and understanding in the therapist will become satisfied with that relationship and so avoid others which may be less satisfactory. Having made one adjustment and worked out one relationship, he will not undertake the risks of other adjustments and relationships. Even with regard to language available to him, the aphasic patient may limit his verbal behavior to situations in which the therapist is involved. Doing so, he reduces the likelihood for disapproval, often more imagined than real, for communicative failure. Unfortunately, this limitation also restricts practice in expression and communication, with resultant undesirable effects for ultimate social adjustment as well as language improvement.

From the point of view of the therapist, a dependency relationship is also undesirable. The tendency for a therapist to become subjectively and personally involved in working with a handicapped individual is understandable. Frequently, such a relationship satisfies a need which the therapist may unconsciously have—a need to be needed. It is, however, difficult for effective therapy to be carried on when a patient's failure becomes one which the therapist shares. When the patient's moods, frustrations, successes, or defeats are felt by the therapist, he cannot do justice to the individual patient whose experience he is sharing subjectively. Nor, under the circumstances, can he work effectively with other patients with whom he has a different relationship.

The therapist must maintain objective interest and avoid subjective involvement. One way of doing this, if the rehabilitative program permits, is to have a team of therapists working with several aphasic patients individually, as well as in a group. If the therapist is in private practice and does not have a group of aphasic patients, he must maintain objectivity though working individually. If he finds this too difficult, in fairness to the patient as well as himself, the patient should be referred to another therapist for treatment.

THE ROLE OF THE FAMILY

Except during the relatively brief and acute period of treatment when the patient is in the hospital, and often even during that period, the influence of the members of the family can hardly be overestimated in the ultimate recovery of the aphasic. Not only language performance, but the patient's outlook for all aspects of recovery are influenced by those who, besides himself, are concerned with his rehabilitation.

From the viewpoint of the family constellation, any adult who becomes severely impaired linguistically, whether or not there are associated motor and/or sensory involvements, produces changes in the roles of the other members of the family. The problems related to role change become especially acute if the aphasic was a key person in the family's economy, or the key homemaker. If it is the husband who is aphasic, realistic projecting and planning is required in terms of what may happen if future gainful employment is highly unlikely, and there are no funds besides welfare to take care of the years ahead. If some employment is possible, then the wife needs to prepare to become a supplementary bread-winner. In more fortunate situations, disability insurance and other insurance programs may soften and ease planning. In any event, there are often role changes in the home, with the husband needing to assume "traditional" duties of the wife if she is the patient, or the wife taking over some of the husband's roles if he is the patient.

In a report by Malone (1969) on attitudes expressed by family members of aphasic patients, feelings of guilt, irritability, oversolicitousness, rejection, and apprehension relative to finances were common. Husband and wives indicated awareness that they were treating their mates as dependent children. These are all real problems which must be faced and talked through but which cannot be talked away. On the other hand, these are often temporary problems, and the attitudes can be modified as the patient's picture becomes stabilized. In any event, counseling is indicated by a person competent for this task.

Another aspect of the problem is the role of the family in language training. Although family members cannot be expected to be objective "teachers," they can hardly be ignored. Because the family will be involved unless the patient is in residence at a rehabilitation agency, the family should be instructed as to how they can be of help to the patient at home. "Homework" assignments can be given to be carried out at home under the supervision of a willing family member. This may constitute good therapy for the family as well as the patient. Certainly the desirability of making no assumption or remark that implies that the patient is a nonunderstanding, intellectually deficient person must be established. On the positive side, the need to continue involving the patient as a vital member who may understand and may communicate should be established.

How much the members of the family should be informed with regard to language depends, of course, on the background and capacities of members of the family. At best, the members might well be given the kinds of information we shall present in our discussions of therapeutic approaches. This suggestion is not intended to have the family members become the therapists, but to have them know what language therapy is about. We have had patients whose relationships with their mates permitted them to become initially active participants and finally the actual language therapists with excellent results. In other instances, after appraising the family attitudes, we advised minimal involvement in therapy, *except to emphasize that an encouraging attitude is in itself an excellent and necessary form of therapy.*

The Place of Psychotherapy

There is probably less question as to the aphasic patient's need for psychotherapy than there is as to whether and how this need can be met. It is fairly obvious that any individual whose thinking and communicative ability have been disturbed and who is aware of these disturbances must reorient and readjust himself to the modifications which they impose. Any person deprived of a means of being economically self-supporting, or who is able to continue only with the help of others to whom he recognizes an obligation, can benefit from psychotherapy to assist him in making the necessary adjustments. If, in addition, an individual is suffering from varying and changing degrees of sensory and/or motor disability, there can be little doubt that psychotherapy, if it can be provided in an acceptable form, is indicated. This includes most, if not all, aphasic patients. There is, however, considerable doubt that psychotherapy can be made available to most aphasics. Nevertheless, we are concerned that in many instances more harm than good is accomplished through most direct attempt at psychotherapy. The basic reason for this concern is the appreciation that, despite the aphasic's need, language—the instrument for direct psychotherapy—is impaired. Without assurance that the patient is able to understand, to reveal the amount of his understanding or misunderstanding, direct psychotherapy is precarious. Certainly, direct psychotherapy should not be undertaken unless the aphasic patient has sufficient language ability to express himself and to understand what is being explained to him as well as the need for the explanation.

The clinician who undertakes to work directly and individually with an aphasic must not only be qualified in psychotherapy but must have specific experience with aphasic patients. The clinician must be constantly aware that he cannot assume that the patient completely understands even on an intellectual level what he is trying to have him understand. The usual test of understanding—an appropriate verbalization—is not to be expected of many aphasics.

Beyond this precaution, there is another which should be observed. The aphasic patient should probably not be given direct psychotherapy if his problems, were he not an aphasic, would otherwise not come to the attention of a psychotherapist. An aphasic patient is entitled to a certain number of problems because he is a human being. As such, he, in common with other human beings, should be permitted to work his problems through for himself. It is only when his problems are too severe, or too numerous, that psychotherapy should be considered.

An essential aspect of therapy for the aphasic, which can usually be worked out indirectly and without the intervention of an especially trained psychotherapist, is the patient's necessary acceptance of himself as himself, disabilities included, on a temporary basis. The patient should be encouraged to postpone a "final assessment" and to make reevaluations of his changing self as language, sensory, and motor improvements take place. The aphasic must be given time to adjust to his disabilities and limitations, and to the attitudes of his family, relatives, friends, and other members of his environment.

Aphasia is not a static condition. Neither should the attitudes be in regard to the aphasic's involvements. Counseling for the family, if only to appreciate this point, may in itself be effective therapy.

Learning Principles and Techniques

BASIC PRINCIPLES

Although we shall use the term *learning* in referring to the reacquisition of language by the aphasic, "learning" does not imply the establishment of new forms of behavior. "Learning" does imply the facilitation of retrieval and so the reestablishment (reacquisition) of previously established behavior—the comprehension and production of appropriate language.[1]

There are some common principles and some similarities between an adult's learning of a new (second) language and the reacquisition of language by an aphasic. However, despite some similarities there are important and critical differences which must be understood and appreciated by the clinician in his rehabilitative efforts with the patient.

Differences between an Aphasic's "Relearning" and Normal Adult Learning of a Second Language

1. The normal adult who learns a new (second) language does so with an unimpaired cerebrum and central nervous system. For the aphasic, projection and/or association areas are damaged. In addition, sensory and neuromotor mechanisms may also be impaired.
2. The normal adult who learns a new language is not disturbed by remnants of what he once knew. He is aware that he is starting with a "clean slate." The aphasic in "relearning" may be hindered as well as helped by what he once knew. Residuals of established habits and old plans may interfere with the establishment of new strategies and techniques for learning.
3. The normal adult in a new language learning enterprise does not expect that patterns and associations will come to him spontaneously. He knows that he must apply himself to establish patterns and associations and to evolve and apply rules for the new language. For the aphasic, some associations do come back spontaneously, and it is understandable that he will hope that spontaneous improvement will continue. This hope may interfere with voluntary efforts at "relearning."

REINFORCEMENT THROUGH "REWARD": CONFIRMATION AND INFORMATION

We accept the position that the adult aphasic's "relearning" is susceptible to the influence of reward to enhance (reinforce) the response to be established. However, the reward, if it is a material one, should not be made too obviously. The chocolate-drop reward (consequence) immediately following an appropriate response may do very well for a child. For the adult, a more mature reward-consequence is desirable. This may take the form of the clinician's verbal response, a gesture of approval, or a brief extension of the patient's product that incorporates what he has said in a related statement. Such a response to a response provides both information and confirmation to the patient that he is "right." After a series of "correct" (appropriate) responses, a general type of reward might be offered the patient in the form of a snack, a drink, or some other pleasant break in the session. However, a break should not be introduced if the patient is doing well and enjoying success, in itself the most potent of

---

[1] We suggest that the reader review the discussions on cognitive function and new learning in Chapter 3, pp. 61–64.

rewards. The clinician, sensitive to his patient, might time the break by asking the patient when he wants one, or at signs of fatigue or tension.

Stoicheff (1960) studied the effects of listener (clinician) instructions and reactions to naming and reading tasks in a population of 42 aphasic patients, 30 males and 12 females, ranging in age from 18 to 80 years. The subjects were required to make oral responses to test items following instructions which were either (1) encouraging, such as "I think that you will find the going much easier today than you have before; I expect that you will do just as well today if not better"; (2) discouraging, such as "I am disappointed with how much you have slipped behind in the short time that I have watched you; this seems to be harder for you each time you try instead of easier"; or (3) nonevaluative, such as "I want you to do the same kind of things as last time; we'll be working on different (words, pictures)." While the subjects responded to the stimuli, the experimenter interjected comments such as "Good," or "You're doing fine" as an encouraging comment, or "You missed that one," or "That's wrong" for the discouraging comment.

Stoicheff's results indicate that aphasic subjects did significantly better with encouraging instructions and comments than with discouraging ones. The nonevaluative instruction showed no difference on the reading task compared with encouraging instructions, but were higher (fewer errors) than for discouraging instruction. For the naming tasks, nonevaluative instructions produced results in between the encouraging and discouraging situations. Beyond this, Stoicheff found that "dysphasic patients rate their performances more poorly under discouraging instruction than do those under encouragement. The implications for these findings for clinicians and others associated with the aphasic persons presents a strong argument for the need for expressing positive attitudes and action, verbal and otherwise, relative to language recovery."

INTENSIFICATION OF STIMULATION

Intensification of stimulation can be achieved through an actual increase in the size or loudness of the material presented, or through repetition of the material, or through both. If visual material is used, the print size, at least at the outset, should be relatively large. Type at least twice the size of the type of this book is recommended. If the material is audible, intensity may be increased simply through talking more loudly than for ordinary conversation. Care should be exercised, however, that increased loudness *does not suggest yelling*. If a patient seems embarrassed by the raised level of the clinician's voice, an amplifying unit may be used. In early stages, especially for patients with auditory aphasia, increased loudness may help to break down the "barrier of auditory resistance." Some patients prefer to have the audible material personalized by listening through earphones. This technique serves as an ego-saving device. When head-set earphones are used, no outsider is aware or disturbed by the intensified level of the speech signals sent to the covered ears of the aphasic patient.

Repetition of stimulation is most successfully employed when it is not too obvious. The child may learn to read by being exposed to a sentence such as "Tim saw the rabbit go hop, hop, hop." The adult prefers to have his "hops" better distributed. More subtle distribution is recommended for all forms of presentation. If, for example, a "new" word is to be added to the patient's functional language inventory, the word should be incorporated in the therapist's responses several times during the course of a session rather than successively repeated. Similarly, the patient should be given several opportunities to produce utterances that incorporate the word.

NEGATIVE PRACTICE

The conscious and deliberate use of an inappropriate word or phrase—the technique of negative practice (Dunlap, 1928)—has for some time been recognized as an effective technique for eliminating unintentional errors. For the aphasic, a modification of the technique of negative practice along the following lines is suggested:

If a patient evokes a wrong response in answer to a question such as "What do you use for cutting meat?" and says *spoon* instead of *knife*, the therapist should explain that "We use a spoon for eating soup. We use a *knife* for cutting meat." This should be followed by presenting the patient with an opportunity to use the word *spoon* as an *appropriate response*, and then by a second opportunity to use the word *knife* correctly. If the word *knife* still cannot be evoked readily, further opportunity for the appropriate use of *spoon*, or whatever other word tends to be evoked, should be offered the aphasic. Through this approach, even though the word *knife* is not forthcoming, the patient has been helped to learn correct associations for the word *spoon*, and an appropriate association has been formed.

DETERMINING THE ORIGINAL APPROACH

The reacquisition of symbolic functioning for the aphasic may be facilitated if the therapist can determine how the content or process was originally established and in what way the product was symbolized or recorded. For example, if a patient learned manuscript writing before cursive writing, it may help considerably if the manuscript approach is used with the patient who has writing difficulty. If the patient learned to tell time by adding the minutes to the hour [6:40 (six-40), 7:10 (seven-10), etc.], he should be "taught" time-telling that way rather than to say 20 minutes to seven, or 10 minutes after seven. In writing numbers for division, some patients used the arrangement $X\overline{XX}$ for both "short" and long division; others used $X\underline{X}$ for "short" division and $XX\overline{XXX}$ for long division; still others used $X\underline{XX}$ for all division. Information about the habit of the patient can frequently be obtained from members of the family. If this information is not available, the age of the patient and his place of education may provide clues as to the likely approach to school learning. Most young patients probably learned to subtract by the additive process so that $\frac{6}{-2}$ will be worked as "Two and what make six? Two and four make six." Older patients may have been taught to subtract by the "take-away" process—"Six minus two is four." If the patient has used the phrase "take-away" instead of "minus," then the therapist should use that term and approach with him.

Essentially, as we have emphasized, most aphasic learning is actually a retrieval or reestablishing of functions. This can usually best be accomplished by determining how the function was initially established rather than by imposing the therapist's own way of organization and association on the patient. There are, of course, exceptions. If the initial intake or output modality is no longer operational, then it should be bypassed. Thus, if it becomes clear that, as Luria (1970, p. 380) points out, a basic or elementary functional system is permanently impaired as a result of a breakdown of an analytic center and attempts at training are not successful, "the only means of compensating for deficits of this type is by transferring the functions to other structures or to other functional systems."

RAISING THE LEVEL OF RESPONSE

Earlier it was pointed out that there is a considerable amount of speech which remains relatively intact for most aphasic patients. These forms include emotionally laden speech content, automatic and serial speech, and social-gesture speech. Use can be made of these low-level productions for "higher-level" speech purposes.

A patient who cannot readily evoke the name of a number can be trained to *count* serially until that number comes up in the sequence, and then to stop at it. Later, he can be taught to say the sequence quickly and silently, and then to utter aloud only the numeral which is appropriate. In this way, patients can learn to give their telephone numbers, their home addresses, the date, and other functionally useful number phrases. Similarly, patients can be taught to evoke a particular day of the week, or a month of the year.

Automatic content, such as prayers, familiar verse, and songs, can be used to evoke significant words and phrase. *Good* and *morning* can be evoked separately through the relatively automatic gesture phrase, "Good morning." A physician, Dr. Rose (1948), who suffered a stroke and associated aphasic involvement, described his own retraining through his recollection and memorization of familiar lines of poetry, psalms, and other material which, according to him, "At one time I could almost say it in my sleep." In the account of his recovery, Dr. Rose explained that he also memorized or near-memorized considerable amounts of "new poetry." He recommends "Read often aloud and you will come close to memorizing. . . ."

Where bodily action is customarily or frequently associated with given locutions, as is often the case with gesture-phrases, the patient should be encouraged to engage in such action as an aid in the evocation of the desired words. Terms of greeting, as well as the single-word responses *Yes* and *No*, can frequently be evoked more readily when associated with bodily action than when attempted alone.

Other techniques for facilitation of responses are discussed by Kreindler and Fradis (1968, Chap. 9). Kreindler and Fradis indicate that facilitation may be achieved through either indirect or direct approaches. Indirect facilitation includes the following:

Correct performances which appear spontaneously, occasionally or isolately, or may be obtained (experimentally) under influence of some affective stimuli, concrete situations, particular stereotypes, and so forth, fall into the category of indirect facilitation . . . In such cases, the facilitatory factor is not acting directly upon the verbal performance which is to be fulfilled, but it is acting upon other factors likely to facilitate these performances.

Direct facilitation includes the following:

Correct performances, obtained in aphasics through a direct action upon the given verbal performance, fall into the category of direct facilitation. For example, to obtain naming of an image, say, that of a key, the patient is given the respective word to read, write or repeat, he is given a key to hold, and so forth: in other words one keeps within the same "dynamic system" . . . that of the word "key," which comprises the various forms (oral, read, written) that this word has in the second signalling system, as well as the corresponding aspects in the first signalling system (the image of a key, the sound produced by a bunch of keys, the keys-handling movements and so forth).

Kreindler and Fradis (1968, pp. 143–144) present the following as schema for facilitation in aphasia:

1. Indirect facilitation —heightening of affective tonus
   —placing in a concrete situation
   —introduction into a verbal stereotype (automatic speech, song, etc.)
   —association of thoughts
   —introduction into the same notional sphere
   —variations in stimulus intensity
   —variations in stimulus rate

2. Direct facilitation —simultaneous (tracing, articulatory movements)
   —successive (deblocking)

How to Begin Training

Training should begin with an evaluation of the patient's assets and limitations. These should include a knowledge of what the patient can do, as well as what he cannot do, at the time the evaluation is being made. This knowledge should go beyond estimating the patient's present linguistic and general "educational performance" level. The complete picture should include an assaying of the patient's health history, his premorbid manner of reacting to illness, to frustration, and to the need to exert intellectual effort. This information will determine, to a large measure, how the patient is likely to respond to his present limitations.

An evaluation of linguistic ability can be made through the use of aphasia inventories, several of which were described in Chapter 6, and selected educational achievement tests. An estimate of premorbid tendencies should come through an interview with responsible members of the family. An evaluation of present behavioral tendencies should come from direct observation as well as from reports from members of the family. When these areas of information are obtained, the therapist will know what the patient is presently able to do, as well as what kind of a patient he has for reeducation. The therapist will then be ready for the next question: "How do I begin specific linguistic reeducation?"

Probably the best broad answer to the question is to begin in an area in which the patient can be stimulated. More particularly, the area will depend on the individual patient's immediate needs as well as his ultimate objectives and the strength of his inner motivation to arrive at the objectives. If these are not known to the therapist, and occasionally they may not even be known to the patient, a trial-and-error, or better, a "trial-until-success," period is indicated. A failure to elicit a favorable response may merely mean that the area or mode of stimulation, for the time being, is not an appropriate one. Another should then be tried.

Frequently, the immediate and obvious needs of the patient may serve as a guide. If the patient is still in the hospital, words such as *nurse, water, comb* or better, phrase-sentences which include such words, might well become an immediate starting point. The patient who can call attention to his needs, and who can thereby save himself embarrassment, has been helped to rediscover how very functional language can be. He can rediscover the magical power of words! The patient who can acknowledge a greeting, who can thereby indicate that he is still a vital human being, will command some respect and will ward off injury to his ego. Language which will help to achieve this end is a good area in which to begin to stimulate a patient.

The patient's less immediate objectives will depend on a number of factors. Among these are the type and amount of sensory and motor involvement, the degree to which these involvements are likely to be permanent, the effect of these involvements on his reemployability, and the language needs of the patient in the light of his vocational goal. If this goal is too remote as a basis for stimulation, then the patient's avocations and hobbies should be considered. A reservation, however, must be made with regard to this area. If the patient's physical disabilities are such that the avocations may forever need to be put aside, stimulation in this area should be avoided. Failure to do so may merely remind the patient of what was and can no longer be, and frustration rather than successful stimulation may be the result.

Some specific examples of what can be done may be of help. One patient with right hemiplegia who had been a golf enthusiast was stimulated to start language training after he was provided with a set of left-handed golf clubs and received instruction in their use. He then was willing to learn to read a manual on how to play golf, to learn to spell and say such words as *hole, tee, fairway, par,* and *birdie,* and to read numbers which approximated "average duffer" golf scores. Another patient wanted most to learn to read his young wife's letters and to be able to say in his own words "How much I love her." A middle-aged woman patient wanted to be taught "how to talk back" to her nurse who was treating her like a child. All very human needs!

THE PATHWAY FOR STIMULATION

In general, the best pathway for stimulation will be the sensory and motor avenues which are intact or relatively unimpaired. Which these are will depend, of course, on the individual patient and can usually be determined after an adequate physical and linguistic examination. The information provided by the neurologist as to sensory and motor abilities and disabilities is essential. Questions of hearing loss, as well as auditory aphasia, apraxic involvements, and so on, must also be answered. With such information, the therapist can usually decide whether the sensory avenue should be through vision, hearing, or possibly through the tactual pathway. He should also be able to decide whether the primary motor expression or output should be through speaking, writing, or the use of symbol-gestures. A selected "initial circuit" may, for an individual patient, be aural for reception and graphic for production; for another it might well be visual for reception and oral for production.

Unless the patient, for reasons which cannot always be determined, rejects the avenues selected on the basis of physical examination, the "initial circuits" should be developed until the patient is able to achieve a fair degree of facility in revealing his moods, attitudes, and thoughts. If the patient rejects or resists the use of these avenues, then the therapist must accept those which the patient himself prefers. In any event, it should be made clear that other receptive avenues and productive modalities are not to be ignored. As soon as possible, practice through other avenues should be provided so that multiple associations may be established and conventional intake and output modalities employed.

Schuell, Jenkins, and Jiminez-Pabon (1964, p. 352) argue strongly that "Techniques for stimulating language are the backbone of aphasia therapy." The techniques "depend upon a barrage of controlled auditory stimulation and upon feedback processes from obtained responses." The method described by Schuell *et al.* (1964, pp. 353–356) is essentially one which employs visual-auditory association, employing a set of 200 to 300 basic vocabulary cards *for adults*. Such cards may be made and individualized for each patient, or they may be commercially available published materials.[2]

The auditory-visual association is established by exposing the picture card to the patient, who is directed to "Look at the picture, and look at the word, as I say it. Try to hear it, and try to think it. When you have it, let it come out, but do not force it." The clinician points first to the picture and then to the printed word, "saying the word strongly and clearly each time, and using about twenty repetitions."[3] It is important that the clinician wait long enough between repetitions to permit the patient to rehearse and evoke the word if it is available to him.

Picture identification by a single word is a first step for the more severely impaired aphasic. For the less impaired, and for those who succeed in this first step, Schuell *et al.* recommend that visual-auditory representations intended to elicit phrases or sentences become the next step. This is exceedingly important so that the patient is not reinforced in the use of agrammatic utterances. So, on the second level, a picture may be associated with the question "What is this man doing?" and an acceptable answer, "He (the man) is driving a car."

We should like to note that although Schuell *et al.* consider their approach basically one for auditory stimulation, we consider it to be a visual-auditory approach with oral (spoken) feedback response. If a patient evidenced oral apraxia, or a severe anomia, we would strongly recommend that he write, print, or select the appropriate response in a controlled multiple-choice situation.

It should not be taken for granted that every aphasic patient is readily available for reeducation. Some patients require a considerable amount of stimulation in order to become available for therapy. Along this line, Wepman (1953) characterizes appropriate stimulation as "any and every kind of outside, external persuasion, used by those in the patient's environment to provide the individual with stimuli to which he may react."

HANDEDNESS CHANGE

For many aphasic patients the need for changing handedness, usually, from the right to the left hand, is an essential and inevitable procedure. If the paralysis of

---

[2] Among the published materials are the Taylor and Marks Rehabilitation and Therapy Kit (1959), the Longerich Aphasia Therapy Sets (1959), and the Picture-Word Series for the Language Master (Moore and Schuell, 1954). We recommend that published cards be adjuncts and that the basic word-picture cards, if at all possible, be made for the patient from magazine illustrations. A patient who is free of manual motor disability may be encouraged to make his own illustrations.

[3] We urge that the clinician reduce the number of repetitions to as many, or as few, as necessary to elicit an appropriate response.

the preferred hand is severe, a shift in handedness must be accomplished if the patient is to relearn writing. For the patient with residual weakness, the desirability of effecting the change has not yet been proven experimentally.

The need for handedness change is frequently resisted by patients who still have some amount of control of the preferred hand. It is probable that the patient's wish to be as much like his former self as possible is responsible for this resistance. We recommend change of handedness for patients with upper extremity paresis because it has become apparent that in most instances both motor control and legibility of writing are improved. To overcome resistance, we suggest to the patient that he write with the nonpreferred hand for a period of a month. If, at the end of the period, the patient wishes to resume writing with the original hand, no objection would be made. Almost all patients who agreed to the month's trial period continued, as a matter of choice, to write with the alternate hand. Some were pleased that they had become "ambidextrous." Several patients admitted that they began to feel more secure about what they were writing, that "things clicked right inside their heads" shortly after they attained some degree of skill with the nonpreferred hand.

The accomplishment of a shift in handedness seldom takes more than three or four weeks—providing that resistance to the change has been overcome. Gardner's (1945) manual for left-handed writing has been found most useful for establishing the new writing technique. Plunkett's manual (1954) is also useful for teaching left-handed writing.

Programmed Instruction

Programmed instruction has been used by Holland (1970), by Sarno, Silverman, and Sands (1970), and by others in experimental studies with aphasic subjects to teach specific content or the ability to generalize from content. Although we are likely to associate programmed instruction with machine teaching, the use of "hardware" is not a necessity. Whether or not "hardware" is employed, programmed instruction does imply the application of Skinnerian learning principles which include shaping, differential reinforcement, and response differentiation.

Holland (1969) succinctly describes the essential characteristics of programmed instruction:

To write a program, the programmer must begin by defining in detail the behavior ultimately to be taught. He must then survey the response repertoire of persons for whom the program is intended, or choose a grossly related response that these persons are capable of emitting. He defines this as the program's beginning. The program moves in small, carefully controlled steps toward closer approximations of the criterion behavior. This is called shaping. A program continuously demands responding from the learner, and at each step of the program correct responses are differentially reinforced.

Programmed instructions make demands on the programmer—the instructor—as well as the subject. The programmer must begin by making an estimate, an educated guess derived from assessment, as to where a program is to begin. This guess is then tested by the subject's performance, and revised accordingly. Essentially what is involved is pretesting, the application of the program, and posttesting to assess the efficacy of the program and, from the point of view of the subject, determining whether the desired behavior has been successfully established.

Holland (1969) reports success in increasing auditory memory span for auditory materials consisting of sequences of digits and progressively longer and more complex units of spoken speech. The subjects were mild to moderately impaired aphasics. Sarno *et al.* (1970) reported no greater improvement than with "more conventional" instruction with a population of severely impaired (global) aphasics. Little progress was made and the little was not significantly greater than the improvement shown by the patients who received no instruction.

Programmed instruction of the kind described by Holland meets the needs of the clinician who has been educated in Skinnerian behaviorism as well as those of aphasics who are comfortable with procedures which involve them in specific step-by-step learning. Each step constitutes a level of achievement toward the final goal of the program. Thus, both patient-subject and clinician know where they are and how much further they need to go to achieve the purpose of the program. When a machine is employed in the programming, a patient who has had the initial advantage of human contact therapy can work on his own. Such "self-teaching" extends the instructional period and so has obvious advantages.

Holland (1970) presents several cases in a population of middle-aged aphasic patients (50–60 years) who received programmed instruction for a variety of language impairments, including dysarthria. Most of the programs were individually developed and prepared on cards, although teaching machines were also, though infrequently, employed. Except for the dysarthric patient, Holland reports encouraging improvement for all of the others. Holland shares some important observations with regard to the efficacy of individualized programmed instruction:

The work has made it clear that programming techniques *per se* are clinically feasible, can result in exacting and creative therapy materials, and are effective in rehabilitation. Further, and this was somewhat surprising, once the principles of reinforcement, shaping, and fading are learned, writing programs for individual patients is relatively easy. The time consumed in the development of a programmed text, for example, is enormous; planning an hour of programmed materials for clinical use seems to be a more flexible and simple procedure once the techniques are firmly in hand.

Programming therapy material generally follows traditional programming procedures. Several features of programming are apparently unique to the problems of aphasia, however, the first of these concerns error rate. Error rates typically viewed as acceptable for programs seldom exceed 10%. In programming for aphasics, such a low rate is extremely difficult to obtain consistently. While this is unexplained, problems such as perseverance and response variability probably are partially responsible. Further, in using these programs, aphasic patients tended to capitalize upon their errors quite ably—to contrast them with the correct answer and to explore alternatives. In a sense, they appeared to "use" the available information in an incorrect response and did not, therefore, try to avoid making mistakes. This probably resulted from their past history as adequate language users, and reflects a basic difference between learning something totally new and regaining something once well known.

The second unique feature also concerns errors, in this case the consequences of an incorrect response. In view of the tendency, just described, to give incorrect response rather than none, patients typically were allowed to move forward in a program once a correct response was achieved, rather than to use a back-up procedure (that is, moving backwards to the last correct item and then repeating the missed item). Backing up appeared to be confusing to patients, since the sense of forward progression seems to become lost to aphasics when the procedure is invoked.

Because it is so necessary for a clinician who opts to program his material to really know about the procedures, the final suggestion is made cautiously. It is probably more practical for the clinician to devote his time to experimental development of his own programmed materials, to understand thoroughly how behavioral principles can be applied to therapy, and to apply them to his own clients systematically, than it is for him to search through others' materials to find what someone else has programmed for aphasics.

In concluding the paper, Holland is emphatic that "Programmed instruction is neither an excuse for relinquishing clinical responsibility nor a panacea for the many problems inherent in adequate clinical treatment of aphasia; but it does have a place, perhaps even a considerable place, in the clinician's repertoire of skills."

We view programmed instruction, especially where "hardware" is employed, as an adjunct to the more conventional forms of patient-clinician contact. If we can generalize from the Sarno *et al.* study previously cited, programmed instruction is not productive in advancing the most severe aphasic patients. We do see it as having advantages for patients who have made some progress, whether as a result of spontaneous improvement or of an initial period of therapy. Programmed instruction, whether or not it employs a machine or is built into a series of cards or a workbook, certainly has advantages for recovering aphasics who are able and willing to work without direct clinical supervision. Such "students" may then begin to feel that they are achieving an important measure of independence. This, in itself, is a help toward recovery.

Preventive Approaches

Earlier we discussed the value of undertaking treatment as soon after the onset of aphasia as possible as a preventive measure for aphasics. Another point of view with regard to prevention is described by Beyn and Shokhor-Trotskaya (1966). The basic principle of their approach is to anticipate what form of speech might recover in a patient's progress and "to reorganize the primary speech defect and thereby to prevent the emergence of secondary symptoms of speech disorders ... the characteristic feature of the preventive method of rehabilitation is its prophylactic nature." Specifically, as applied to a group of patients with motor aphasia, the investigators laid the foundation for the future development of a normal grammatical system in a group of patients who would be expected to develop agrammatisms by *regulating the content of the words* introduced into the patient's speech by external control.

We took into consideration the well-known proposition of the psychology of speech that inner speech derives its content from external speech. Therefore, in contrast to the usual methods, in the early stages we *excluded* the communication from the outside of any nominative words, since these could only aggravate the pathology of inner speech peculiar to patients with motor aphasia (i.e., the disintegration of its predicative system). It seemed to us that only those words which were most closely connected with the utterance as a whole could successfully resist this pathological tendency. Our task, therefore, was to select for the speechless patients the simplest possible words which could function as a whole sentence.

In accordance with this theoretical position, the investigators started with words (first and second weeks) which were "partially verbs and partially interjections," such as "No," "There!" "Here," which served as predicatives and, with appropriate intonation and gesture, constituted "sentences." Pronouns were next introduced (third and fourth weeks) to constitute utterances such as "I want to stop," "I shall eat," followed by longer utterances such as "I am going for a walk" and "Give me a drink." We should note that up to this point, although nouns are used, they are in the objective and not in the nominative form. When nominative form words are first introduced, they are of generalized denotation, such as *man, woman, boy, girl.*

Beyn and Shokhor-Trotskaya report that none of 25 adults trained with the preventive approach employed telegraphic speech even though 16 of the group continued after considerable training to be unable to produce grammatically acceptable utterances. Nine of the group, interestingly, continued to have difficulties in the use of prepositions.

We do not know whether preventive training which implies the *control of utterances* will work with most patients. The basic notion, however, that *supplying a patient with a model for correct utterance before errors are produced is consistent with learning principles.* We can certainly recommend reinforcing that which can be correctly evoked as a principle for aphasia therapy.

References

Beyn, E., and Shokhor-Troskaya, M. 1966. The preventive method of speech rehabilitation in aphasia. *Cortex*, 2:1, 96–108.

Dunlap, K. 1928. A revision of the fundamental law of habit. *Science* 67, 370.

Gardner, W. 1945. *Left Handed Writing*. Danville, Ill.: Interstate Press.

Holland, A. L. 1969. Some current trends in aphasia rehabilitation. *ASHA*, 2, 3–7.

_____. 1970. Case studies in aphasia rehabilitation using programmed instruction. *Journal of Speech and Hearing Disorders*, 35, 377–390.

Kreindler, A., and Fradis, A. 1968. *Performance in Aphasia*. Paris: Gauthier-Villars.

Longerich, M. 1959. *Aphasia Therapy Sets*. Los Angeles: Longerich.

Luria, A. R. 1970. *Traumatic Aphasia*. The Hague: Mouton.

Malone, R. L. 1969. Expressed attitudes of families of aphasics. *Journal of Speech and Hearing Disorders*, 34, 146–150.

Moore, P., and Schuell, H. 1954. *The Language Master Handbook for Aphasia*. New York: McGraw-Hill Book Company.

Plunkett, M. B. 1954. *A Writing Manual for Teaching the Left Handed*. Cambridge, Mass.: Manter Hall School.

Rose, R. H. 1948. A physician's account of his own aphasia. *Journal of Speech and Hearing Disorders*, 13:4, 294–305.

Sarno, M. T., Silverman, M., and Sands, E. 1970. Speech therapy and language recovery in severe aphasia. *Journal of Speech and Hearing Research*, 13, 607–623.

Schuell, H., Jenkins, J. J., and Jiminez-Pabon, E. 1964. *Aphasia in Adults*. New York: Harper & Row.

Stoicheff, M. L. 1960. Motivating instructions and language performance of dysphasic subjects. *Journal of Speech and Hearing Research*, 3, 75–85.

Taylor, M., and Marks, M. 1959. *Aphasia Rehabilitation and Therapy Kit*. New York: Saxon.

Wepman, J. M. 1951. *Recovery from Aphasia*. New York: Ronald Press.

_____. 1953. A conceptual model for the processes involved in recovery from aphasia. *Journal of Speech and Hearing Disorders*, 18, 4–13.

_____. 1968. Aphasia therapy: Some "relative" comments and some purely personal prejudices. *Proceedings of the Conference on Language Retraining for Aphasics*. Columbus Ohio State University, pp. 97–106.

10

Specific Techniques

It is not possible, and probably not desirable, to present numerous specific techniques for the rehabilitation of aphasic patients. The best techniques are those which are designed for the individual patient. The therapist will find some useful advice and information in texts and articles on the subject of remedial education. We should not, however, assume that teaching a person to *read again* presents the same problems as teaching a poor reader, or a slow-to-get-started-reader, how to read in the first place.

At all times, the therapist must bear in mind that his patient is going to relearn (reacquire) considerably more language than he can possibly be taught directly. The basic job of the therapist is to get the patient going, to help him to realize that he can "relearn." Once the patient appreciates this, neither he nor the therapist will be surprised at the large amount of spontaneous linguistic recovery which takes place.

The literature on training approaches for aphasics has grown large since World War II. Much of what has been published should probably best be regarded as description of approaches that have been found to be helpful to individual patients which have been generalized to "types of patients" with comparable language impairments. Most clinical aphasiologists are by no means certain about the rationale for their approaches, except that what they recommend has been found to work. Exceptions, perhaps, are Soviet aphasiologists such as Luria (1970) and Beyn (1964) and others influenced by their position. They do seem confident about the relationship of their therapeutic principles and practices to their theoretic concepts of aphasia.

With these reservations in mind, we should like to emphasize that the approaches and technique about to be considered are to be regarded as suggestions and not as prescriptions.

Therapeutic Techniques for Intake Disturbances

AGNOSIAS

Visual agnosias, as we indicated earlier, must be determined if the patient manifests any reading disability or, more generally, a disability in responding appropriately to visual configurations. An agnosia for visual form may explain a patient's inability to read. Occasionally, a patient will fail because the size of the configuration is too small. In keeping with the principle of intensification of stimulation, it is recommended that larger configurations be tried. When recognition is established with the larger ones, then the therapist should introduce smaller configurations until ones approximating those most commonly found are used.

If the patient demonstrates an agnosia for flat representations of forms, but can recognize three-dimensional forms, he should be given practice in associating one with the other. Such practice might consist of his placing three-dimensional configurations on sheets which have two-dimensional ones. That is, he is directed to place a rectangular block on a rectangle, a triangular block on a triangle, and so on. When he succeeds in doing this, the process should be reversed, and the patient should be directed to place a cutout of a two-dimensional figure on the actual object. A final step should be the appropriate and ready selection of the flat figure as it is named by the therapist.

Visual agnosia becomes a significant problem for aphasics if it involves *letter recognition*. In not all cases, however, are the two necessarily related. We have examined many patients who could recognize and read aloud whole words but who apparently could not recognize or at least identify individual letters of the words. It is possible that these patients learned to read by the word- or sentence-recognition method. For them, individual letters do not have the same significance as for persons who have learned to read by building up words from synthesizing letters and sounds. Because of this, the attitude of the patient may be such that he finds no reason for concerning himself with letter recognition. In effect, such persons manifest a disinclination rather than a disability in a recognition function.

For patients with actual *visual letter agnosia*, remedial procedures along the following lines may be tried. An alphabet book, or a series of alphabet cards, with pictures or pictures and words for each letter may be arranged. Children's alphabet books are not recommended because the representations are on a level which might cause ego insult. It is usually no great problem to get colored illustrations from magazine advertisements. Each picture should be edited so that the representation to be associated with the object is most readily evident. If possible, a single object representation should be used. So, a single picture of a book and the word *book* should be associated with the letter *B*. If it is possible to find common object-pictures the form of which suggests the letter, as, for example, a telegraph pole for the letter *T*, such pictures are especially worthwhile. The patient may be directed to copy these letters. If he cannot copy, then he should be asked to trace them, and later to copy them when tracing is easily accomplished. Again, the principle of intesification of stimulation may be used, with the ultimate objective of decreasing the intensity (size) of the letter to usual book-size print. The final step, of course, is for the patient to learn to write letters from dictation.

Some patients who were not readily able to learn to recognize words by the approach just described were helped through body pantomime. For example, a large letter *T* was attached to the corner of a large mirror before which the patient and therapist stood. The therapist stretched his arms out at shoulder height, said "*T*" and asked the patient to imitate the action he saw in the mirror. Later, the patient was able to respond with pantomime to the picture of the letter *T*. Finally, the patient learned to recognize the letter without resorting to pantomime.

These techniques, it is again emphasized, are suggestions. The therapist, using his own resources, should be able to invent suitable ones for his individual patients. Discussions of other successful techniques for dealing with the problem may be found in such texts as those of Goldstein (1932), Granich (1947), Wepman (1951), and Longerich and Bordeaux (1954).

READING DISTURBANCES (DYSLEXIA)

Although some of the techniques of remedial reading for children may be employed with modification with adult aphasics, there are some fundamental differences between the reading disabilities of the child and the impaired reading of the adult. First, we must bear in mind that the aphasic, unless illiterate, was once able to read. If the aphasic was illiterate, then reading disability should not be considered part of his remedial problems. Reading impairment is rarely if ever the only difficulty presented by the aphasic. Other impairments are likely to be present which may compound the reading problem.

With these precautions in mind, the following approach to "remedial" reading is recommended:

1. Begin work at the patient's level of ability.
2. Build up sight identification of words, phrases, and short sentences.
3. Use the sound out (phonic) approach for words that are not easily read, *providing* that the patient has no dysarthria or inclination to paraphasic errors, or evidence of auditory aphasia.
4. Comprehension rather than oral style is the objective. Check comprehension by eliciting an oral or written response from the patient.
5. Secure interesting reading material at the patient's level of competence.

6. Upgrade the level of material as the patient progresses.
7. Make reading materials available that may be read by the patient *solely for enjoyment* and which will not become the content for instruction.

To begin at the patient's level of ability requires an evaluation of that ability. The usual standardized tests for reading achievement may be used for this purpose, with the recommended modification that the time allowance for testing be ignored.

Eisenson's *Examining for Aphasia* (1954) includes a series of reading items which are usually sufficient for preliminary purpose for moderately dyslexic disturbances and are sufficient for evaluating the reading level of severe alexic patients. Schuell *et al.* (1964, p. 171) offer a series of questions to serve as a guide for assessing level of reading comprehension.

Building up of a readily functional sight vocabulary should be determined in part by the patient's needs and interests as an adult and in part by the provision of words selected from lists incorporating words and phrases most frequently found in the patient's language. The Thorndike-Lorge list (1944) has become a source for word selection for many books on reading. A list of spoken words (Jones and Wepman, 1966) based on responses to the Murray Thematic Apperception Cards provides another source for vocabulary selection. We would like to reemphasize, however, that published lists can only suggest words the aphasic *should* know. In the final analysis, aphasics should be helped to recognize and read the words they *need* to know according to their situations and their objectives.

The use of a card with an "exposure slot" is helpful for many aphasic patients in the early stages of reading reeducation. Many patients become overwhelmed when confronted with large amounts of material. They tend to respond better when a small amount is presented at one time. The card serves the purpose of helping patients to believe that they are making progress, a little at a time, and reducing the size of the task. For some patients, pointing to each word as the word is read serves the same purpose. Ultimately, of course, the patient should be encouraged to try to do without this kind of an aid. It is well to remember that, for the aphasic, security and accuracy of comprehension are more important than speed of reading. As training progresses, speed of reading may be improved through the use of flash cards, or by having phrases or short sentences exposed for brief periods on a screen.

Many patients enjoy building up their own stock of reading cards. These may be prepared by the patient with illustrations cut from magazines. A sentence relating to the picture, with the most significant word or words underlined, may be typed under, over, or to one side of the picture. A key word or phrase may be typed or written in one corner. If the patient is able to write, his own writing may appear under the printed material. The patient, in adding to his card list, may go over them by himself, or review them with a relative, friend, or another patient. Periodically, the stock may be separated into cards he can always read easily and correctly, ones he usually read easily and accurately, and others "not yet" read easily and accurately. Through this device both the patient and the therapist can estimate improvement in single-sentence reading based on material selected by the patient.

Vocabulary-building cards such as the Dolch Sight Vocabulary Cards and Sight Phrase Cards can be used to considerable advantage. Although these sets of cards were prepared primarily for teaching children to read, their small size and general appearance make them suitable for adult use.

The development of comprehension cannot be taken for granted merely because a patient learns to read words and sequences of words aloud. It is essential—even more so than for children who do not read well—that comprehension be checked constantly. This may be done by having the patient indicate *in some form most readily available to him* that he understands what he has read. The patient may retell the content in his own words, complete sentences with key words, or even use gestures to reveal his comprehension. As the patient improves, he may enjoy taking self-administered reading tests, such as are provided in many primers and in texts for teaching language to foreign-born persons. Considerable use can also be made of reading paragraphs and test materials of standardized reading scales.

Securing reading material at the present level of the aphasic is frequently a real problem. If the patient's alexia is severe, something comparable to a primer is needed. Primers, however, are infantile both in content and in format. The author undertook to "translate" a primer story for use with his patients. He found the task of using a simple vocabulary and casting the words and ideas into an adult form a much more difficult one than he anticipated. The results, however, were rewarding. In his "translation" he used black-line drawings and photographs to replace the multicolored pictures of the primer. The story, including illustrations, was then bound in hard covers. The aphasics did not suspect that they were reading a paraphrased primer story, and seemed pleased that they had a "book" prepared especially for them.

Probably the best type of initial reading material is that which is prepared especially for the individual patient. As patients improve, edited (rewritten) news reports are useful. They have the advantage of being timely, and so are usually of immediate interest.[1]

[1] We have found general acceptance by aphasics of specially prepared newspapers such as *Young America* (Eton Publishing Co., Silver Springs, Md.) and the special *Reading Skill Builder Series* (Reader's Digest Educational Service, Pleasantville, N.Y.). Among other books prepared for special groups of readers which we recommend as useful for aphasic patients are the following.

The *Everyreader Library Series* (Webster Publishing Co., St. Louis, Mo.) includes classics and biographies adapted by remedial reading experts for use with slow readers. A basic vocabulary and simple sentence structure are employed. Titles include *Ivanhoe, A Tale of Two Cities, The Gold Bug, Cases of Sherlock Holmes*, and *Simon Bolivar*.

The *Oxford English Course* (Oxford University Press, New York) consists of a graduated course intended for persons for whom English is a second language. The vocabulary for each course is based upon a selected list of essential words. The entire series includes language books for presenting basic vocabularies and teaching grammar. *Language*, Book One, Part One, introduces the alphabet arranged for reading and writing. The supplementary readers include simplified versions of the classics which employ limited (basic) vocabularies. Titles which employ vocabularies of from 1500 to 2000 words include *The Tempest* and *The Purloined Letter*.

Auditory Disturbances. It is fortunate that most aphasic patients recover spontaneously considerable auditory comprehension in the early stages of their aphasic involvement. It is probably also true that patients and clinicians both tend to overestimate the amount of recovery which seems to have taken place. Much of what we say to patients in conversation, regardless of specific content, can frequently be answered by a single word, or a nod of the head. A patient who has just the merest hunch of what is said to him can frequently determine by observing the speaker's face whether a "Yes" or "No" is expected. Often the patient catches the rudiments of what is said, but if no specific response is expected of him he does not have any check or test of how much he really understood. Some patients stop listening, or become "functionally deaf," when they cannot readily understand what they hear. By doing this they avoid the challenge, the effort, and the possible frustration of trying to comprehend. One of our patients, a highly social person, almost always took the initiative in conversational situations. He spoke with relevantly fluent circumlocutions and seldom permitted other persons in a conversational group to say much in response to him. By controlling the conversation, the patient seemed to understand conversational speech. When this patient's device of taking the initiative was evaluated for him, he accepted the evaluation and began to listen as well as to speak. By doing so, the first principle of training for a patient with auditory disturbances became established: *patients must learn to listen if they are to learn to understand what they hear.*

In our discussion of therapeutic problems and approaches in Chapter 9, the technique of intensification of stimulation was considered. The auditory aphasic needs intensification. He also needs constant encouragement and reassurance that in time comprehension will come and two-way communication will be reestablished.

For the auditory aphasic, television observation is strongly recommended, especially for dramatic plays. The frequent close-ups, permitting the patient to concentrate on the facial movements of speech, which may be associated with the total background situation, constitute excellent therapy as well as educational recreation. Newscasts, whether on television or radio, are also highly recommended. If possible, a discussion between patients and clinician should follow listening to news broadcasts. Such discussion, which should be held informally, will serve as a reinforcement of understanding. If a given newscast involves a matter about which there may be differences of opinion, then the patients may be encouraged to give their reactions or opinions about what was said.

For more formal teaching situations, Schuell (1953) offers a number of suggestions for determining whether a patient understands what he hears. Schuell emphasizes that the only way to be certain whether an aphasic patient understands what he hears is to ask him to respond in some way. The nature and particular type of response which the patient should be encouraged to make will depend on both the patient's productive abilities and the specific situation.

Among the type of responses which may be elicited, Schuell suggests the following:

1. Identifying objects in a picture. This may be used in going over illustration in magazines, books, or specially arranged cards.
2. Following directions.
3. Answering questions, formally or informally, in conversation with the therapist.
4. Completing sentences intentionally left incomplete by the therapist.
5. Answering specific questions presented by the therapist.
6. Identifying, by pointing, underlining, or naming specific words or sentences for a given context.
7. Paraphrasing in the patient's own words, or in words he recalls, what the patient heard.
8. Writing answers, especially if the patient can write more readily than he can use oral speech.
9. Presenting oral opposites of single words, phrases, or sentences: for example, high—low; come here—go away; it is early—it is late.

To this list, which is merely a list of suggestions, the therapist can and should add his own devices to ensure the second basic principle of therapy for the training of a patient with auditory disturbances. The principle is that *the patient must understand what he hears*.

Auditory aphasics who show impairment in phonemic discrimination or *discriminative hearing* (Luria, 1966, pp. 103–113) present a special problem. Such patients, by virtue of their auditory disturbance, are likely to have difficulty in differentiating between words which have sounds not separated by wide distinctive features, such as *boat* and *coat, coal* and *goal, path* and *bath*. Such difficulties become apparent when contextual meanings do not bring out differences in word meaning. Fortunately, as Luria observes, patients with disturbances in phonemic hearing do not usually have any related disturbance in melodic hearing. This observation, plus "the characteristic of sensory (acoustic) aphasia is the fact that all functions not related to the defect to sound analysis and synthesis are usually preserved" (Luria, 1966, p. 112) provide the basis for therapy. The patient must direct his attention to the overall meaning of an utterance, to visual components of articulation, to the inflection, stress, and intonation to compensate for impairment in phonemic discrimination. As Luria points out, "Assistance from kinesthetic and visual-spatial analysis and synthesis may therefore be used for rehabilitation of patients in this group." More detailed rehabilitative writings on methods are outlined in Luria's writings on the rehabilitation of aphasic (Luria, 1948, 1970).

Therapeutic Techniques for Productive Impairments

At the outset it is important that we appreciate that productive impairments as well as receptive (evaluative) ones are seldom found as pure or isolated disabilities in the adult. Not infrequently, the patient's concern with one aspect of his impairment may make him oblivious to other aspects. Without thorough examination, areas of evaluative as well as productive defects may not become apparent either to the clinician or to the patient. This statement is not intended to imply that the clinician or therapist has an obligation to "reveal all" to the patient just as soon as "the all" is discovered. It is intended to imply that the ultimate object should be improvement, to whatever degree seems possible, in all areas of disability.

NONVERBAL APRAXIAS

It is obviously important, as indicated earlier, to determine whether a particular productive disturbance is one related to the symbol *per se*, or to the motor act *per se*. In the case of writing disturbance, it is essential to know whether the patient's basic difficulty is in knowing how to use a tool external to the body—a pen or pencil—intentionally and meaningfully, or to use the arm-hand-finger tools intentionally or meaningfully. For the most part, the speech therapist is not likely to be concerned with the patient's use of tools which are not part of the body. Such training is likely to be provided by other members of the therapeutic team. It may, however, become necessary to teach the patient how to handle writing equipment such as pencils, pens, chalk, the blackboard, and so forth.

Probably the best initial approach to the handling of tools is to have the patient imitate the therapist's act as a whole in a relatively simple movement. The first tool should be large, easy to grasp, and one that offers little resistance. Soft chalk and a large blackboard, soft black crayons and a large sheet of paper mounted on a blackboard, are good instruments for a start. If the patient cannot directly imitate the writing of a simple word outline such as *cat* then the therapist may try placing the writing instrument in the patient's hand and moving the hand for the execution of the word outline. From soft chalk or crayon, the patient should progress to using a large, oversize pencil. If the patient finds it difficult to grasp a pencil, its width and tenability can be enhanced by tying multiple-strand string around the bottom of the pencil. If the notion of grasping itself needs to be established, the use of a half-filled bean bag or a sponge-rubber ball is recommended.

In clinical situations, the occupational therapist can be of considerable help in teaching the patient the use of tools, including those required for writing.

DYSARTHRIA

Dysarthria, an impairment in articulation, is sometimes associated with aphasic involvements, and, more rarely, an isolated residual defect. It may also be found as a relatively severe form of productive impairment without associated aphasia. Schuell *et al.* (1964, p. 362) report: "There is a minor category of aphasic patients who show a mild aphasia accompanied by persisting dysarthria." Common defects in articulation include the phonemes *s, sh, ch, j, r,* and *l*. These sounds, interestingly, are among the last established by children in their speech sound development. Consonant blends such as *st, kl, gr, pr, pl,* and "triple blends" such as *sks* and *sts* are also difficult for patients with dysarthria.

Control of articulatory activity may be enhanced by emphasis on the visual aspect of articulation. An approach we recommend requires imitation by the patient of simple articulatory movements made by the therapist. Imitation may be direct, with the patient observing the therapist, or it may be mirror imitation, with the patient observing the therapist and himself in a large mirror. The use of photographs or video play backs to enable the patient to imitate himself is also suggested.

From single sounds such as *ee, oo,* and *a* (ah) which, fortunately, have some word value in English, the patient should move to consonant-vowel combinations. To begin with, the readily visible consonants should be taught. The sound *p* is a good one because of its distinctive lip movement and breath characteristics. It can be combined with each of the vowels mentioned above to constitute three word forms. The patient then is not only making sounds, but to a degree may be making sense. It is not recommended that the sound *m* follow the teaching of *p*. The partial similarity in lip activity may confuse some patients. Instead, a sound produced differently, such as *t* or *n*, should be taught next. Fortunately, *t* plus each of the three vowels adds at least two more word forms for most American speakers, and three word-forms for American speakers who use Standard Eastern or British (London) dialect.

The concept of voiced and unvoiced sounds should be established after sound as such is appreciated. If the patient does not vocalize sounds spontaneously, the patient's hand may be placed at the therapist's larynx while the therapist produces voiced sounds. We have found that frequently all that is necessary for the patient to produce vocalized sound is to place his (the patient's) hand on his own larynx in imitation of the therapist. In this way, differences between cognate sounds are usually established readily.

The next step is to establish speech sounds which are not readily visible, such as *s, z, r, k,* and *g*. These again may be taught in isolation and in combination with vowels in addition to the first three which have been suggested. Wherever possible, chosen combinations should be ones which are word-forms rather than nonsense syllables. Word-forms may be used and recognized as speech.

As soon as possible, the patient should be encouraged and provided with opportunity to incorporate his troublesome sounds into words and phrases. Schuell *et al.* (1964, p. 362) recommend having the sound to be established made part of a syllable or short word with different (long and short) vowels. For example, for a patient who needs to control the *l, the combinations may be la, lay, lee, lo, loo.* Phrases might include

Lay—lay it away
Lip—upper lip; lower lip
Loan—a loan; alone
Load—a big load; a heavy load

Except for the severe anarthric patient, it is seldom necessary to teach a patient all sounds, or very many combinations of sounds. Once the idea of articulatory activity is established, most dysarthric patients progress by themselves in controlling additional sounds, and in moving from sounds to words, from words to phrases, and then to longer utterances.

Severe Dysarthria. For the severely dysarthric (anarthric) patient, we recommend a procedure based on knowledge of speech acquisition in children. Our assumption is that children develop proficiency in the control of sounds that are easiest for them, and presumably the same order should facilitate reestablishment of control in the dysarthric adult. The basic objectives are (1) to establish a sequence of articulatory movements that will produce the desired sound or combination of sounds in a syllable, and (2) to reduce "random" movements which may result in "jargon" production. In our recommended procedure, the initial attempts are made with the clinician and patient facing a mirror so that the patient has an opportunity for direct imitation of the desired oral activity. If videotape equipment is available, the activity may be recorded and played back for the patient so that, when successful, he may continue practice by imitating himself as well as the clinician.

The order of sounds, first presented in isolation and then followed by a consonant-vowel (CV) syllable, follows:

Order of Sounds Approximating Normal Acquisition

m, n, ng[a]	*k, b, d, g, r*	*t, th* (unvoiced), *v, l*
p, f, h	*s, sh, ch*	*th* (voiced), *z, zh, j*
w, y		

[a]The ng does not occur as an initial sound in English. The establishment of this sound, if it does not occur "spontaneously" would be reserved for CVC syllables, or words such as bang.

The recommended order need not be followed rigidly. The patient may begin to demonstrate control of sounds after a few are established through training. We would also make use of what the patient may produce in his own substitutions of sounds. For example, if the patient produces a *th* for an *s*, we would establish the *th* by providing him with materials and opportunity to produce appropriate *th* syllables and words such as *thin, thick, thigh, thumb,* and *thing.*

We would move quickly from the production of the isolated sound to a CV syllable, using different vowels to combine with the consonant. Thus, we would combine the *m* with *a* to produce the syllable *ma* and then *m* with *oo* to produce *moo.* If the patient has difficulty in combining the consonant and the vowel into a syllabic product, the sounds may be separated into *m–a* with an interval between. As soon as possible, however, the continuous syllable sequence should be established.

When the patient establishes control of CV syllables, we suggest going to CVC combination, with the same sound in first and third position, for example, *mam, moom, meem, peep*, and so on. When such combinations are established, we would include a different consonant, initially from the same level of the list, for example, *man, mean, hop, heap*, and then combining sounds from the approximate levels.

Early in the training program we would introduce words and incorporate them into short phrases or sentences employing a carrier phrase such as "I want," or "give me," or "that is." Following is a list of short words that have no more than five phonemes that can be used in phrases and sentences:

I	walk	up	and	can
me	run	down	if	do
my	what	away	to, two	am
you	when	under	kick	read
we	why	over	hit	book
is	now	soon	see	candy
has	later	there	sing	food
come	go	here	move	read

Rhyme phrases such as "kick the stick," "candy is dandy," "look at the book," "fell into the well," "high in the sky" may be used as a challenge for the patient to indicate that he has control of word productions that are nearly alike. Rhyming also provides an opportunity for auditory discrimination and perception.

The clinician should note the rate of articulation that permits the patient to produce utterances with maximum proficiency. If a normal rate results in error, then the patient should be directed to slow down to a rate of minimum error. The clinician may find that slowing down his own rate to correspond to the patient's most proficient one is a better procedure than the direction to "slow down." However, it is important that the appropriate intonation (melody of utterance) be maintained.

ORAL (SPEECH) APRAXIA

Johns and Darley (1970) distinguish between the dysarthric and oral (speech) apraxic patient. They designate the speech apraxic as a person who demonstrates "aberrations in programming of articulatory movements in volitional speech in the absence of significant impairment of language comprehension and muscular weakness. ... " The speech productions of the apraxic are characterized by "a high degree of inconsistency of errors; predominance of substitution, repetition, and addition errors as opposed to distortion errors of dysarthria; marked prosodic disturbances without phonatory and resonatory changes; increase of difficulty from spontaneous to oral reading to imitative speech conditions. ... "

Johns and Darley found, in the course of examination, that speech apraxic patients improved when presented with auditory-visual stimuli (speech models from a visible examiner) rather than stimuli from an auditory tape playback or from a written stimulus. They also found that patients improved when given the opportunity to perfect their responses by repeating the stimulus word three times without interruption by another presentation of the model.

The approaches we have presented above for dysarthric patients are, we believe, appropriate for the oral (speech) apraxic. We certainly would emphasize the visual-auditory imitative stimulation procedure. For such patients videotape recording and playback to permit seeing *and* hearing is especially important.

WRITING (AGRAPHIA)

We shall begin with the assumption that the patient has no external tool apraxia, or has overcome this form of disability and now must be trained to learn to form letters and to write words and sentences. If the patient has a hemiplegia or a severe paresis which involves his preferred hand, a change of handedness is essential. The use of Gardner's or Plunkett's manual for this purpose has already been indicated. Visual disturbances, especially those involving visual field, must also be considered. It is essential that the patient be able to see as well as feel the materials he is to use. If the material is to be copied, it should be placed so that it can be seen easily. If this can be accomplished, almost all aphasic patients can succeed in copying. Retraining might well begin with copying material on a blackboard. Next steps might include copying with a soft crayon on a large sheet of newsprint, copying with a pencil, and copying with a pen. Many patients are able to proceed directly from blackboard to pencil and paper. It is again emphasized that the therapist must assume the responsibility for the good working condition of the equipment. Mechanical difficulties should not be permitted to aggravate the patient's efforts at improvement.

If a patient cannot copy readily by looking at material above his writing space, he may be helped by placing letters underneath thin, transluscent paper, through which the letters underneath may be seen. The letters should be clear and simple in outline. If possible, they should be enlargements of the kind of writing the patient himself habitually used. Almost always, some specimen of the patient's own writing may be obtained from a member of his family.

Occasionally, a patient, for reasons not always apparent, has persistent difficulties with one or more letters. It frequently helps to personalize these letters. One patient learned to write the letter *I* by standing straight and tall, with his hands close to his sides, so that he looked like an *I*. Another, who was fond of smoking a pipe, associated the letter *P* with the picture of a pipe placed so that it suggested the letter *P*. The resourceful clinician may arrive at his own devices which meet the needs and interests, as well as the disabilities, of his particular patient. For further suggestive techniques, the clinician is referred to texts by Granich (1947) and Goldstein (1932), and to an article by Smith (1948).

Copying should be followed by writing from memory after visual presentation. The time period of stimulation presentation should be reduced progressively to a brief period, sufficient only for the patient to read what is presented. Following this, the patient should be encouraged to write from dictation, beginning with single words and proceeding, as early as possible, to short phrases and short sentences. Eventually, short paragraphs should be used for dictation material.

In his attempts at writing, the patient should never be required to struggle for the letter or word he cannot evoke from memory. The elusive word should be made available to him so that he can copy what he cannot recall.

Spelling disability, in the sense that the appropriate sequence of letters cannot be recalled for a given word, is not an apraxic disturbance as the term *apraxia* has been used in this chapter. It is a higher-level symbolic disturbance, and therefore is classified as agraphia. Many patients with writing disturbance have this form of difficulty. Some have both apraxic and spelling involvements. A few will have little difficulty with spelling as such once they overcome their apraxic disability.

For the patient with both forms of writing disturbance, practice in copying and writing from dictation has incidentally provided practice in spelling. Continued practice may be given in flash-card presentations, and in spontaneous writing with word lists available for copying when necessary. If it is determined, as is sometimes the case, that the patient's oral spelling is more accurate than his written efforts, then the oral approach should be emphasized. Similarly, if the patient seems to learn better through the auditory than through the visual avenue, the words should be spelled aloud for the patient, and he should practice writing while he spells aloud.

In teaching spelling, the selection of words to spell should be determined primarily by what the patient will need to write. The essential objective for spelling instruction, for aphasic adults as for children, is to equip them to write what they need and want to write. The needs of a carpenter and a lawyer are likely to be more divergent for the building of a writing vocabulary than for a speaking or reading vocabulary. This, however, should not overlook the possibility that some carpenters have avocations which include the need to write and spell to a greater degree than some lawyers.

Spelling lists serve as a guide to ultimate objectives. The lists previously suggested for basic reading vocabularies obviously may be used for spelling as well. These lists should be supplemented by special ones that are related to the patient's interests, and should include vocational and avocational vocabularies if the patient is likely to return to them.

It will frequently be found that many patients' spelling difficulties are similar to those usual with children. Devices such as enlarging the letters of the troublesome parts of the word, or writing the letter in colored ink or crayon, may be of help. The patient should be encouraged to keep his own list of troublesome words, written in a fashion best suited to help him learn the correct spelling of the words. In this regard it is hoped that the patient will pride himself on a list decreasing rather than increasing in size.

PARAPHASIA

Paraphasic errors—errors of omission, substitution, or transposition of sounds or words—frequently constitute a final therapeutic problem for both the patient and the therapist. These, together with word-finding (anomic) difficulties, may persist as residuals of aphasic involvement. In some instances, there is little to do but to become resigned and adjusted to their continued presence, especially under conditions where intellectual vigilance is reduced.

For patients who are motivated to make themselves understood, it is of some help to record their oral speech and to play it back. Then the patient may be asked to indicate what words he omitted that another speaker is likely to use to convey the same meaning. The patient is then encouraged to fill in the omitted words. The author has found that it may also be of help to reduce his own speech to telegraphic style when speaking to the patient, so that the patient can appreciate that such speech is difficult to understand. Where possible, this exercise should be given to a group of patients who may correct one another. Written speech may be corrected by having the therapist indicate the places within a sentence where words were omitted. The patient is then encouraged to fill in the omitted words. If he cannot do this, the words should be inserted for him, and the patient is then directed to rewrite the sentence with all words in conventional order.

Errors of sound reversal may be treated in a similar way. For some patients, the technique of negative practice may be used with success to create awareness of error. Fortunately, for most aphasics, severe paraphasic errors tend to disappear as general improvement takes place. If paraphasic errors are relatively infrequent, it may not always be worthwhile to correct them. It is well to remember that even normal nonaphasic persons sometimes commit paraphasia. We call them slips of the tongue. Their psychodynamics, from which aphasics are not free, are, as Freud indicates, a matter of the psychopathology of everyday life.

AGRAMMATISM

Some patients evolve oral and written speech which is characteristically agrammatical. Their speech suggests the economical form of a message prepared as a telegraph or a cablegram. So-called "unessential" words—the connectives, prepositions, and conjunctions—are often omitted. A sentence such as "Let us go for a walk" may be reduced to "Go walk" or simply to "Walk." According to Goldstein (1932), many patients lose their attitude toward grammar and need to be reoriented to grammatical practices. This reorientation is not always possible, especially with a patient who has accepted his disabilities and the immunities associated with them. For such a patient, his new point of view seems to be "I am a patient, and I have many disabilities. It is up to others to make adjustments to me and to exert effort to figure out what I mean."

There are, however, other aphasics whose agrammatism should not be attributed to a disinclination to bear the responsiblility for conventional linguistic formulation. Goodglass and Mayer (1958) say of them:

They have lost the ability to find the melodic-syntactic models which correspond to their concepts. Being deficient at this level, their choice of grammatical words is limited to those which belong to the few sentence models which they know, or represents an artifical recourse to knowledge of the "rules" about making sentences. They do not have the benefit of automatized "feel for sentences" to aid them in the selection of the grammatical words, except within their restricted repertory of sentence schemata.

Goodglass and Mayer summarize their findings for five agrammatic and five nonagrammatic aphasics who were administered a sentence repetition and a word-substitution test. Their results showed:

(1) the agrammatic group tended to revert to one of a small number of simple syntactic models; (2) the agrammatic group made more errors of omission and substitution of grammatical morphemes; (3) the agrammatic group showed more stereotyped repetitions of the same errors; (4) the agrammatic group made more total errors; (5) there is a tendency for the agrammatic group to have less word-finding difficulty.

The implication of these findings is that the problem of many agrammatic patients requires direct attention and training. Holland and Levy (1971) approached the problem through a teaching-machine program of instruction based on the teaching of a simple declarative sentence. They found seven agrammatic aphasics made significant improvement in their ability to use the sentence "The man opened the door," and sentences similar in syntactic structure. The subjects also showed a generalized ability to use the interrogative form of the sentence but no generalized ability to use either a negative or a passive transformation for the basic sentence. Holland and Levy state:

The generalization data thus support the following conclusions: Aphasics can relearn, at least for immediate recall, what they are taught. Further, generalization insofar as syntax was defined, trained and measured in this study, appears to accrue to interrogative transformations, but the structurally complex negatives and passives did not follow suit. It strongly suggests that the nature of the retraining tasks one assigns to aphasic patients must be carefully considered in order to capitalize on the aphasic's limited ability to generalize.

If these findings can be generalized for their implication, it is that agrammatic patients need to be taught syntactical forms and transformations by direct examples and opportunity for practice in appropriate situations. Fortunately, our own experience indicates that many agrammatic patients show continued improvement when given such training.

Ingram and Eisenson (1972, Chap. 9) developed a program for establishing grammatical structures in developmentally aphasic children. The program, which can be adapted for adults, is based on model constructions that incorporate a variety of syntactic features. The order of presentation approximates their acquisition in the normal child.

The program begins with two-word noun plus verb constructions—such as "Hit ball," "Cut paper"—and moves progressively forward to other model constructions that incorporate features such as the possessive form, the use of the demonstrative *that*, the pronouns *I, it, me, my,* and *you,* and the use of prepositions, articles, and conjunctions (functional words). The final level of the program incorporates negative modal constructions, such as "The boy can't ride the bike." Other features include the use of the copula verb form, such as "The man is tall," the progressive form, such as "The man is running," and longer model constructions that include the use of a relative clause, such as "The girl is eating the ice cream that she enjoys." Model *wh* and *how* questions are also presented, such as "Who is driving the car?" and "How do you wind the watch?"

WORD-FINDING-DIFFICULTY (ANOMIA)

Both logical and psychologically, the aphasic patient's language needs are greatest for oral speech, and training should, wherever possible, begin here. Unless he is an extremely withdrawn person, a patient can learn to get along without all other forms of productive language except oral speech. Word-finding difficulty is both the most common characteristic of the aphasic's disturbances and the most persistent even after considerable overall improvement has taken place. It is the form of difficulty most likely to return under conditions of tension, excitement, or fatigue. For many, and perhaps for most aphasics, it is to some degree a permanent residual problem. Sometimes, the substitute word may not readily suggest, in sound or meaning, the desired word. Some patients prefer to say something, in the remote hope that they may guess right, or because of an attitude that saying something—anything—is better than saying nothing. Most patients are able to recognize their errors and try to correct them. If, as indicated earlier, the word evoked in error is one which may be functionally useful, an attempt might be made to establish that word. If this is not the case, the therapist should return patiently to trying to establish the originally selected word.

In establishing a name of an object, the function of the object should be demonstrated, and the object should be named. The patient may then be asked to repeat the name after the therapist. If he can write, he should be asked to write and say the name, alone if possible, otherwise with or after the therapist. Finally, the patient should be given an opportunity at some later time in the therapeutic session to evoke the name by himself.

Once the naming process gets under way for descriptive action, as well as for nominal terms, progress may be accelerated and considerable spontaneous improvement may be expected. Improvement as a result of direct training may also be more rapid. Most patients, however, will continue to find that a few words are always elusive and will not be theirs for ready evocation. Some patients will learn to speak slowly, as if they are always hunting for words. Others will become adept in using synonymous terms and phrases. Still others will indulge in lengthy circumlocutions to suggest the meanings of the precise words which will not readily roll off their tongues.

The "tip of the tongue" experience is one which may be fruitfully employed with the anomic patient. He should be encouraged to say the word, even though he is aware that it is not the precise one he seeks, and then try to "close in" by saying another word "closer to the mark." If the elusive word is evoked, the patient should incorporate it into a phrase or sentence, and then write it or have it written for him, for later review. We suggest a card with the word on top and a sentence below it.

As soon as possible, and at the very outset *if at all possible*, the patient should be urged to incorporate the words which have become established, or which are being established, into conventional oral sentence form. All too frequently patients become satisfied with naming as a sentence function. This device, though economical of effort, does not help the individual concerned, or others, to think of him as a recovered person rather than as a patient.

ARITHMETIC DIFFICULTY (ACALCULIA)

Arithmetic disturbances may arise because of linguistic aspects *per se*, or because of the special processes involved in calculation and problem solving.

Fortunately, much of arithmetic effort is entirely automatic by the time the individual becomes an adult. Because of this, many aphasics can arrive at correct results without being able to name the numerals or tell what they did to arrive at their results. Speed of calculation can be enhanced by making the patient aware of automatic arithmetic series, and by showing him how he can make use of them. After relative automaticity is established, the patient may be shown the rationale of the various arithmetic tables. For example, the patient may be shown that the series 2, 4, 6, 8, . . . is arrived at by adding the amount 2 to each previous amount.

The need for reteaching arithmetic in a manner as close to the one in which the particular process was originally learned has already been discussed under Learning Principles and Techniques, pp. 154–156. Additional suggested approaches to calculation difficulties may be found in texts which deal with the teaching or the remedial teaching of arithmetic.

As with other symbolic functions, the amount and kind of calculation to be taught should be determined by the individual patient's immediate needs and later objectives. If the patient is ambulatory, counting sums for payment of purchases and making change should probably have priority.

References

Beyn, E. 1964. *Aphasia and Methods of Its Elimination.* Leningrad: Meditsina.

Eisenson, J. 1954. *Examining for Aphasia.* New York: Psychological Corporation.

Gardner, W. 1945. *Left Handed Writing.* Danville, Ill.: Interstate Press.

Goldstein, K. 1932. *After Effects of Brain Injuries in War.* New York: Grune & Stratton.

Goodglass, H., and Mayer, J. 1958. Agrammatism in aphasia. *Journal of Speech and Hearing Disorders*, 23:1, 99–111.

Granich, L. 1947. *Aphasia: A Guide to Retraining.* New York: Grune & Stratton.

Holland, A. L., and Levy, C. B. 1971. Syntactic generalization in aphasics as a function of relearning an active sentence. *Acta Symbolica*, 2, 34–41.

Ingram, D., and Eisenson, J. 1972. Aphasia in children. New York: Harper & Row, Chap. 9.

Johns, D. F., and Darley, F. L. 1970. Phonemic variability in apraxia of speech. *Journal of Speech and Hearing Research*, 13, 556–583.

Jones, L., and Wepman, J. M. 1966. *A Spoken Word Count.* Chicago: Language Research Associates.

Longerich, M., and Bordeaux, J. 1954. *Aphasia Therapeutics.* New York: Macmillan.

Luria, A. R. 1948. *Rehabilitation of Brain Functioning After War Traumas.* Moscow: Academy of Science Press.

———. 1966. *Higher Cortical Functions in Man.* New York: Basic Books.

———. 1970. *Traumatic Aphasia.* The Hague: Mouton.

Plunkett, M. B. 1954. *A Writing Manual for Teaching the Left Handed.* Cambridge, Mass.: Manter Hall School.

Schuell, H. 1953. Auditory impairment in aphasia: Significance and retraining techniques. *Journal of Speech and Hearing Disorders*, 18, 14–21.

Schuell, H., Jenkins, J. J., and Jiminez-Pabon, E. 1964. *Aphasia in Adults.* New York: Harper & Row.

Smith, M. 1948. Teaching an aphasic how to write again. *Journal of Clinical Psychology*, 4, 419–423.

Thorndike, E., and Lorge, I. 1944. *Teachers Word Book of 30,000 Words.* New York: Bureau of Publications, Teachers College, Columbia University.

Wepman, J. M. 1951. *Recovery from Aphasia.* New York: Ronald Press.

11

Group Therapy

Group Therapy: Genesis and Purposes

The history of group therapy for aphasic patients suggests that often the treatment of patients other than on a one-to-one basis was usually born of necessity rather than planned with specific purposes and objectives. Sometimes groups came into being as "holding companies" for patients when clinical time for individual therapy was not available. Other groups generated from casual coffee-break meetings or from interchanges between patients in a waiting room. Whatever the genesis, there is fair agreement today that there are values in group therapy that are different and not likely to be achieved if a patient's sole avowedly therapeutic contacts are only with a therapist. Godfrey and Douglass (1959) describe the origin and some of the gains observed in a therapeutic group in a Toronto, Canada, hospital.

With the serving of coffee and the creating of an informal setting, it became obvious that a socio-psychotherapeutic process was in fact operative. Because they were so involved and enthusiastic about the project, the two occupational therapists were anxious to learn more of aphasia-therapy principles, but it was felt that their very lack of sophistication in this respect was in fact an asset rather than a deficit, and so they were not encouraged to acquire the complex technical terminology and concepts current in the literature on aphasia and clinical psychology. Implicit within the speech-social group climate was an enthusiasm and initiative on the part of the therapists which had a "natural" and "warm" character and which might only too easily become a studied and self-conscious effort with the acquisition of technical knowledge in these matters. There could be no doubt that patient-therapist relationships were of such a nature that the patients were responding to this factor, gathering from it support and strength in consequence of which there were obvious signs of markedly reduced anxiety, lowering of defensive attitudes, less withdrawal from human relationships and lifting of depression. Although in some cases language functions themselves did not particularly improve, the patient's ability to accept the limitations of disability, and to acquire relatively objective unemotional attitudes and to relate to others was a striking and impressive feature.

It is important to appreciate that the group described by Godfrey and Douglass was conducted by "minimally trained" occupational therapists rather than by language therapists. Hence, the observation that "Although in some cases language functions did not particularly improve . . . " may hardly be considered an indictment of group therapy as far as language rehabilitation is concerned. On the other hand, the note that " . . . the patient's ability to accept the limitations of disability, and to acquire relative objective unemotional attitudes and to relate to others, was a striking and impressive feature" must be considered a positive aspect of group therapy.

As a practical matter, few clinicians in private practice are likely to have a large enough clientele of aphasic patients to make group therapy, whatever its values, a serious consideration. For the most part, group therapy is possible only in centers that have clinics for the treatment of aphasic patients. Such centers are usually found in urban areas and in hospitals with specialized neurological services.

The literature on group therapy presents "testimonials" and clinical observations, almost always favorable, rather than controlled studies in which individual patient progress in groups is compared with progress in a one-to-one therapeutic relationship. This observation, not intended as a negative criticism, is inherent in the nature and dynamics of persons functioning as members of a group. Most reports on group therapy (e.g., Blackman, 1950; Aronson, Shatin, and Cook, 1956; Friedman, 1961) emphasize the gains in social adjustment and reduction of patient anxiety as positive values. It seems appropriate, therefore, to accept Schuell, Jenkins, and Jiminez-Pabon's (1964, p. 343) basic premise that "individual therapy and group therapy are two entirely different classes of events, and should not be confused." In order to avoid confusion, the therapist working with patients in a group situation has the responsibility of knowing the objectives he has in mind for the group as a whole, and for individual members of the group. An objective may be simply to have the members learn how to make social responses to one another, or to have a particular reticent person lend his voice to a group response, or to have a ventilation and gripe session in behalf of one or more members of the group. Whatever the objective the therapist has in mind, he must also be alert that a patient's need may change the goal for a given session and so must use his judgment as to whether and how the change may be achieved.

In broad terms, group therapy may have one of three objectives. The first and perhaps more important is providing psychological support for individuals within the group. The second objective is providing an opportunity for the practice of communicative interchanges, social and propositional, in an accepting social setting. This may include the practice of language "learned" by the patients in their individual therapy sessions. A third objective may be the actual teaching of some content—reading, writing, or arithmetic—in the equivalent of a small classroom situation. The objectives are by no means separated or exclusive. Furthermore, the objectives for a given member of a group may be different from ones for other members. Properly managed, each member of a group can take from it what he most needs at a given time. A well-trained leader sensitive to the needs of the constituents of a group, or of individuals working in a group setting, can enhance the likelihood that each member is given an opportunity to derive some gain according to his particular needs at a particular time.

It should be apparent that group therapy is not for all aphasic patients nor for all therapists who work with aphasics. A clinician who is also a group therapist must have special sensitivities to all members of the group, must be able to keep the overall situation under control, and must not permit his concerns for any member or members of a group to be expressed in his own anxieties. Not all clinicians, however effectively they can work with individual patients, are able to work with groups. Those who cannot, should not!

Group therapy cannot be justified solely on the basis of economy of effort or of expense. It can be justified as an adjunct to individual therapy, providing that the adjunctive values can be achieved better in a group setting than on an individual basis, and better in a "structured" arrangement than in some other informal social situation.

One of the initial and important values of group therapy is that it permits the patient to become aware that his is not an isolated and unique problem, that there are others "in the same boat." This very recognition, however, constitutes a basis for care in the situation and maintenance of the members of a group. If an aphasic assesses improvement in terms of how severe other patients' limitations may be after a period of training, rather than of how much progress the others may have made, then a group experience may have negative effects for him. The decision as to whether a patient is to participate in adjunctive group therapy must be made on an individual basis, and usually on a trial basis, with the effects carefully observed and evaluated by the responsible clinician.

Values of Group Therapy

When feasible, and with the precautions expressed above, group therapy as an adjuct to individual rehabilitative training is recommended for the following possible values:

1. Group training provides an opportunity for socialization. The aphasic patient, because of his communicative impairment, cannot easily socialize with verbally normal persons as an equal. As a member of a group of similarly handicapped persons, socialization becomes more possible. In setting up a group, it is essential that a relaxed attitude prevail. Blackman (1950) set up a group situation for aphasics and was able to report that the individual aphasic lost his feelings of isolation and apparently enjoyed the friendly competitiveness and social acceptance of the others. Activities that may successfully be employed to increase socialization and group belongingness include singing of both well-known and current popular songs; practicing "social-gesture" speech such as acknowledgments of greetings, introducing a new member to a group, and leave-taking from a group. These activities provide situations for the practice of linguistic formulations which most aphasic patients can evoke with relative facility.

In these group activities, the patient must be encouraged to do as well as he can. If he cannot sing with words, but can hum or whistle a tune, then the humming or whistling should be approved. One way of establishing group approval for nonverbal expression is to begin by setting up a musical situation in which, initially, some individuals are asked to hum, some to whistle, and some to sing the words of the song. In response to a greeting, if the patient finds it difficult to respond with a "Fine, thank you" to a "How are you?" or "How do you do?" then a gesture or a simple "O.K." plus a gesture should be encouraged.

When the group has "jelled" and the members have built up an *esprit de corps*, then more ambitious projects such as skits, charades, and quiz programs may be included. With an advanced group, discussions of current problems may be introduced. Such discussions may be preceded by a reading of highlights of the day's news or a period of listening to or viewing a news broadcast. It is important to bear in mind that in the early stages of group work, participation and not accuracy of information is the objective. As the individuals of the group find participation becoming easier, other aspiration levels and objectives may be set.

2. Group training provides an opportunity for *motivation from peers* rather than from the superior clinician. It is easier for an aphasic to try to evoke a response or read a phrase if another patient has tried, failed at first, and succeeded after a second or third attempt. The motivation of "You can do it, Joe. You saw me try and finally get it" coming from one aphasic is more readily acceptable to another than when it comes from a therapist who has no linguistic impairment.

3. The group approach provides a situation in which awareness of certain aphasic *speech "habits,"* such as telegraphic and agrammatical language structure, become apparent. The aphasic who uses telegraphic speech, who omits prepositions and conjunctions, will appreciate the difficulty of understanding such language when he hears it from others. Such appreciation should provide motivation for improvement. The verbalized "I don't know what you mean

when you talk like that," or the implied failure of comprehension which one aphasic can read from the faces of others who are listening and trying to understand him, should stimulate an attempt at a more conventional language pattern so that "I-fish-Sunday" may be changed to "I'm going fishing next Sunday."

4. Group training provides an aphasic patient with an opportunity to observe the techniques of other aphasics for evoking speech and for getting speakers to make themselves understood. The individual patient also has in the group a ready-made and sympathetic audience for the testing of his own techniques for oral expression. The techniques which prove to be successful can then be used outside of the group. The unsuccessful techniques can be delayed for outside use until further testing indicates whether they are inappropriate for the given patient and should be put aside for others. In brief, the group provides an opportunity for vicarious as well as active learning. The aphasic can learn by observation without direct ego involvement and risk of failure.

5. Still another advantage of group training is that it provides the aphasic with an opportunity in a learning situation to respond to more than one manner of speech and language usage. The clinician has habits of speaking which are peculiar to him. The aphasic whose learning is associated with one person becomes accustomed to the manner of this person. When others are introduced, learning is not limited to one speaker, and adjustments to others are not so difficult to make as they may become without group training.

6. The last of the advantages of the group approach to be considered is the opportunity it provides for *ventilation of feelings and airing of grevances*. Aphasic patients, in common with most handicapped persons, often develop feelings of hostility and aggression. Some of these are, undoubtedly, realistically justified; others are not. The expression of these feelings as well as their evaluation can be accomplished in a group situation. The knowledge and assurance that an aphasic patient gains when he learns that others feel or have felt like him, and have to a large extent gotten over their feelings, is of invaluable help. This consitutes psychotherapy without imposition. With it, the aphasic is likely to feel less isolated, and in time, less hostile to the nonaphasics with whom he must live.

Shortcomings of Group Therapy

As we have indicated, the group approach is not without some possible disadvantages. For the most part, the disadvantages to be considered can all be overcome with skilled handling on the part of the clinician directing the group, or in individual sessions with the patient.

1. Withdrawn patients may find it difficult to attempt expression as members of a group. They may inhibit even the small amount of speech available to them rather than risk faulty expression before a group. Instead of attempting speech,

as they may be encouraged to do in individual treatment, withdrawn patients may develop techniques of avoiding response, or may "hide behind" talkative ones and limit their own production to simple gestures of agreement or disagreement.

2. Group pressure may provoke some patients into talking about personal problems before they are entirely ready for such revelations. Patients not adequately able to define their problems may find their explanations misunderstood or improperly evaluated. The impact of such a reaction may set the patients back considerably in their rate of progress. Although an alert group therapist tries to avoid this situation, avoidance is not always possible.

3. The rate of a group is usually slower than the best member can manage and somewhat faster than the weakest member can progress. Patients who have made considerable improvement may be irked by having to slow down. Patients who are slow learners may find the pace uncomfortable, become confused, and cease trying to maintain the group's pace.

Despite these possible shortcomings, our experience with patients working in groups has been generally favorable. We cannot be too emphatic, however, that group training is recommended to supplement and not to replace individual training. If proper precautions are exercised, and no aphasic patient is introduced into a group until he has shown that he is ready for this experience, the advantages of group training will far outweigh any possible disadvantages.

References

Aronson, M., Shatin, L., and Cook, J. 1956. A sociotherapeutic approach to the treatment of aphasic patients. *Journal of Speech and Hearing Disorders*, 21, 352–364.

Blackman, N. 1950. Group psychotherapy with aphasics. *Journal of Nervous and Mental Diseases*, 111, 154–163.

Friedman, M. H. 1961. On the nature of regression in aphasia. *Archives of General Psychiatry*, 5, 252–256.

Godfrey, C. M., and Douglass, E. 1959. The recovery process in aphasia. *Canada Medical Association Journal*, 80, 618–624.

Schuell, H., Jenkins, J., and Jiminez-Pabon, E. 1964. *Aphasia in Adults*. New York: Harper & Row.

12

The Recovered Aphasic:
Residual Problems and
Vocational Implications

Our primary concern in this chapter will be to consider the implications for vocational readjustment associated with the sequelae of brain damage. Some of the sequelae are directly related to the individual's history of recovery from aphasia, the person's own way of responding to his linguistic impairments, and to the sensory, motor, and psychological changes as well as to the changes in his own special environment related to the effects of becoming aphasic and recovering from aphasia. Other consequences of brain damage are those which are associated with the cerebral insult *per se*, and which may also be found in persons who did not have any significant or readily observable language dysfunction associated with the cerebral damage. Still others may be associated with the process of aging, which may have brought about behavioral modifications and necessary adjustments even had there been no sudden and dramatic episode following a localized brain lesion.

We shall not dwell on those broad categories of adjustment problems related to failure in making any significant language recovery, or only a limited amount of recovery which precludes the possibility of return to previous vocation or, realistically, to any form of gainful employment except in protected or sheltered situations. Problems of rehabilitation for such persons are considered in publications such as *Psychology and Rehabilitation* (Wright, 1959) and *Vocational Rehabilitation Problems of Patients with Aphasia* (Social and Rehabilitation Service, U.S. Department of Health, Education and Welfare, 1967). We shall assume then that our discussion will be concerned essentially with persons who have made a sufficient improvement in their language functioning to be regarded as recovered or postaphasic individuals.

The Recovered Aphasic

The person we identify as a recovered or postaphasic individual is one who has improved sufficiently from his linguistic impairments to be able to engage in spoken or written communication—to listen with good comprehension and to speak, read, and write—without discernible difficulty compared with his premorbid level of accomplishment. The postaphasic individual may, in fact, have to spend more effort to maintain adequate communicative functioning than he did prior to his aphasic involvement. Indeed, he may even have periods when, because of fatigue, stress, or anxiety, his best level of performance is not maintained. However, his experience has taught him that under what are for him more optimal conditions—a reduction of stress, or a period of rest to overcome his fatigue—he will again return to his usual level of linguistic functioning. It may well be that even before the aphasic involvement comparable periods of communicative difficulty may have been present, as they are occasionally for almost all of us. However, since most persons are inclined to attribute deficiencies to a given episode or cause associated with major changes, the postaphasic is not immune from such assumption.

From a social and interpersonal point of view, the recovered aphasic should be given insight and, when necessary, counseling to see to it that he is not exercising the privileges, powers, and occasionally the outright tyranny that all too often accompany or characterize the behavior of the aphasic person as a patient. Within the limits of his intellectual capacity and sensory and motor disabilities, should these exist, the postaphasic should be motivated to carry his share of the burden of communication as well as his responsibilities as a member of his household and his community. In terms of physical activites, the postaphasic should do whatever he can that needs to be done and, conversely, should not insist on doing what he cannot do and, prior to his involvement, might not have attempted to do.

RECOVERED OR RECOVERING APHASIC: ANXIETY

Perhaps the terms recovered aphasic or postaphasic should be replaced by *recovering aphasic*. Recovery is an ongoing process for the life of the individual. Once a person has incurred a cerebral insult he is likely to live with more apprehension about the possibility of a second episode than is the person who had no first episode. Anxiety and its effects are likely to set in more rapidly and to last longer for the brain-damaged person than for one who has not had to overcome or adjust to cerebral insult. The apprehensions of a person who has had a history of seizures cannot readily be talked away. In these respects, as well as in adjustment to the lability of level of linguistic performance, recovery from aphasia is a continuous process regardless of how high a level of linguistic proficiency the individual may have reached.

Eric Hodgins, a professional editor and author of *Mr. Blanding Builds His Dreamhouse* and, as a postaphasic, *Episode: Story of the Accident Inside My Skull*, lectured on his own experiences as a person recovering from a stroke. In one of his lectures, "Outwitting Ben Casey" (Hodgins, 1965, p. 15), he addressed himself to his awareness that people, including those in the medical and paramedical professions, do not understand the multiple problems faced by the aphasic. Hodgins says: "For one thing, the subject scares the daylights out of them. For another, they are still too likely to equate brain damage with mental defect and although this *can* be a true equation, the public's fear, ignorance, and confusion work here a terrible and unjust discrimination upon those for whom the equation is not true: those whose *neurological* pathways may have gone awry, but whose *psychological* pathways remain straight and clear.... "

McKenzie Buck, a professional speech pathologist and a recovered aphasic, writes with insight about the anxieties of aphasic and postaphasic persons. Buck (1968, pp. 42–43) observes: "Oddly enough, moderate levels of functional anxiety often contribute to positive stabilizations. Many times anxieties help the patient to become realistically cautious. Tensions are often protective and contribute to safety as he walks down a stairway or routinely tests the heat of his coffee before he 'gulps' it down. Brain-damaged clients possess some realistic anxieties. They are in the process of reestablishing an appropriately protective self-concern."

Along much the same line, Douglas Ritchie, author of an autobiography of his recovery from stroke, also indicates that anxiety and fear may be used constructively. In reviewing reasons and situations conducive to eliciting relatively good language production, Ritchie (1961, p. 162) observes:

"I am inclined to think that the psychological reason is by far the most important reason of the lot. This is not to say that concentration or mere tiredness count for little, but it is the mood that counts for most. I have been right when I said that it is the stranger who makes me talk rather than my wife. This is because strangers are frightening to me and fear ranks above tiredness or lack of concentration as a stimulus. If I get into a bus, something makes me say "Sixpence" to the conductor, and the something is fear. Fear of the other passengers, who may think me dumb or mad, of the conductor, who won't know where I want to go to. In the same way it is fear, strangely disguised as friendship for D'Arcy, Sam, or Barbara, that makes me talk. Fear of being thought dumb, fear mostly of boring people because I am so slow of speech and of comprehension."

Residual Deficits and Related Problems from the Point of View of the Recovered Aphasic

Before discussing the residual problems of the postaphasic and their implications for vocational readjustment as seen by the professional clinician, we shall permit several persons who by all objective standards have made excellent recoveries to speak for themselves. At a meeting of professional aphasiologists—physicians, psychologists, and language pathologists—the author asked several postaphasics to tell the other participants what aphasia, and the recovery from aphasia, meant to them. Following are several of their evaluations (Burr, 1964, p. 4). One said, "My aphasia was not being sure of what I had to say. It was not being sure of what I heard so I had to beat around the bush until I did figure things out, only I never could be sure, *and I'm not sure today*."

A second said, "Aphasia is not finding the right words or not knowing whether I could find just the right words and put them together in just the right way."

Another opinion: "Aphasia was frustrated thinking and being frustrated in telling others what I thought. I got the ideas okay, and if only I would have done something instead of saying something I would have stayed out of trouble. Aphasia happens when you have to tell people instead of having to do something. Aphasia is not knowing what in the hell I should say when someone asks me a question, even though I always knew, or thought I knew, what I should say if the question was addressed to somebody else."

Another point, another patient, another expert: "Aphasia is the difficulty I had in getting along with people, with my wife and with my kids, because they thought I had become feeble-minded. It was trying to keep control of myself when I became angry because people thought me stupid. It was also a terrible fear, a suspicion that maybe they were right."

One more evaluation: "Aphasia is finding myself saying, or thinking, or doing something over and over again when I know I shouldn't."

Let us add to these evaluations one of the highly literate author, Eric Hodgins, who said, in an address to specialists in the field of rehabilitation (1965, p. 9): "Whatever the size of the dead spot inside of the skull of today's luncheon speaker, it has had the following effects, which have not remitted in five years time: Some difficulty with speaking, writing, spelling, and word finding—but no new troubles with syntax, which seems to belong to a different jurisdiction.

Douglas Ritchie (1961), in his autobiography of his expereince as a stroke and aphasic patient, wrote: "Victims of aphasia did want to regain the powers of language but, above that, nearly all of them unconsciously craved for some emotional balance of which they had been robbed by the stroke." Further, Ritchie wrote: "A publisher's reader, on reading the manuscript of this book, said: 'He had a pretty poor time of it. But my heart goes out to his wife. She deserves the George Cross.' "

The special and multiple problems of the patient whose aphasic involvements are associated with stroke are summed up by Eric Hodgins (1965, p. 3):

As my own day-of-discharge crisis approached I did not show all the fear I felt—because, if you please, I was afraid to! But the question, what is to become of me?—short range, middle range, long range—hammers and hammers and hammers inside the head of the patient who has had a stroke, and there is no one to give him a *con*clusive or *in*clusive answer—nothing *con*clusive because the patient always asks for bread when only stones are ready; nothing *in*clusive because of course the problem of stroke is not exclusively medical. It is all mixed up with the patient's family life, with how he earned his living, with the economic and social brackets which used to enclose him, and even with the racial group to which he belongs. No physician can ride herd on these hosts of problems, but the doctor who blandly pretends they do not exist or who has not the social imagination to ponder them will not, as I see it, be outstandingly successful in the after-care he gives the stroke patient.

Although in this essay Hodgins speaks of the problems immediately subsequent to his discharge from the hospital and his status as a patient, the fear he entertained continued for many years to be part of his "postpatient" adjustment problems. So also did the special fear that something mentally, intellectually, may have gone awry. Douglas Ritchie (1961, p. 30) recalls, "I did not know how much the paralysis had affected me, but even more I did not know how much the mind was coming adrift."

VARIABILITY OF PERFORMANCE

How well a person speaks and how well a person—any person—listens varies considerably with the state of the individual at the moment of communication interchange. Factors such as motivation, specific interpersonal relationships, "what's on one's mind," as well as environmental noise and fatigue, all contribute to an individual's ability to communicate for reception as well as production. We do not always understand what we are trying to read even though the material is well within our capacity for comprehension. We do not always write with the same degree of fluency and facility for indicating what we have in mind. Even our spelling varies, for reasons which are usually not readily apparent.

McKenzie Buck (1957), in writing of his own recovery from a stroke and aphasia, makes a significant observation about the variability of his ability to communicate in relationship to the listener:

The days that followed initial hospitalization, made me aware that the vascular accident was not as severe as it could have been, even though I experienced an almost complete paralysis to the musculature on the right. I could still follow the line of relative conversations but had difficulty in responding quickly as a conversationalist. At this point. I would like to report an interesting observation: individuals who seemed to have little or no knowledge of what actually was existing within my makeup were the easiest individuals with which to communicate. As I stated earlier, this may have been in part a reaction of patient to environment, but could readily be a result of various attitudes demonstrated by the people with whom I was associated. I am sure that there were more aphasic symptoms in terms of expressive communication with those individuals who had a more thorough knowledge of the disorder than there was with those who were less well informed.

Although Buck is here recalling the early stage of his recovery, variability of performance, greater than for nonaphasics, is a continued feature in the postaphasic. Awareness helps, especially if it is shared by listeners!

Modifications and Implications for Vocational Adjustment

GENERAL CONSIDERATIONS

A basic problem that must be faced by the therapist and the recovering aphasic is the vocation to which the "patient" may return, or the vocation or vocational changes that must be considered when physical and language recovery so dictate. It is obvious that physical limitation in the instances of persons whose aphasia is associated with stroke would require vocational changes for some persons. So would sensory limitations for others. In some instances, persons in the middle-age and older age ranges who might in any event have begun to look forward to retirement or semiretirement might want to consider such adjustments rather than to return to former employment even if this were possible. Indeed, in some instances the cerebral episode associated with the aphasic involvements may be considered a contributing cause of the problem, and possibly to its solution.

The problems indicated or implied above are, we believe, appropriately the concern of the vocational rehabilitation counselor. Realistically, however, the patient's needs and wishes are often first revealed to the language clinician. McGeachy (1967, pp. 16–17), recognizing this, makes several observations relative to the role of the clinician (speech pathologist) in the vocational adjustment of recovering or recovered aphasics:

1. During the course of therapy the clinician should learn whether the patient is willing or interested in returning to work on a different and perhaps lower level or is insistent on attempting to return to his previous position.
2. In some instances the patient may prefer to change his job, or his place of employment, even if his recovery is sufficient to permit him to undertake his previous position.
3. If language recovery is not complete, or adequate for the patient to return to his previous position, he should be directed into a new area in which he can function competently despite his language deficit.

4. In a rehabilitation setting, the speech pathologist and the vocational counselor must work in close rapport to fulfill their responsibilities to the patient whose rehabilitation includes job retraining.

Specifically, with regard to language training, McGeachy says: "Once the decision has been made as to the aphasic patient's employability, then future sessions should be arranged to assist him in developing and maintaining those language skills which are necessary for his contemplated job. He may have to learn a whole new "work jargon," or amplify his present language for use in a job situation. Whatever the decision, he must have repeated reassessment, and sometimes therapy, to maintain his language level over the years."

Sarno, addressing herself to the older persons and to their counselors, makes the following pertinent observations (1967, p. 20):

The aging process itself, even in the absence of aphasic impairment, brings avocational problems to many. They are complicated and aggravated when aphasic impairment exists. The speech pathologist, often confronted with the aging aphasic patient, I believe, would like to see a broadening of the counselor's scope to include not just those problems where vocational training and placement are the goals. A concept of counseling as a service which might bring to the patient activities in lieu of work for earnings, to provide the same self-esteem, "pride and pleasure-in-doing" that work gratification can bring.

Although McGeachy and Sarno have addressed themselves to problems of persons whose language recovery may be far from "optimal," their observations also pertain to persons with objectively minimal or residual language involvements. In the succeeding pages we shall be concerned primarily with those persons who have made "optimal" language recovery and for whom the ability to communicate in social situations would not, *per se*, be a seriously limiting factor.

The Need to Exercise Vigilance. Recovery from aphasia is, as we have suggested earlier, an indefinitely ongoing process that includes reorganization of language patterns and language habits. This process continues even for those persons who, objectively, may be restored to premorbid levels of verbal proficiency, or so close to this level that only the person who has suffered the cerebral insult may be aware of the difference in his pre- and postinsult levels of functioning. Brain damage, whether or not it is accompanied by aphasic involvement, tends to reduce vigilance.[1]

The implication for vocational adjustment relative to the increased need to exercise vigilance—greater awareness and greater conscious control of verbal expression—is that the person should not be exposed to working conditions that require immediate perception and comprehension and verbal expression and

---

[1] Clinically and operationally, vigilance may be defined as a need for maintaining a high level of attention and a rapid activation of perceptual and motor structures to carry out a required performance. For discussions of changes in the state of vigilance associated with brain damage, see Luria (1966, pp. 550–556) and De Renzi and Faglioni (1965).

verbal commitment without ample opportunity for second thought and an opportunity for correction. The desirable working situation should permit opportunity for unhurried expression of thought. The postaphasic who learns how to take his time may even establish a reputation for being a "deep thinker" who refuses to make snap statements and quick judgments. All things considered, it is a good reputation for anyone to establish. It is a necessary reputation for the postaphasic with responsibilities for what he has to say and what he has said.

To apply the above to a given profession, we would and have advised trial lawyers to spend their time in their offices, researching cases, preparing briefs, and consulting with their clients at leisure. When dictating, it is frequently better to talk to a recording apparatus rather than a secretary. The recorder is under the control of the speaker, and can be played back without embarrassment. Moreover, there is no pressure to "get on with it" which the presence of a secretary may provoke.

Reduced Intellectual Efficiency. Most recovered aphasics, and especially those who have incurred temporo-parietal damage, are likely *to manifest some degree of reduced intellectual efficiency*.[2]

For practical purposes, reduced intellectual efficiency (*intellectual inefficiency*) often becomes manifest as an intellectual decrement. There is, however, an important semantic difference between inefficiency and decrement. By intellectual inefficiency we mean that the individual can, under optimal conditions, work up to or close to his level of intellectual potential. Such conditions include a minimum of "noise," of factors that might serve to distract attention or impair concentration. Fatigue and anxiety are personal factors which have negative values. Decrement, on the other hand, implies an irreversible loss even under optimal conditions.

Conditions that exist in busy and competitive environments may quickly and significantly reduce the level of intellectual efficiency of the postaphasic person more so than the same conditions might have affected him before his cerebral insult. Thus, the postaphasic requires optimal working conditions to perform effectively. In a controlled environment, free of noise and other factors that are distracting, a postaphasic may be able to function in a productive and satisfying manner. Perhaps we should be mindful of an observation made by Hughlings Jackson (1879) that an aphasic person is "lame in his thinking," but that this does not imply he is lacking in his wits or deficient in his intelligence. The recovered aphasic may also, on occasion, be "lame in his thinking." When conditions are well controlled, such "lameness" disappears. However, the potential for circumstance to produce "just a little limp" may be present for an indefinitely long time, and more so for the postaphasic than for most persons of comparable age and education who have not suffered cerebral insult.

[2] For a review of the broad question of intellectual efficiency associated with aphasia, see Zangwill (1964).

Perceptual Dysfunctions and Perceptual Defenses. Many older persons incur some degree of hearing loss as part of the process of aging. Cerebral insult, especially to the temporal area, may also produce difficulty in auditory perception for speech.[3] These losses constitute a basis for a superimposed or secondary problem which, perversely, probably has its origin as a technique or device for avoiding a problem. The device, often used by normal persons but probably more so by persons with organic impairment, is the use of *perceptual defense*. Under conditions of stress, or under any of the conditions which are associated with reduced perceptual and intellectual efficiency, a postaphasic person may have increased difficulty in hearing, or perhaps more accurately, in *listening* (deriving meaning from auditory stimuli). If the postaphasic tries to listen and, because of the nature of the circumstances, has difficulty in comprehending—difficulty he has not yet learned to expect—he may "turn off" the speaker. By this "turn off" he avoids, at least for a while, the need to face his problem of failing to comprehend what a speaker is saying.[4]

A defense against failure to understand is *not to listen*. Sensory hearing loss, even if no greater than that associated with aging, combined with actual perceptual dysfunction, however minimal, plus perceptual defense, creates a serious problem even though it may be only of a transient nature. The implication of such a problem for vocational adjustment should be apparent. The language clinician and the vocational counselor should help the postaphasic to recognize the conditions under which he may be inclined to exercise perceptual defenses. The counselors must make certain, or as reasonably certain as the implications of the term *recovering* permits, that the potential employee—the recovering aphasic—is able not only to hear or see, but also to *perceive* in the environment in which he will have to function. If the demands of the working situation are excessive, and likely to be conducive to the exercise of perceptual defenses, the situation should be avoided. However, the potential employee can be helped by "dry run" and actual trial on-the-job experience to increase his capacity for the working conditions. On the other hand, the recovered aphasic should be given insights as to any tendency he may develop for resorting to perceptual defense at the first suggestion of difficulty.[5]

Perseverative Tendencies. Most persons who have incurred brain damage, and so most aphasics and many recovered aphasics, continue to show evidence of

---

[3] Miller (1960) found that hemiplegic patients, with or without aphasia, tended to show greater threshold losses for speech than for pure tones.

[4] There are, of course, parallel problems in comprehending written language. However, in reading the material itself does not have the dynamic, generative power to produce anxiety and embarrassment as does the presence of a speaker. Almost all of us have on occasion "stared" at a printed page or even moved our eyes over the page without deriving any meaning from it. For reasons usually not readily appreciated, we "cut off" for a while and though we "see" a page of words, we do not perceive or derive meaning from what is before us. Postaphasic persons, more often than previous to their involvement, are inclined to look and not behold, to "hear" and yet not listen.

[5] Our own observation is that the tendency to make quick use of defenses is often a premorbid habit, recurring more frequently and in prolonged and exaggerated form following cerebral insult.

neural lag. Under stress, they manifest an increased tendency toward perseveration, to maintaining a response rather than modifying it according to the demands of changing events. Even under relatively comfortable circumstances, recovered aphasics perform better when there is no pressure for rapid changes of mental set. A tendency for excessive perseveration has at least three vocational implications.

The first is that the recovered aphasic needs help to deal with situations that might be conducive to stress. The second is that the recovered aphasic needs help to develop insights into the manner and circumstances of his performance and so to avoid becoming involved in situations that require rapid changes of set and quick changes in type of activity. The third implication, happily, is a positive one. There are kinds of activities that permit an individual to work at his own rate without needing to be concerned about environmental pressures or competition. There are also many repetitive activities in which the postaphasic can perform relatively well.

Perseveration may and can be avoided. If it is avoided, anxiety, feelings of inadequacy, and occasionally even catastrophic behavior, such as fainting, sensory loss, and aggressive reactions, will not chronically become part of the behavioral patterns and the "new" personality of the recovered aphasic.

Tendencies Toward Concretism and Ego Orientation. In the process of recovery, many persons tend to exercise what may have been a premorbid inclination toward concretism and ego orientation. Such persons often fail to make the necessary adjustments to environmental demands, especially with regard to their understanding of other persons' spoken and written language, as well as with regard to their own production of language. Their thinking, their needs, the way in which language is used, may become modified and governed by limitations that are expressions of their own excessive egocentricity.

In a very real sense, and despite physical recovery, such persons continue to be patients. They function with expectations that the members of their environment will put out and adjust to them. Thus, their interpretation of what goes on in their personal environment has limited meaning and restricted significance. Such partially recovered aphasics should not be in vocational positions where flexibility of thinking and ability to appreciate the intent and needs of others are important ongoing considerations.

PROBLEMS DIRECTLY ASSOCIATED WITH LANGUAGE IMPAIRMENT

The problems and the vocational implications arising from aphasic language involvements are obvious and need little consideration. There is, however, one aspect of the problem that deserves mention. We have on many occasions been impressed with an attitude of unwillingness by some recovering aphasics to assume a fair share of responsibility in making themselves understood to listeners. We are concerned about an expression of attitude that because of a history of aphasic involvement, an adult, usually an older adult, may behave as though it is the listener's task to figure him out, to divine his mood, his intent, as well as his words. Although this attitude is not peculiar to adults who are or have been aphasic, it constitutes a greater problem in dealing with aphasics and postaphasics because most of us are more likely to accept the added burden of communicative responsibility than would be the case with nonaphasics. The danger for recovering aphasics is that if we accept too large a load of communicative responsibility we may reinforce a mode of verbal and affective behavior that in the long run will make a chronic patient of someone who might otherwise have become an adjusted postaphasic.

References

Buck, M. 1957. Life with a stroke. *The Crippled Child*, December.

———. 1968. *Dysphasia*. Englewood Cliffs, N.J.: Prentice-Hall, Inc.

Burr, H. G., ed. 1964. *The Aphasic Adult: Evaluation and Rehabilitation*. Charlottesville, VA.: Wayside Press.

De Renzi, E., and Faglioni, P. 1965. The comparative efficiency of intelligence and vigilance tests in detecting hemispheric cerebral damage. *Cortex*, 1:4, 410–429.

Hodgins, E. 1965. *Having a Stroke and Getting Over It*. New York: Eric Hodgins. (Pamphlet available through Zrike, O'Brien and McNulty, 51 W. 52nd St., New York, N.Y. 10019.)

Jackson, J. Hughlings. 1879. On affectations of speech from diseases of the brain. *Brain*, 1, 304–330.

Luria, A. R. 1966. *Human Brain and Psychological Processes*. New York: Harper & Row.

McGeachy, D. J. 1967. The role of the speech pathologist and/or speech clinic in dealing with the vocational rehabilitation problem of the aphasic patient. In *The Vocational Rehabilitation Problems of the Patient with Aphasia*, Washington, D.C.: Social and Rehabilitation Service, U.S. Department of Health, Education and Welfare.

Miller, M. M. 1960. Audiological evaluation of aphasic patients. *Journal of Speech and Hearing Disorders*, 25:4, 333–339.

Ritchie, D. 1961. *Stroke: A Study of Recovery*. Garden City, N.Y.: Doubleday.

Sarno, M. 1967. The role of the vocational rehabilitation counselor as seen by the speech pathologist in providing services for the aphasic. Washington, D.C.: In *The Vocational Rehabiliatation Problems of the Patient with Aphasia*. Social and Rehabilitation Service, U.S. Department of Health, Education and Welfare.

Social and Rehabilitation Service. 1967. *Problems of Patients with Aphasia*. Washington, D.C.: U.S. Department of Health, Education and Welfare.

Wright, B. ed. 1959. *Psychology and Rehabilitation*. Washington, D.C.: American Psychological Association.

Zangwill, O. L. 1964. Intelligence in aphasia. In *Disorders of Language*, DeReuck, A., and O'Connor, M., eds., London: J. & A. Churchill.

Appendix I

Excerpts from Eric Hodgins' Having a Stroke and Getting Over It

Eric Hodgins, editor and author of several books, including Mr. Blanding Builds His Dream House *and* Episode, *suffered a cerebrovascular accident and a stroke in 1960. Hodgins had left-sided paralysis and aphasia. He made an excellent recovery from his aphasia but was left with residual left-sided weakness. Hodgins, it is of interest to note, was originally left-handed.*

The excerpts that follow are from four addresses to professional audiences concerned with problems of rehabilitation. In these addresses, Hodgins raises a number of relevant and challenging questions, and provides his own answers to a few, that are important to persons in the field of rehabilitation, to patients in their process of recovery, and to members of the family and their friends.

Stroke as the Patient Sees It

Stroke is so manifold in the ways it presents itself that not even a patient can call it *it*. Nevertheless, I am going to call it *it* tonight, on the understanding that this is for grammatical convenience only.

The first thing to be said about *it*, is that it is like nothing else on earth. But if some Alice-in-Wonderland comparison were forced on me I would have to say, "*It* has more in common with a traffic accident than with a hot appendix." The victim-patient is confused, or stunned, or shocked, or unconscious. Whatever his state he is not in good condition to give any fellow layman a clear and coherent account of what happened. Perhaps he can talk—perhaps not. Even with speech, he can't say "It hurts"—because it probably doesn't. So, Stroke exists in no focal plane the uninitiated layman can understand or recognize, or on which he can practice his own brand of differential diagnosis. Thus, as with the traffic accident, a variable period of total confusion elapses after the stroke has struck before the cry goes up, "Somebody get a doctor!" . . .

There was nothing off-hand about the treatment I received from my stranger-doctors—far from it. Yet in treating a stranger some things *do* get overlooked. It was only after a consultant's searching neurological examination, my third night in hospital, that some local Dr. Kildare stuck his head back in my doorway and asked, obviously as a cover-man for an embarassed senior: "By-the-way, are you right-handed or left-handed?"

It was a good question, but overdue. The left side of my body was affected *but so was my speech*, yet I showed no overt signs of being left-handed. Even mid-nineteenth century physicians knew that all three of these things could not co-exist or be fitted together correctly, for the brain area governing speech lies in the brain's "dominant" hemisphere, whichever it happens to be. So: which brain-hemisphere had experienced the lesion? Or was it maybe a bilateral lesion? The true and slightly extensive answer to young Dr. Kildare's question was: I had been born a left-hander but had been forcibly switched in boyhood because when William Howard Taft was President left-handedness was disreputable, except in baseball parks.

Unlike other patient types I can think of, the stroke patient goes to the hospital with profound relief, and gladly. Although he is probably not in pain, he is in considerable fear—more than he can express. Something has gone very, very wrong, but "Somebody will fix it": this child-like phrase describes the depth of the patient's need for support and reassurance. He looks to the physician and the hospital for the alleviation of his fear. And, *up to a point*, they provide it. Then, as things go today, they stop. After a few weeks this rapport is lost. Why?

My own view is that the doctor's concern for the patient and the patient's concern for himself run on completely different timetables. The doctor's concern is highest in the beginning: if the patient is not worse within the first 48 to 72 hours, he is probably not going to get worse—medically—so the doctor feels justifiable satisfaction: "We pulled him through." But the fear the patient felt in those early days is nothing compared to the dark foreboding he feels when he faces what, in most other illnesses, is a time for celebration—his day of discharge. For the Stroke patient this is *the* crisis of crises, although medically it is not a crisis at all. Yet as I see it, the day of transfer out of the receiving hospital to "go home" and begin, very slowly, the task of refitting himself into the jig-saw puzzle of his former life—this is the very day when the care and management of the stroke patient is most likely to get very seriously boggled. . . .

Despite the paramount position of American medicine in the world today, the United States has become a dismaying country in which to be ill—whether from Stroke or anything else disabling. Ironically this springs from the very fact of our affluent society. As the tides of higher and higher costs and prices—and fees—continue to sweep in, the disabled find themselves driven into a smaller and smaller area of high ground these flood waters have not reached—yet. The skills in today's surgery, the technical advances in today's medicine, are breath-taking. But in the midst of this magnificent record of invention, innovation and accomplishment there is a dead spot, if not a zone of silence. Americans have yet to agree on the proper social-economic invention which will pull us alongside, humanly, with the technical best we have—which is so inhumanly good.

Outwitting Ben Casey

Perhaps the most useful function I can serve is in trying to help people without brain damage understand what it is like to have *some* damage. I think I can do this with one short anecdote called *The Paper Cup*.

The point is that I can't drink from one. Why not? It's feather-light; indeed, there's the trouble. Drinking fountains are usually arranged so that the right hand turns on the water while the left hand pulls the paper cup from that metal tube on the wall. Both these operations are a cinch. But the reason I can't drink out of a paper cup is that I crush it to death in my left fist. The lack of feedback from my left finger-tips, plus the muscles that don't know *quite* what they're doing, plus some other X-factor—these account for the throttling grasp I give the cup with my left hand—and mind you, the left side is the one that is medically described as "weak." But in The Case of the Paper Cup the true fact is that my left side doesn't know its own strength. . . .

People have come to understand "rehabilitation." They have come to understand that the handicapped—the paraplegic, the polio victim, the amputee, the halt, the maimed, the deaf and the blind—can be absorbed into our modern urban and industrial society and that this, not favors, is what they passionately want. But people have *not* come to understand brain damage. For one thing, the subject scares the daylights out of them. For another, they are still all too likely to equate brain damage with mental defect and although this *can* be a true equation, the public's fear, ignorance, and confusion work here a terrible and unjust discrimination upon those for whom the equation is not true: those whose *neuro*logical pathways may have gone awry, but whose *psycho*logical pathways remain straight and clear.

Function Is as Function Does

In speaking of the problem of Stroke, I speak as a layman but from personal experience. There was not a hint of medical mismanagement in my case, despite the heavy starting disadvantage that physician and patient were total strangers to each other and had been brought together only by the emergency of the stroke itself. But was there *good* management? This is a different question altogether, and to this I feel the answer is quite uncertain. Stroke, which begins as trouble within the cardiovascular system, manifests itself to the surviving patient as trouble in his neuromuscular system, but that is only the beginning of stroke's ability to ignore the boundaries set forth by medical textbooks: the "convalescent" stroke patient stands a good likelihood of becoming, in this misnamed phase, a person deeply in need of a psychiatrist. For if the patient's personality, his work, and the residual disabilities with which his stroke has left him—if these three factors line up adversely enough, then a depressed and perhaps despairing human being has now supplanted, in February, someone who, in January, was earning his living, supporting his family *and*—very important—paying his taxes. A community asset is now a community liability, reconvertible into an asset, probably, given the best of management, but not next week, not next month and *perhaps* not next year.

In my own case I found it both depressing and infuriating that I encountered no physician with the willingness or capacity to say, as my acute symptoms subsided, "I freely concede you are in a jam—in fact, in several jams. I have no ready-made solutions—but I will help you think your way out of your jams, because I conceive it part of my job, my *medical* job." Perhaps it is a contentious suggestion that medicine should reach this far out from its examination rooms and its prescription pads to help the stroke patient. But in that case, whose job is it?

View From the Patient's Head

How can we straighten out our words—to say nothing of our thoughts—so that the other fellow knows what we're trying to talk about? Discoordination and disobedience among muscles on one side of the body is *not* paralysis or hemiplegia; speech stumbles, occasional disconcerting word losses and curiously random spelling difficulties do *not* add up to aphasia. This patient can, however, testify that they subtract heavily from his psychic reserves, already depleted by shock, fear and confusion. But ships at sea seldom sink from direct or simple loss of buoyancy. Those that sink first lose stability; not unless they have heeled over so far that water begins to pour through the deck openings, are they doomed. So it is with human beings, too, I should think; if those who are caring for the stroke patient can preserve in him sufficient stability, the problem of buoyancy may then prove relatively simple.

What I am saying, of course, is that I think the emotional problems of stroke patients are now the ones least well studied, the ones least comprehended; in fact the ones most thoroughly and systematically neglected.

As a stroke patient whose vintage year was 1960, I have had ample time to forget some things, but some other things can never be erased. I think, for example, of the first time, post-stroke (about four months), when I tried to read and comprehend a manuscript. It was quite short, but it had been heavily edited, with many hand-written deletions, or additions to the typewritten copy. And I could not comprehend it. I could not follow the editings. I could not follow the prose, I could not follow the reasoning; I could not, in fact, discern the subject. This awful example of incapacity at my profession of forty years faced me on the afternoon of that same day whose morning had seen me at my doctor's office, where he had said, "You are really coming along quite well." So I thought to myself in despair, "If this is what it means to be 'coming along quite well,' then I think I want no more of it." Now, looking back on things with a five-year perspective, I have the impression that it took two and a half years to re-stabilize me and make me accustomed to my neurological deficits. In retrospect, this is not so much; in prospect, alas, it seems an eternity.

A view from this patient's head today reveals the neurological deficits to be principally three: civil disobedience in the small muscles of the left hand, loss or distortion of tactile sensation on the left side, and loss of the proprioceptive sense. The patient can perceive each of these separately, but I think it's important to say that *operationally* they form a triad and that so far as daily life is concerned, no useful purpose is served by considering them one-by-one. They are lock, stock and barrel. But I continue to hear what are, to me, fool remarks based on the separate consideration of one or two.

The last five years, having seen their enormously heightened appreciation of the treatment of Stroke by medical men, therapists, and by men and women specializing in physical medicine and rehabilitation, the lay public must now get busy—very busy. It is quite true that "Stroke is not exclusively a medical problem." But where health is concerned there is no such thing as an "exclusive medical problem."

All illness involves the community in which it takes place. Does this sound like an ABC copybook maxim? If so, why are we being so slow to learn it? We learned it about infectious and contagious diseases in the 19th century: indeed, we broadly call them "communicable." I think it is time now that we broadened things out to say, "All illness is communicable," and to ask ourselves, why does society react so differently to acute and to chronic situations?

Appendix II

Case History of Herbert Packer, A Recovered Aphasic

Herbert Packer, a professor of law, at age 44, was admitted to the hospital in March, 1969, with complaints of severe headache and transient right-sided paralysis. Three days after admission he suffered a second cerebrovascular accident which was associated with right hemiplegia, oral apraxia, and expressive aphasia. He was unconscious for four days. Informal examination on recovery of consciousness revealed that H.P. could understand conversational speech and could read a newspaper, but he could not speak or write with either hand.

H.P. had a course of language therapy and made rapid progress. He rejected learning to use his left hand for writing and preferred to use the typewriter. Within six months H.P. returned to academic duties on a limited schedule.

In October, 1971, H.P. suffered a sudden "blackout." After three or four days he recovered to the status before his "blackout." His only new difficulty was in coordinating breathing and speaking. This difficulty was corrected after a brief period of speech therapy.

H.P. recalled that his chief problem was in a tendency to speak telegraphically. He recognized that his "terse" efforts at communication often failed to give the listener enough information to permit ready understanding. However, H.P. also recognized that he was inclined to be terse in speaking previous to his cerebrovascular accidents, so he was surprised at the failure of listeners to

Professor Packer died on December 6, 1972. Up to the time of his death he was actively engaged in teaching and in writing. His last writings included a Report to the Carnegie Commission on Higher Education on the subject of legal education and a co-authored book with Thomas Ehrlich on *New Directions in Legal Education* published by McGraw-Hill in 1972.

209

understand him. Another difficulty was in speaking, and especially in lecturing extemporaneously. He began to write out his lectures and to read verbatim from his prepared material. This method of presentation did not suit his style. He was also aware that he had become reluctant to "field" questions from his students. In retrospect, H.P. indicated that a lack of confidence, rather than an impairment in ability to speak extemporaneously, was accountable for his difficulty. He regained confidence after discussing the matter with his speech therapist. At the time of the interview with the author (May, 1972), H.P. believed that he had overcome his apprehension and was again lecturing and "fielding" questions in his accustomed pre-cerebro-accident style.

The excerpts that follow are from an interview with reporters from the Stanford Law School Journal and Professor Packer. The interview, published May 11, 1972, and reproduced here by permission of Professor Packer, had as a headline, "Professor Packer Gives Views on Politics, Law, and Wine." Professor Packer also presented his views on the effects of his stroke on his philosophy of life and his awareness of responsibilities and relationships that, prior to his illness, he had taken for granted.

We should also note that H.P. was aware of the difficulty he had in speaking extemporaneously. At the time of the interview with this author, extemporaneous speaking was no longer a problem. H.P.'s language was forceful, whether on a propositional or subpropositional level. He had no special difficulty in presenting abstract ideas, or in providing precise examples to support the arguments and positions he takes. Yet H.P. had problems. Some were residuals of his stroke and aphasia. Others, as H.P. indicated, were ones that existed prior to his strokes, but had become more challenging in their management than before his involvement.

Journal Editors' Note: Prof. Herbert Packer is one of the nation's foremost scholars in criminal law. His recent book, Limits of the Criminal Sanction, *won the Order of the Coif Triennial Award in 1970 as the outstanding work of legal scholarship of the prior 3 years.*

Born in 1925, Packer received his LL.B. from Yale in 1949. After serving as clerk to Judge Thomas Swan of the 2d Circuit Court of Appeals (1949–50), he worked in a Washington law firm until coming to Stanford in 1956.

Prof. Packer volunteered for this interview, and suggested the opening question which follows.

Journal: What's a crippled guy like you doing on our faculty?

Packer: Good question. I taught here for a good many years, and then in 1969 I had a stroke. Well, that knocked me out for a good long time, and I've only just really recovered.

J: Were you Vice-Provost of the University at the time?

P: Not at the time. I'd resigned before my stroke.

J: I've heard it said that the stroke was the result of the stress of that job.

P: I think it may have been. If you had been here in 1968 you would know what I mean. I got flak from students and everybody else.

J: Did you resign because of the flak?

P: Hell, no. I'd never resign because of flak. I like flak. I thrive on it. But I just decided that I wanted to get back to doing what I felt like doing—teaching and writing, mainly writing.

J: Are you doing any writing now?

P: I sure am. I'm doing a history of the U.S. Court of Appeals for the Second Circuit. That's sort of a long-run project.

J: Do you do any traveling to interview people for the project?

P: I do travel occasionally. Actually, I've only just recovered enough to be able to travel by myself. I had my first trip alone about three weeks ago, out to New Haven. My stroke knocked me out for a good long time. I started teaching again in 1970, but I've only just regained the capacity to talk extemporaneously. That's one of the reasons I suggested this interview. I say "just" but that really isn't accurate. I've just proven to myself that I can do it.

It was really a long process of getting back. I went through a lot of physical therapy, designed to help me regain my muscular capacity. I had to learn how to walk over again.

J: Did the stroke affect your mental abilities at all?

P: As far as I know, my mind is as good or not as good as it used to be. A period of disability enhances your ability to contemplate. You really don't have anything else to do, so you have to sit and think. And I say that's a very valuable experience. I thought about everything, including suicide. I had a real period of depression, but I think I'm out of it now.

J: Didn't you have another stroke more recently?

P: That was last fall. For a few days it made things worse, but it turned out not to be at all serious actually. In fact I think it really helped me. Having gone through it twice, I just decided, goddammit, this stuff just can't kill me, so dammit, I better recover.

J: Why did you begin teaching in 1970 though you didn't yet feel comfortable speaking extemporaneously?

P: Well I felt I had to, to prove to myself that I shouldn't retire. Retirement was a strong thought in my mind. I wasn't really pleased with the experience of teaching again. It was, I think, a really lousy teaching job, and I apologize to all the students. What I did was, I wrote out everything I was going to say, and then I read it. I fielded some questions from the class, but not many. I really apologize to all those students. I really don't think that they had a decent criminal law course.

J: There was some complaint after the exams about the low grades that you gave, and later you raised them all substantially. What was the reason?

P: I decided they were too low. The thing is, I should never have turned those first grades in. That was my big mistake. Actually, I always make that sort of mistake. I just shoot from the hip. It's not a good idea. . . .

J: From 1964 to 1969 you, along with several others now on the Stanford faculty, were a reporter for a proposed revision of the California Penal Code. In 1969 you were all fired en masse by the legislature. Did your own recommendations on revising sexual conduct statutes contribute to this result?

P: I think they did. My proposals were essentially to de-criminalize homosexual acts. I don't know if the legislature didn't like the proposals, but the Chairman, Senator Grunski, sure didn't. Sandy Kadish and I wrote him a very hot letter which was published in the *Stanford Law Review*. You should read it. The other recommendations also contributed to our being fired. I'm sure that John Kaplan's marijuana proposal played a part. And I agree with his proposal.

There are other areas of the criminal law which need revision. Heroin should be de-criminalized. Both use and sale. I think we should go to the British system. The British have public clinics to which a registered addict can go and get his shot. That of course kills any chance for a black-market. I believe it is better than the Methadone system. I say that if somebody wants to take heroin, let him. Let him go to hell in his own way.

J: It seems to me that that amounts to legalizing suicide. Do you believe that suicide should be legalized?

P: I sure do.

J: But I just realized there is no way we can punish someone who has committed suicide.

P: But you can punish attempted suicide, which of course is a terrible idea. Imagine, putting a man in jail because he attempts suicide.

J: Should heroin be legalized for all age groups?

P: Well, as far as I'm concerned, any sale to someone under 18 should continue to be criminal. But possession should be completely legal for everybody. . . .

J: Are there any other areas of the criminal law besides drugs and sex which you believe need revision?

P: All sorts of areas. Gambling, for example. I'll generalize it even further. Any area concerned with one's personal morals, the criminal law has no business in at all. A lot of jurisdictions have started to move this way. New York, of course, has legalized abortion and also homosexual conduct. Illinois has legalized homosexual conduct.

J: Do the effects of this that are being perceived tend to support your thesis?

P: I don't think that anybody has been able to judge that. I think empirical research is awfully difficult. Empirical research into the effects of law is just about impossible. I tend to just say, to hell with it, you just can't do it.

J: Then how do you verify the premises upon which you build your system?

P: What I try to do is think it through, as I think I did in *The Limits of the Criminal Sanction*, using history. Take Prohibition, for God's sake, that's a real lesson.

J: You're saying we should eliminate regulation of the moral conduct of others. But why has there been this regulation throughout history? Your proposals are quite radical breaks with past trends of history.

P: I don't think they're radical at all. Look at foreign policy. There, the lesson is exactly the same. Your commitments should never outstrip your capacities. And of course in Vietnam you have a good example of a case in which we did allow our commitments to outstrip our capacities.

J: I think the question meant to say that there's a general societal urge to penalize certain types of conduct, but your thesis is that this urge should be repressed. How do you justify its repression given the societal urge in that direction?

P: That's a very metaphysical question. I'm afraid I can't answer it. As the waiter said when asked the time, "I'm sorry, this is not my table."

I think that the main job of the criminal law is very simple. It is to prevent people from using force against others and from taking other people's property. Aside from that the jobs that it can do are very limited.

J: There are certain things that may not fit into the criminal law, but I'm curious whether they fit anywhere else. Can the civil law deal with some of these areas, or do they get shoved under the rug?

P: Shoving things under the rug is always a bad idea. Take so-called civil commitment, for example. That is real punishment, that's criminal, I think. There's no excuse for it at all. We similarly sweep the treatment of juveniles under the rug. It's a good idea to bring things out into the open, and the criminal law, thank God, does that. I don't talk about rehabilitating people in the criminal law. We don't talk about children being in need of protection, and that sort of crap. The juvenile courts, are, in my judgment, a real menace. That's one area in which I do feel some competence to talk. That's a quasi-criminal area, and I tend to agree with those people who say the whole process should be brought out into the open and made manifest.

J: Why does someone get so concentrated in one area of law? Why did you get so interested in criminal law?

P: I don't think it's a narrow interest at all. I think it's about as broad as all out of doors. I first got into it through a series of happenstances. When I joined the Stanford faculty, back in 1956, they needed a man in criminal law. So I said I'd be glad to teach it, I'd try it out. Actually, at that time I felt my main field was going to be anti-trust, which I also taught. Then two things happened. One, I found I just couldn't ride both horses at the same time. And the criminal aspects of the anti-trust law interested me a great deal—and they still do. One of these days I'm going to write something about it.

So I dropped the anti-trust course, but I did pick up legal process, which I happen to think is really a superb course.

J: In conception or in practice?

P: In conception, and when I taught it, it was pretty good. I used the Hart & Sacks material, which I think came under unjustified criticism. I like the course because it gives you a chance to examine the way law works, which is what jurisprudence ought to be about. Actually, jurisprudence to me is just a lot of words. But I like what I call applied jurisprudence, which is jurisprudence at work. Deciding, for example, what sorts of things a court can do, what sorts of things a legislature can do—that really is what the legal process course is all about.

J: I'd like to disagree with you. It seems that's the kind of information you can get from a political science course.

P: Oh hell no, for God's sake, not political science! What the hell do those jokers know about law—nothing! And I would repeat that to any political scientist whom you want to come up with. There's a role for the theoretical aspects of political science, definitely; the behavioral aspects, no. Behaviorism is really a dead end. It's the great art of knowing what is not worth knowing.

J: To what do you attribute the success of polls, and other evaluations of opinion today?

P: What success? Polls? Sure, polls maybe can help tell who may win an election. But that's nothing. They can't tell you anything really important, I don't think.

J: Couldn't you take a poll that would help you estimate, for example, what the reaction to your revisions of the criminal law would be among the public?

P: Hell, no! You can't design it, in the first place. I have yet to see a poll that could accurately ask somebody whether he favored or didn't favor some proposal. Maybe we could just terminate this by saying that I have a closed mind on this subject.

J: How would you react to a couple of propositions. First, you were remarking that civil commitment was a horror, juvenile process a similar horror, and to a certain extent prisons have proven themselves to be a similar horror. What would you say to the proposition that these phenomena are to a certain extent a consequence of people classifying the mentally ill, juveniles, and prisoners as classes apart from society, so that they don't perceive injuries to these exterior classes as injuries to their society?

P: That's one of many reasons, actually. I think it's an awfully good one and I agree with it totally. Take civil commitment. The medical profession as a whole is just so damn backward. . . . They just want to play God. And I don't like people who play God. If there is one thing that I came away from my stroke with, it's the conviction that doctors who play God are just no use at all; in fact they are worse than no use, they are a real handicap.

J: If I may change the subject, you were once on the curriculum committee of the Law School, and you recommended, among other things, changing from the quarter system to the semester system and doing away with requirements after first year.

P: Sure, I really take credit for having freed the slaves.

J: In connection with that, you were quoted as saying that the faculty were much more innovative than the students, who were rather conservative. Is that still true?

P: My God, did I say that? Well, since then I've discovered how conservative faculty people are. When their own interests are at stake, both groups are very conservative.

J: Are you happy with the faculty and students here?

P: Very happy with the faculty. I think our faculty is probably the best in the country right now. Now let's talk about the students. I do not think that our students are better now than they've ever been. It's a real mistake to tell students how good they are. It just inflates their damned egos. It can be a mistake to inflate faculty egos too, but since most of your readers are students, I don't think you have to worry about that.

J: How would you compare today's students with your contemporaries when you were in school?

P: I can't quantify it. There's always some good ones and some not so good ones. I do think that idealism plays a much bigger role now than it did. I think students are a great deal more activist, as a whole, and I sort of regret that, because I think it leads them into anti-intellectualism. I don't think activism is necessarily incompatible with intellectualism. I think that people ought to be active. I tried to be active all my life. Unfortunately, I have a weakness for ideas. I like ideas—more than I like power! A great Faustian struggle goes on in everybody between power and ideas.

J: You said you began your opposition to the Vietnam war in 1966. Are you pleased to be in the majority now?

P: Sure I'm pleased. It doesn't happen very often, though. I'm accustomed to being a loser. In politics I grew up a loser. Adlai Stevenson took my virginity— twice!

J: Do you give the sort of political activists you criticized before any credit at all in winding down the Vietnam war?

P: They've played a very substantial role. I give them credit for that. What I don't give them credit for is their damned rhetoric and their anti-intellectualism.

J: I've heard you characterized as liberal in general political matters, but very conservative as far as the University is concerned. Is that true?

P: Sure, it's true. I'm a political liberal mainly because I always have been. Very early in life I became a John Stuart Mill liberal and I've remained that ever since. As far as the University is concerned, now we're talking about my own interests, my personal interests, and of course I'm conservative there. That may or may not be a sufficient explanation of it, but it's certainly a necessary one. Look, when I feel threatened, I just get very conservative. I've felt very threatened by what's gone on at the University—not in a personal sense, just institutionally. There were several years around here when I felt very threatened. . . .

I envision the threat as being as follows. Society will just stop supporting universities, and that was a real possibility for a while, I think. I don't think we're over the hump permanently, but we seem to be making quite a comeback. I say "we" meaning, of course, people like me. But I do not feel the threat no longer exists; it's just dormant at the present time.

J: It seems to me that the things that are going on here are not much of a viable threat, because there are so few people doing them.

P: Boy, don't you believe it! Take this damn crisis about recruitment. Two years ago the Faculty Senate would probably have supinely lay down and said, sure, war recruiting has to go; and that would have really put us in the soup. That's what I mean by feeling my own interests to be at stake. Apart from that, I also think that there are principles that one ought to follow as long as he finds it possible to do so. The principle that I follow is roughly this. Let every guy do exactly what he wants to do so long as he doesn't hurt anybody else.

J: What do you do when those two things conflict? War recruiting is a good example.

P: That's very easy for me. War recruiting doesn't hurt any individuals. But the capacity of people to decide for themselves what they want to do, what sorts of jobs they want to have, whom they want to talk to, seems to me just so transcendently important, there's no use even talking about this stupid war recruiting business.

J: War recruiting does injure individuals, but it's just that the injury is connected to the act of war recruiting by a very long, complex process.

P: A terribly long, complex process—so much so that how can you possibly say that war recruiting is bad when somebody has been kept from talking to a guy whom he wants to talk to.

J: Perhaps what you're saying is, where the connection between one injury and this situation is so attenuated and another injury and this situation is so direct, that we should protect against the direct injury rather than the long, complex chain of indirect injuries.

P: Of course we should. "Harm to others," which of course was John Stuart Mill's great phrase, is capable of causing great confusion, because obviously, any policy is going to hurt somebody. The question is what the chain is. Is it going to hurt him directly or immediately, or is he going to be hurt as the result of a combination of circumstances. That's why I think that freedom is the big virtue. It's important to be free just so long as one does not directly hurt other people.

J: Does your analysis of freedom extend into the free market area also?

P: It sure does. But I do think that economics can be overvalued, and the free market can be overvalued too. Life does not consist of microanalysis.

J: What are some of your avocations?

P: I'm a great reader, I spend a lot of time reading. Also, my wife and I happen to enjoy collecting wines, and we've built a couple of wine closets in our house. We buy the wines and lay them down. We have some California wine, though I obviously prefer the European. I'm really looking forward to drinking some Chateau Latour in 1984.

J: I have a very personal question. Do you feel that because of your stroke you had difficulty communicating with your children? Did it put a barrier between you?

P: For a while it did, but now I find that barrier's been overcome. Actually, I'm happier now than I think I ever was. You were asking me earlier whether I thought the results of the stroke had impaired my ability to do things that I wanted to do. Well, what's happened is that I've changed my wants.

J: Would you recommend tailoring one's desires to one's capabilities to people in general?

P: I sure would. For me, the Faustian struggle is over. A really catastrophic accident can determine the outcome for you, and it did for me. But it took me a long time to realize that.

By the way, I really enjoy talking to law students. What I do is leave the door to my office open when I'm free. You see, I have a secretary, and the main entrance is through her office, room 105, but actually, it's a lot simpler for students just to walk into my office, which is 104. So anytime that door is ajar, that means that I'm not working, and free to be interrupted. I just evolved that policy. For the last 2 or 3 years I hadn't been doing it; I'd been licking my wounds in private. Since I'm not as agile as I used to be, I don't go climbing all over the building, so I'm almost always here in my office. . . .

J: Why does the far left feel that you are an enemy?

P: I guess because they think that a guy in my position, which I guess they would label 'social democrat,' is the real enemy of the left. The same story as was in Germany just before Hitler came to power. The Communists really waged war on the social democrats and I think exactly the same thing is going on in this country today. Any totalitarian is bound to think that a social democrat, which I define as being somebody who believes in individual freedom and who also believes that the government has to control the economy, is the real enemy. The social democrat is the enemy of any totalitarian, be he left or right because of his essential belief in individual freedom. They are my enemies and I know it.

As will be noted from the interview above, Professor Packer was not slow to form or to express his opinions on his experiences. Following are his notes and his views about two speech therapists, the differences in their attitudes and approaches and in his attitude toward them.

Herbert Packer's Notes on His Speech Therapy

After my stroke in 1969, I underwent speech therapy. The therapist was an inexperienced young lady who made up for her own lack of confidence by trying to assert herself in our relationship. Toward the end of our therapy, she insisted on giving me exercises in remembering series of numbers. I objected strongly to this because I did not think that remembering series of numbers was at all relevant to my condition. She also gave me some exercises in spelling words. One of those sessions occasioned the following incident, in which she is represented by the letter C and myself by the letter P:

C: Spell "banister."

P: B-a-n-i-s-t-e-r.

C: That is wrong; it has two n's.

P: (Silence. My self-confidence was gone, so I did not tell her to look it up.)

C: Well, let's just go on. (The dictionary gives the spelling as "banister" with "bannister" as an occasional alternative.)

C: Spell "barrister."

P: "B-a-r-r-i-s-t-e-r."

C: Please use it in a sentence.

P: She broke her ankle sliding down a barrister.

C: That doesn't make sense to me.

I had remembered an old joke, which I used to get some revenge. The therapist did not understand that she had been one-upped. Shortly after this session, she phoned my wife and said that she would like to talk with her about my case. My wife, whom I had told about the preceding incident, met with the therapist, who complained that my wife was undermining her—the therapist's—relationship with me. In fact, the therapist had succeeded in destroying the relationship. Not long thereafter, I terminated the therapy. The therapist did a technically competent job, but she struck out because she did not know how to "handle" me. That I would suppose was how she would put it. As a former patient, it still makes me bridle when therapists talk about "handling" people.

After the "blackout" in the fall of 1971, I decided, with the help of my neurologist, whom I like and trust, that I perhaps could use some more speech therapy. The second speech therapist was a more mature and understanding person. She diagnosed my problem very quickly. It was that I was breathing through my nose rather than through my mouth.[1] This accentuated my tendency to speak telegraphically. The therapist gave me some exercises to aid me in breathing through my mouth. But more than the exercises, her attitude helped me. She was very supportive and told me that, so far as she could determine, my real trouble was a lack of self-confidence. By harping on that theme, she (with some aid from a psychiatrist whom I was then seeing) aided me to recover my self-confidence, to the point where I was able to speak extemporaneously before a large and critical audience. It was then that I decided to give the interview that Dr. Eisenson has edited.

[1] The reference to breathing refers to *breathing while speaking*.

Appendix III

Aphasic Language Modifications as a Disruption of Cultural Verbal Habits[1]

A speech clinician who has had several years of extensive and intensive experience with aphasic patients is likely to have made observations that would permit the grouping of aphasics according to their linguistic recovery. Such grouping might well fall into four general categories: (a) Some patients recover rapidly and beyond the expectations of the clinician so that "spontaneous" recovery must be considered a factor in the improved picture. (b) Some patients recover slowly but steadily with measurable increments during the first year of training so that both patient and clinician are encouraged by the progress. (c) Some patients improve more slowly, but fairly steadily with the constant help and motivation of the clinician. (d) An appreciable minority of the patients make little or no objectively measurable linguistic improvement after a year or more of clinical training.

We have no ready answer or explanation for these variations in rate and degree of language recovery among aphasic patients. To be sure, individual clinicians have developed their own practical criteria for their patients. It may well be that the judgment of the individual clinician is an unwitting or unconscious appraisal of his own inclination and ability to work more effectively with some patients than with others. It would be extremely useful and economical in time and effort, for both patient and clinician, if we could determine the necessary attributes of a clinician to work successfully with aphasic patients in general, or with some kinds of aphasic patients in particular. It may well be that if we could and would match patients and clinicians in terms of personalities, attitudes, and

[1] Reprinted from Jon Eisenson, *Asha*, 5:2, 503–506.

approaches to working out day-to-day problems of living and specific problems that call for specific learning of information or the establishment of skills, we could arrive at a new and effective concept of a therapeutic team. In the present context I use the term "team" to mean the combination of a patient and a clinician.

Patients other than aphasics are known to seek out professional help for their physical or mental ills on the basis of needs that do not readily yield to objective evaluation. In my own experience as a director of training in speech and language clinics in military, as well as in civilian settings, I have encouraged exchanges of patients among clinicians. Often the patients showed an acceleration in rate of improvement following such exchanges. My impression is that the clinicians also showed evidence of recovery on their own part. I believe that the reason for the sudden enhancement of therapeutic effort is that the exchanges resulted in an improved therapeutic team. Thus, a patient who needs to be treated with firm authority does well with a clinican who can be authoritative. Another patient who may have struggled against too much authority before his aphasic involvement may do better with more permissiveness and less obvious authoritativeness. Patients who enjoy drill work do better with clinicians who are patiently able to provide opportunity and supervision for drill than they do with clinicians who find repetition of an activity burdensome and even abhorrent.

Practical Prognostic Criteria

Are there any conditions and traits among aphasics that can be used as practical working criteria for clinicians who must screen their potential client case loads to arrive at a number with the most helpful prognosis? I believe there are. These practical criteria have not all been scientifically evolved; yet they tend to corroborate the judgments of experienced and well trained clinicians, and so they merit consideration.

Motivation

The will to do well and the belief that he can and is doing well underlie both the immediate and the ultimate improvement of the aphasic patient. Motivation of the aphasic patient involves his family, his clinicians, all his associates, as well as the reactions the patient makes to himself in the light of his modified physical, emotional, and intellectual circumstances. It is difficult to objectify familial attitudes to patients in the light of their own self evaluations, but the judgments of many respected clinicians attest to the detrimental effect of some aspects of the behavior of persons in the aphasic patient's environment. On the positive side, many clinicians have attested to the favorable changes in the aphasic's recovery following encouragement and attempts at constructive motivation. Fortunately, we have some recent experimental evidence relative to the effects of specific motivating remarks during a controlled instructional period with aphasic patients. Stoicheff (4) found that aphasic patients subjected to discouraging instructions do significantly more poorly on language tasks than those who receive encouraging instructions. Beyond this, Stoicheff found that the aphasics who received discouraging instructions rated their performances more poorly than did those whose instructions were encouraging.

The effects of motivation can be also assessed from highly personal considerations. At most clinics we find patients who can be reached, almost literally, only through their purses. We have worked with aphasics who regularly blocked in arithmetic except as the arithmetic content helped them to compute and check on their welfare and pension allowances. I worked for considerable time with one patient who could not overcome an impairment in reading until the mate brought suit for divorce. Then the patient learned unerringly to identify words such as alimony, lawyer, judge, divorce, separation, and trial. The patient was able to arrange these words in sentence form, pick them out of long sentences, and find them in lengthy paragraphs. Shortly after the end of World War II, I worked with several veterans who seemed unable to learn to read until the Veterans' Administration announced a policy that a disabled veteran would be provided with an automobile free of cost if he could demonstrate ability to drive and to meet his state driving license requirements. In New York such requirements include a test that involves some ability to read. A few patients who had had severe to total alexia made quick and fruitful improvement in reading ability and, incidentally, in their ability to obtain their automobiles as a gift from their grateful government.

Manifest Personality

Just about anybody may incur brain damage, but the effects of the damage vary considerably with the personality of the individual who has incurred the damage. Let us accept as an operational definition of personality that "A personality is as the person does." Let us assume further that what a person does is fundamentally related to his inclinations. These assumptions should help us to understand much about the aphasic's behavior, his retained abilities, his immediate disabilities, and his maintained impairments. Most of us engage in a considerable amount of behavior not in keeping with our basic inclinations. In doing so, we yield to influences and drives which are culturally determined and have on-going forces as levelers of behavior. We often do what we think our culture expects us to do so that we will be acceptable and accepted. The aphasic, often by virtue of his motor and sensory involvements, has less need to yield to cultural impositions. His brain damage and the consequent sensory, motor, and intellectual modifications are the factors that determine his immediate adjustment drives and needs. In a very real sense, the aphasic, at least at the initial stage of his involvement, is relatively free of cultural impositions. Thus, an aphasic who may have been—and in the privacy of his home frequently was—a rigid, concrete minded, compulsive individual is likely to yield to the forces of these traits and so present what may seem to be a "new" personality. Cultural pressures, for a time at least, have become secondary influences as determinants of behavior. Even the language the patient at first recovers and employs shows inclination toward high individuality and egotistically determined expression rather than culturally determined practices and expressions. I believe that in a very fundamental way the ego-oriented aphasic is asserting "World, figure me out. I no longer have the need to behave according to your image. Figure me out as best you can, if you can, but don't count on too much help from me!"

Are the implications of this view of the personality of aphasics applicable to all of these patients? Certainly not! Certain aphasics are out-going and relatively easy-going, can readily place themselves at the disposal of the clinician or of another patient, and have no difficulty in adjusting themselves to group and environmental demands. These, however, are the patients who tend to do well, who make good progress in therapy, and who often improve spontaneously with or without direct therapy. These are the persons who do not long need to be considered patients. Their strivings are to the external world, and they try to the best of their present abilities to make fair adjustments to the demands of the world. They view the demands as proper requirements rather than impositions. Somehow they get along, and in doing so they adapt themselves to the ways of the world in which they live. Much of this adaptation is to resume the verbal habits of their culture. But a minority of aphasic individuals continue as patients throughout their lives. Among this minority we are likely to find three sub-groups. One consists of individuals who were pre-morbidly inclined to be at odds with their environment and their cultures. A second group consists of persons who discover such gains in their new state that despite its limitations and impairments, they are loathe to surrender the gains. A third sub-group consists of individuals with diffuse cerebral involvement who are intellectually deteriorated or deteriorating and for whom adjustment is both physiologically and intellectually impossible.

Linguistic Modification as a Disruption of Culturally Imposed Verbal Habits

Let us now project these observations and see where they may lead us in formulating a theoretic explanation of maintained aphasia. Suppose we look upon the linguistic modifications in aphasic involvement as a disruption of culturally imposed linguistic habits. The language rules we call grammar are in essence a pattern of verbal habits. The parts of speech we use in speaking and in ordinary writing that we somehow manage to dispense with in sending telegrams and cables are also verbal habits. A person who is accustomed to going bareheaded regardless of weather and who nevertheless answers the question, "What do you wear on your head?" with the words, "A hat," is one who accepts cultural intention. The YOU of the question does not really refer to the person addressed. Most of us accept that *you* as an impersonal word, and the question as a whole to be equivalent to "What is the name of the article usually worn on the heads of persons who wear things on their heads?" The individual who accepts the intention of the question and replies "A hat" is playing the game of verbal expectations in terms of his and his environment's verbal habits. Such a speaker is adjusting his reply to the inquirer's frame of reference as far as the speaker is able to estimate it, as well as to the speaker's level of abstraction. But some individuals, and they are not necessarily those with aphasic involvements, may instead choose to say, "I don't wear a hat." The answer given is related more to the listener's ego needs than to the intention of the question. Along similar lines, we have occasional patients who can repeat a sentence such as, "I drink coffee for breakfast," but cannot repeat, "I drink tea for breakfast," because the first is in keeping with his factual world and the second is not. Such patients may have no difficulty in saying "I do not drink tea for breakfast" because indeed they don't. These reality bound patients reveal a disinclination toward the assumption of any orientation or attitude that is not ego oriented. This is probably an aspect of Kurt Goldstein's characterization of aphasic involvement as constituting a primary impairment of abstract attitude. Patients who cannot enter into verbal games that call for pretending may well be manifesting the limitation described by Goldstein (1).

Laura L. Lee discusses such patients in her papers of "Brain Damage and the Process of Abstracting" (2) and "Some Semantic Goals for Aphasic Therapy" (3). In these papers, she emphasizes her thesis that aphasic patients must be helped "to re-establish the cultural patterns of thought" on which all language depends. Lee accepts Goldstein's generalization—which I consider to be a decided overgeneralization—that aphasics as a population suffer from an impairment of abstract attitude. She says "A person with a background in general semantics cannot help but see the clinician's work as general semantics training in reverse" (3, p. 262). The aphasic is specific in his thinking and is concrete minded; he has difficulty in making inferences, at least of the order this culture expects him to make, and in expressing the inferences in language, or in appreciating the inferences of the language to which he must respond.

Lee is so nearly correct that I wish it were possible to endorse her thesis without reservation. But there is room and need for considerable reservation. Most aphasics do not suffer from a severe impairment of abstract attitude except as such impairment is related to a general reduction in their intellectual proficiency. Beyond this, most aphasics, in common with most nonaphasics, are better able to think privately and to act on the basis of their thoughts than they are to translate these thoughts into conventional language for another person or persons to understand.

For the moment, the matter of the aphasic's manner of abstraction deserves more consideration. We must be careful not to confuse level of abstraction with the basis for arriving at an abstraction. Nor must we confuse rigidity of attitude, once an abstraction is made, with concretism or the inability or disinclination to arrive at or to employ an abstract attitude. If an examinee fails to accept the examiner's notion of how several of an assortment of objects should be grouped, it does not necessarily mean that the examinee's grouping is inferior to the one in the mind of the examiner or the mind of the author of the examination. It may be possible that the examinee will not group a bundle of pink wool with one that is deep red because he believes that a Red is subversive and a Pink lacks courage. In his (the examinee's) mind the basis for abstraction and generalization has become more individualized and less culturally determined than an examiner might have anticipated. But the generalization is still not devoid of cultural influence. Perhaps it would be more nearly consistent with the performance of the aphasic to conclude that many aphasics are more likely to generalize in terms of their immediate needs, interests, and drives than those of the examiner. I have often been at a loss, as I observed aphasics being assessed, to decide whether the examiner was more rigid and more controlled by the materials at hand than the patient. It was almost always clear to me that the examiner was usually behaving with greater conformity to cultural expectations than the examinee. This observation and evaluation did not, however, provide me with a basis for deciding who of the two was more or less operating on an abstract level or who of the two was behaving on the higher, or even more appropriate, level of abstraction.

The Essence of Aphasia

I wish, as a final note on my commentary on the psychological aspects of aphasia, to indicate what I consider to be the essence of the aphasic's impairment. In any communicative process the participants necessarily become involved with the need to translate their private thinking into culturally determined linguistic products. These products are a selection of words that meet the needs of the situation. A bilingual participant may translate from one linguistic system, with its verbal habits, into another if the other participant is known to be a monoglot. A flexible person with a rich vocabulary would select a different arrangement of words for a child than he would for an adult. Aphasics in general have great difficulty with this task. Their private thinking, their internal verbalizations, and their overt nonverbal behavior related to such thinking is usually more proficient and appropriate than the expected conventional, culturally determined language associated with their internal behavior. This disparity is, of course, not peculiar to aphasics. Many of us can come to conclusions and act on conclusions that are appropriate to the demands of the situation much more proficiently than we can explain our conclusions or justify our behavior. The disparity between the inner formulations and the nonverbal behavior and the expected conventional linguistic formulations and expressions is much greater for the aphasic than it is for the rest of us. Here, I believe, we have the essence of aphasia, both of the receptive-evaluative and manifestly of the expressive-productive involvements. In terms of intake, the disruption of the patterns of behavior we call aphasia does not readily permit the translation of symbol situations from the conventional to the individualized and then again to the conventional. In terms of production, the disruptions we call aphasia do not readily permit the translation from private to conventional formulation and expression. The aphasics who improve spontaneously and quickly are those who are able to make the transitions and the translations. Most aphasics who make a fair amount of recovery during the first year or two after the onset of their disruptive involvement are able to show ability to readjust to the verbal habits of the culture. Along with such readjustment is an acceptance of what members within a cultural group think about the events with which they are involved. The aphasics who recover more slowly in the absence of on-going cerebral pathology are for some reason or reasons unable to accept cultural impositions. My belief is that these patients always had such difficulty, but met the demands, however begrudgingly, in a fashion that permitted them to get along. Some might even be considered poets of the group that insist the poet's task is done when he has evoked some words and it is up to the listener or reader to figure out just what the "poet" meant or might have felt by the uttered or spoken words. Certainly, much of the paraphasia and neologisms of the aphasic have a "poetic" quality. Images are condensed, analogies implied, and there are even verbal repetitions on the order of "a rose is a rose is a rose."

The chronic aphasic, it seems to me, is a person who, because of his premorbid inclinations, becomes unequal to the extreme demands for reorganization of behavior patterns, including verbal behavior, brought about by the disruptions consequent to the cerebral insult. Cerebral lesion produces disruption and loss of control. Recovery is primarily a process of reorganization and resumption of control and of adjustment to some losses and impairments, both physical and intellectual.

It is not too surprising that some aphasics, even though their physical status has become "stabilized," are nevertheless unable to make all the adjustments necessary to overcome the forces of disruption. In the absence of on-going organic pathology, the aphasics who do not make appreciable improvement with ordinary motivation are those who are trying to accomplish reorganization through ego-orientation. Their inclination, their needs, their interpretations become the dominant ones. Thus, verbal expressions have limited meaning and restricted significance. This approach to reorganization of behavior may be contrasted with persons who accomplish considerable recovery within a few months of the onset of their cerebral insults. The ones who make good recoveries are those who adjust to the behavior of the others in their environment, including the ways of people with words and, we would guess, the ways of words with persons who use them.

Summary

In the first part of the paper the writer reviewed several factors that may account for the differential rates and degree of improvement among adult aphasic patients. Emphasis was placed on nonorganic factors that included motivation, the premorbid personality traits of the patient, and the matching of patient to clinician. The second part of the paper presented a theoretic exposition of the relationship of the patient's personality and his difficulties in accepting and reorienting himself to the cultural verbal habits of his community. Aphasia is viewed as a disruption of behavior patterns, especially those involving language. The chronic aphasic is one who continues to have difficulty in the translation and transmission of his individualized inner symbol formulation to conventional linguistic products. This impairment is related to the aphasic's premorbid and postmorbid personality traits.

References

1. Goldstein, K., *Language and Language Disturbances.* New York: Grune and Stratton, 1948.
2. Lee, Laura L., Brain damage and the process of abstracting. *ETC: A Review of General Semantics*, 16, 1959.
3. Lee, Laura L., Some semantic goals for aphasic therapy. *ETC*, 18, 1961.
4. Stoicheff, M. L., Motivating instructions and language performance of dysphasic subjects. *J. Speech Hearing Res.*, 3, 1960.

Appendix IV

The Family and the Recovering Aphasic

With the exception of military personnel who may spend considerable time in veterans' hospitals, most aphasic patients return to their homes soon after recovery from the acute stage of cerebral insult. Some aphasics become outpatients in rehabilitation centers where they may receive a variety of treatments for their physical and linguistic disabilities. Occupational therapy and possibly even therapy in anticipation of a need for a change of occupation may be included in the treatment program. A few aphasics may become resident patients in special treatment centers. But the greatest number are likely to return to their homes, out of choice or out of necessity, for the postacute period of recovery. Realistically, therefore, it is the environment within the home, and the extended environment of the home, that will be all-important in the aphasic's recovery. As Wepman cautions (1968), "What is so often overlooked . . . is the role of the patient as a convalescent in his family endeavor, the attitudes and personality of the people closest to him and their ability to turn the world, not just their homes, into a therapeutic agency."[1]

Home environment therapy for the aphasic must be designed and directed to establishing behavior, and to changing behavior when necessary, toward making

[1] Wepman, J. M., "Aphasia Therapy: Some Relative Comments and Some Purely Personal Prejudices," in *Proceedings of the Conference on Language Retraining for Aphasics*, Ohio State University, 1968.

We should note that an effective therapeutic agency should not be confused with a clinical-medical agency. The "hospital look" should by all means be avoided or reduced to the absolute minimum required for the physical well-being of the convalescing member of the family.

the convalescing person as self-sufficient and adequate as his circumstances permit. As circumstances—degree of physical recovery, locomotion, linguistic improvement—change, they should be met with new expectations as to appropriate and adequate behavior. If this is done, then excessive and chronic dependencies can be avoided. Matters such as a rearrangement of furniture to remove objects that might constitute obstacles for a person who has difficulty in walking, or in the easy use of a wheelchair, help to establish independence of action. Self-care in personal hygiene, within the limits imposed by physical condition, reduces the likelihood of ego-insult and infantalism. Such care can be taught directly by a physiatrist or physical therapist before the patient has left the hospital. However, as the patient's conditions improve, additional teaching in the home setting should help to maximize the patient's potential for self-care. In most instances, it is better for the mate or other "supervising" relative to help carry out instructions for self-care than to do the instructing.

Dependency, we must caution, is a two-way avenue. The mate of an aphasic, sometimes out of impatience and sometimes out of self-need, may do more than the circumstances require. It is true that some aphasics may exercise a "tyranny of silence" and manipulate and control a whole environment, or particular members of an environment, by unspoken demands and expectations. On the other hand, the emotional needs of a mate, possibly engendered by feelings of real or imagined guilt, may be satisfied by overdoing and keeping the mate dependent. It is probably unrealistic to expect a husband or wife, emotionally involved in the welfare of a mate, to appreciate the existence or implications of an excessively dependent relationship. In some instances, such relationships may have been present prior to the illness of a mate, and may have been mutually satisfying. If, however, because of the change in relationship, new and excessive dependency, interferes with the rehabilitation of the aphasic, then family counseling is in order. Such counseling should be provided by a trained professional person rather than by a well-meaning relative or friend. Preferably, counseling should be obtained by a counselor especially trained in rehabilitation psychology.

Language therapy for the aphasic who has returned to his home should be given, if at all possible, in a setting away from his home. There are too many anxious ears at home for the aphasic's comfort. An individual who may be willing to risk formulating a statement or asking a question when a professional clinician is the only other person involved, may be reluctant or apprehensive to do so when a member of the family is or may be eavesdropping. What the family may do, as we have previously indicated, is to carry out instructions and help the aphasic with his "homework," providing that such activity does not produce emotional upset. However, and because we need to be realistic, many aphasics do not have professional help, and the family becomes the resource for therapy. If this is the case, language therapy should be carried out by the member of the family who is least likely to become emotionally upset, or to upset the aphasic. With this in mind, we have selected a list of readings (Appendix V) and materials intended to be of help to families and friends of aphasics. We hope that if language therapy is a home activity, the family member or friend appreciates that the recipient of the therapy is an adult. The materials used—the books, illustrations, and so on—should be ones that do not suggest a child's primer. Rote repetition, of doubtful value for a child, is likely to be of negative value for an adult. In Chapter 9, "Therapeutic Problems and Approaches," and in the selected Annotated Bibliography that follows, we have included materials that are used by professional clinicians and have been found to be acceptable to aphasic adults.

Appendix V

Selected Annotated Bibliography of Books and Materials for Families and Friends of Aphasics

These are admittedly a token selection of a considerable amount of material that has become available since the 1950's. The selected items are intended to help members of families and friends to understand the multifaceted problems of the recovering aphasic.

Agranowitz, A., and McKeown, M. R. 1964. *Aphasia Handbook.* Springfield, Ill.: C. C Thomas.

A book of materials that should be used selectively with adults. Some of the materials are intended for children and may be "ego-insulting" if presented to adults.

Boone, D. R. 1965. *An Adult Has Aphasia.* Danville, Ill.: The Interstate.

This booklet is primarily for the family of the aphasic patient. The problems of the aphasic are explained. The booklet includes a list of "Do's" and "Don't's" to be observed by the family.

Buck, M. 1968. *Dysphasia.* Englewood Clifts, N.J.: Prentice-Hall, Inc.

This book is autobiographical. The author, a speech pathologist, presents his experiences and emotional problems during the period of his recovery from stroke and aphasia. He provides insights that are important for the family of the recovering aphasic.

Farrell, B. 1969. *Pat and Roald.* New York: Random House.

An account of the recovery from stroke and aphasia of the actress Patricia Neal. The mutual understanding between wife [Pat] and husband [Roald] and the efforts each contributed to Pat's recovery.

Hodgins, E. 1964. *Episode.* New York: Atheneum.

An autobiographical account of the episode—stroke and aphasia—and the process of recovery.

Hodgins, E. 1965. *Having a Stroke and Getting Over It.*

A series of lectures on the author's experiences with stroke and aphasia. The author, a professional writer and editor, addresses his lectures to physicians and other professional persons who are, or should be, concerned with the multifaceted problems of the stroke patient. The lectures provide important insights for the families of stroke patients.

Keith, R. L. 1971. *Speech and Language Rehabilitation.* Danville, Ill.: The Interstate.

This is a workbook designed for the family of aphasic patients who are unable to receive continuous therapy from professional speech pathologists. The underlying premise of the book is that, of necessity, much of the work of rehabilitation takes place within the family unit.

Kingdon-Ward, W. 1969. *Helping the "Stroke" Patient to Speak.* London: J. & A. Churchill.

A professional approach to language rehabilitation in stroke-aphasic patients. Useful for family members who may supplement or take over language therapy.

Knox, D. R. 1971. *Portrait of Aphasia.* Detroit: Wayne State University Press.

A husband's account of his wife's recovery from two episodes of stroke and aphasia. Sensitive treatment of husband-wife relationships as well as those of patient and physician. The account includes approaches in reestablishing spoken and written language.

Martin, B. R. 1962. *Communicative Aids for Adult Aphasics.* Springfield, Ill.: C. C Thomas.

A concise and practical handbook that includes instructions on how to obtain and develop useful materials for the initial stages of therapy with adult aphasics. The materials emphasize reading and vocabulary building.

McBride, C. 1969. *Silent Victory*. Chicago: Nelson-Hall.

An account by the wife of a stroke patient of the emotional problems and barriers that are frequently associated with aphasia. The silent victory was won despite the husband's limited language and physical recovery.

Ritchie, D. 1961. *Stroke: A Study of Recovery*. Garden City, N.Y.: Doubleday.

A diary of an aphasic's recovery. The author discusses the emotional changes that preceded and followed his stroke. Considerable attention is given to feelings of guilt and resentment directed at persons who provide professional but not always understanding care.

Taylor, M. 1958. *Understanding Aphasia*. New York: Institute for Physical Medicine and Rehabilitation.

This booklet is a guide for members of the family and friends of the aphasic patient.

Taylor, M., and Marks, M. M. 1959. *Aphasia Rehabilitation Manual and Therapy Kit*. New York: McGraw-Hill Book Company.

Clinical materials that may be used, with guidance, in the language rehabilitation of aphasic patients.

Index